Oracle PL/SQL Programming

Guide to Oracle8i Features

Oracle PL/SQL Programming
Guide to Oracle8i Features

Steven Feuerstein

O'REILLY®

Beijing · Cambridge · Farnham · Köln · Paris · Sebastopol · Taipei · Tokyo

Oracle PL/SQL Programming: Guide to Oracle8i Features
by Steven Feuerstein

Copyright © 1999 O'Reilly & Associates, Inc. All rights reserved.
Printed in the United States of America.

Published by O'Reilly & Associates, Inc., 101 Morris Street, Sebastopol, CA 95472.

Editor: Deborah Russell

Production Editor: Madeleine Newell

Printing History:

October 1999:   First Edition.

This book is printed on acid-free paper with 85% recycled content, 15% post-consumer waste. O'Reilly & Associates is committed to using paper with the highest recycled content available consistent with high quality.

ISBN: 1-56592-675-7

*I dedicate this book to the thousands of
unjustly incarcerated men and women —
particularly those on Death Row (and of those,
particularly Mumia Abu-Jamal)—trapped in
the vast prison system of the United States.
Perhaps one day justice will truly be blind in
this great nation—blind to the color of a
person's skin and blind to the power
they hold or lack.*

—Steven Feuerstein

Table of Contents

Preface

2700 pages and still writing! Sometimes I feel like the Energizer Bunny of PL/SQL. But Oracle keeps the features coming, and after all these years, I'm still enthusiastic about what PL/SQL can do to improve the quality of life for developers. Even with the coming of Java™ in Oracle8*i*, I believe strongly that the future is bright for PL/SQL developers.

This short book is something of a departure for me—those of you who have read my larger tomes may wonder if I've found a ghostwriter! Now that Oracle8*i* is here, it's my intention to update *Oracle PL/SQL Programming* (now in its second edition) to cover the new version of the Oracle database. Along with developing a third edition of that book (with my coauthor Bill Pribyl), I'm taking a critical look at all of my books to make sure that the O'Reilly & Associates PL/SQL series offers a comprehensive resource for PL/SQL developers.

For now, though, PL/SQL developers need current and useful information about the latest PL/SQL features; there are a lot of them, and some represent major changes in the language. This small book is intended to get you started on understanding these features and using them to best advantage.

For many people, the big news about Oracle8*i* is Java, and the big question for many PL/SQL developers is how (and whether) to use Java in conjunction with PL/SQL. Chapter 9, *Calling Java from PL/SQL*, is a roadmap showing PL/SQL developers how to employ Java right now. It doesn't attempt to teach you the basics of Java—there are many other books that serve that purpose—but it does teach you how to access Java from within PL/SQL.

Structure of This Book

This book is divided into ten chapters and one appendix, as follows.

Chapter 1, *Oracle8i: A Bounty for PL/SQL Developers*, introduces Oracle8i and summarizes the new PL/SQL-related features.

Chapter 2, *Choose Your Transaction!*, describes autonomous transactions. This feature lets PL/SQL developers execute and then save or cancel certain statements without affecting the overall session's transaction.

Chapter 3, *Invoker Rights: Your Schema or Mine?*, describes a new feature of PL/SQL that lets you decide at the time of compilation whether a program, or all of the programs in a package, should run under the authority of the definer or the invoker of the program.

Chapter 4, *Native Dynamic SQL in Oracle8i*, unveils a powerful replacement for (or at least an alternative to) the use of the DBMS_SQL built-in package.

Chapter 5, *Bulking Up with PL/SQL 8.1*, describes bulk binds and collects. Bulk binds let you bundle DML operations (via the new FORALL statement) for bulk passing to the SQL layer; bulk collects let you retrieve multiple rows with an absolute minimum of context switches.

Chapter 6, *New Trigger Features in Oracle8i*, discusses how Oracle8i has expanded the use of triggers to perform database- and schema-level operations and "publish" information about events taking place within the database.

Chapter 7, *New and Enhanced Built-in Packages in Oracle8i*, describes the new built-in packages available in Oracle8i and discusses changes to existing packages.

Chapter 8, *Deploying Fine-Grained Access Control*, examines a new Oracle8i feature that allows you to implement security policies with functions and then use those policies to implement row-level security on tables and views.

Chapter 9, *Calling Java from PL/SQL*, takes a look at what many people think is the most exciting feature of Oracle8i—the interface to Java. This chapter focuses on how you can call Java stored procedures (JSPs) from within PL/SQL.

Chapter 10, *More Goodies for Oracle8i PL/SQL Developers*, describes a variety of new features and performance improvements that don't fit into any other category.

The appendix, *What's on the Companion Disk?*, explains how to install and use the software on the companion diskette.

About the Examples

I've been writing intensively about PL/SQL since 1994, and I have had a great time doing it. At the same time, I must admit that I have simultaneously grown a little bit bored with using the same set of examples again and again (yes, those infamous emp/employee and dept/department tables), and very concerned about the state of the world as we approach the end of the twentieth century. Sure, things could be worse, but things could be a whole lot better (with my examples and the world).

Given these twin preoccupations, I have decided to offer examples that are decidedly different from the usual. I'll be talking about topics ranging from the state of health care in the United States to the strength of the gun lobby, from wage structures to environmental issues. I believe that even if you don't agree with the positions I have on a particular issue, you will find that this "breath of fresh air" approach will help you engage with the technical material.

I would also be very happy to hear from you—whether you agree or disagree!— and I encourage you to visit my web site, at *http://www.StevenFeuerstein.com*, where you can read more about my life and viewpoints and can get in touch.

About the Disk

You'll find a Windows disk included with this book. This disk contains the Companion Utilities Reference for the *Guide to Oracle8i Features*, an online tool developed by RevealNet, Inc., that gives you point-and-click access to the source code I developed while writing this book. (Many of the code examples are also printed in the book.) I've included this code to give you a jump start on writing your own Oracle8*i* PL/SQL code and to keep you from having to type many pages of PL/SQL statements from printed text.

In addition to the code examples, I've included a trimmed-down version of the PLVtmr package. I use this package in my testing of program performance. This package is part of the RevealNet PL/Vision code library. You can download the free, Lite version of PL/Vision or try out a fully functioned Professional version by visiting *http://www.revealnet.com*. The version of PLVtmr on the companion disk can be installed independently of the rest of PL/Vision.

Throughout the book, disk icons (see the "Conventions Used in This Book" section) indicate that a code example shown or mentioned in the text is included on the disk. The appendix, *What's on the Companion Disk?*, describes how to install the Windows-based Companion Reference. You can run the software in any Microsoft Windows environment (95, 98, NT 4.0). If you are working in a non-Windows environment, you can obtain a compressed file containing the utilities on the disk from the RevealNet PL/SQL Pipeline Archives at *http://www.revealnet.com/plsql-pipeline*.

Conventions Used in This Book

The following conventions are used in this book:

Italic

Used for file and directory names and URLs, and for the first mention of new terms under discussion.

`Constant width`

Used for code examples.

Constant width bold

In some code examples, highlights the statements being discussed.

`Constant width italic`

In some code examples, indicates an element (e.g., a filename) that you supply.

UPPERCASE

In code examples, indicates PL/SQL keywords.

lowercase

In code examples, indicates user-defined items like variables and parameters.

Punctuation

In code examples, enter exactly as shown.

Indentation

In code examples, helps to show structure (but is not required).

-- In code examples, a double hyphen begins a single-line comment, which extends to the end of a line.

/* and */

In code examples, these characters delimit a multiline comment, which can extend from one line to another.

. In code examples and related discussions, a dot qualifies a reference by separating an object name from a component name. For example, dot notation is used to select fields in a record and to specify declarations within a package.

... In code examples, an ellipsis indicates code that's been omitted because it's not relevant to the discussion.

[ ] In syntax descriptions, square brackets enclose optional items.

{ } In syntax descriptions, curly brackets enclose a set of items; you must choose only one of them.

| In syntax descriptions, a vertical bar separates the items enclosed in curly brackets, for example, {IN | OUT | IN OUT}.

The disk icon indicates that the code example described in the text appears on the companion disk.

Indicates a tip, suggestion, or general note. For example, I'll tell you if you need to use a particular Oracle version or if an operation requires certain privileges.

 Indicates a warning or caution. For example, I'll tell you if Oracle does not behave as you'd expect or if a particular operation has a negative impact on performance.

Comments and Questions

Please address comments and questions concerning this book to the publisher:

O'Reilly & Associates, Inc.
101 Morris Street
Sebastopol, CA 95472
800-998-9938 (in the U.S. or Canada)
707-829-0515 (international or local)
707-829-0104 (fax)

You can also send messages electronically. For corrections and amplifications to the book, as well as for copies of the examples, check out O'Reilly & Associates' online catalog at:

http:/www.oreilly.com/catalog/ornewfeatures/

See the ads at the end of the book for information about all of O'Reilly & Associates' online services.

If you have any questions about the disk supplied with this book, contact Reveal-Net at *http://www.revealnet.com.*

As I mentioned, you can also contact me directly at my own web site at *http:// www.StevenFeuerstein.com.*

Acknowledgments

This may be the smallest book I have ever written, but that doesn't mean I didn't need any help getting it done! A number of Oracle professionals took time out of their busy schedules to review various chapters, and I am deeply grateful to each and every one of you for your efforts: Richard Bolz, Darryl Hurley, Dwayne King, Vadim Loevski, Vasanthi Nagareddi, Rudresh J. Rana, Chuck Sisk, Kasu Sista, and

Solomon Yakobson. Bill Pribyl, my coauthor on *Oracle PL/SQL Programming*, read every chapter closely and identified numerous opportunities to improve the text—thanks, Bill! The Oracle PL/SQL development team improved the quality of this book through their feedback and prompt responses to my inquiries; many thanks to Usha Sangam and the other developers out at Oracle HQ who looked over this text: Chandrasekharan Iyer, Neil Le, Kannan Muthukkaruppan, Chris Racicot, Ajay Sethi, and Ian Stocks.

On the O'Reilly side of the aisle, this book was shaped and guided to publication by my friend and editor, Deborah Russell. We've been working together since 1994, and she never fails to impress me with her devotion to the Oracle line at O'Reilly and her insights on how to tighten up and focus a technical book. Steve Abrams of O'Reilly also worked hard to get this book done on time and to support both my writing and training activity.

1999 has been a long, intense year for me (and it sure ain't over yet!). I have been reminded of how important it is to lead a balanced life and to live it fully. Man (this man) does not live by PL/SQL alone. As I begin to cruise through my 40s, publish my fourth full-length text on PL/SQL, and put finishing touches on my fifth (*Oracle PL/SQL Programming: Developer's Workbook*), I thank my wife, Veva Silva, and my children, Chris and Eli, for the continual flow of challenges and happiness into my life.

In this chapter:
- *What's in Oracle8i Release 8.1?*
- *And Then There's Java*
- *New PL/SQL Features Roundup*

1

Oracle8i: A Bounty for PL/SQL Developers

After long delays, Oracle8*i* Release 8.1 went into production in 1999. Oracle8*i*, the "Internet database," is packed with an astounding and intimidating array of powerful new features—and I don't even work for Oracle any more! Hey, I don't have to use exclamation marks to describe all the great things you can do with Oracle8*i* Release 8.1!

Whew. Got that out of my system. Do you ever have trouble separating the marketing from the reality with Oracle Corporation? The name of their latest release brings that issue to the fore like never before. "Oracle8*i* Release 8.1"—what does all that mean? Here is how I see it: "Oracle8*i*"—that's the marketing piece touting the first database for the Internet. "Release 8.1"—now they're talking my language, the actual database version. I started with Oracle 5.1 and have been steadily pleased with the improvements through Oracle6 (quickly, please) and then Oracle7. Oracle 8.0 was a .0 release and, as a result, many, many organizations around the world paid very little attention to it. Now, finally, we have Oracle 8.1 and I expect that many organizations will move relatively quickly to this release level.

What's in Oracle8i Release 8.1?

What do you get with Oracle 8.1? The list is very long and very impressive ("more than 150 new features," says Oracle). Here are some of the features I have heard about:

- The Aurora Java™ Virtual Machine (JVM) right inside the database

- Support for Java stored procedures (JSPs)

- JDeveloper, a Java™ Integrated Development Environment

- *i*FS, the Internet File System (not currently available at the time of publication)

- Support for the Linux operating system

- *inter*Media

- Support for SQLJ and JDBC™ (Java Database Connectivity)

- WebDB

- Autonomous transactions

- Invoker rights model

- Many performance improvements

 Throughout this book, Oracle 8.1 refers to Oracle8*i* Release 8.1, and PL/SQL 8.1 refers to the Oracle8*i* Release 8.1 version of PL/SQL.

The Oracle8*i* documentation has a section titled "Getting to Know Oracle8*i*"; the table of contents for new features is 259 lines long! Is that more than mere mortals can deal with? It sure is more than I can deal with. So I am going to stick with what I know best: PL/SQL. This book focuses almost exclusively on new Oracle8*i* features that have a direct impact on (or are implemented by) the PL/SQL language. As you will see, even if the focus is constrained to PL/SQL, there are many, many new techniques and technologies to learn, absorb, and then leverage in application environments.

And Then There's Java

Before I dive into my feature roundups, allow me to reflect for a moment on the PL/SQL language and its future in the Oracle environment. Why would I feel the need to do this? I can answer with one word—Java.

Contrary to popular belief, I do not hate or fear Java. I hold no animosity for a language that has at least the potential to unseat PL/SQL as the dominant (used to be only) programming language inside the Oracle database. I have begun to study Java and have found that it's very different from PL/SQL and much more powerful.

There is no doubt that we will all need to be proficient enough with both languages to be able to:

- Decide which language is best used to solve a particular problem

- Call Java stored procedures from PL/SQL, and vice versa

So yes, Oracle supports interoperability between these two languages, and we need to be ambidextrous when it comes to "left brain" PL/SQL and "right brain" Java.

The big question or rumor that has floated around the Oracle world lately, though, is a more troubling one: will Oracle simply abandon PL/SQL for Java? Not only would that put me out of business, it would also cause tremendous upheaval in the Oracle customer world. It is simply not going to happen, and the best way to demonstrate that fact is to see the forward motion in the PL/SQL language.

When object technology was first introduced in the Oracle database and in PL/SQL (in Oracle 8.0), a debate raged within Oracle headquarters: should PL/SQL become a full-fledged object-oriented language? Should it remain focused on what it does best? Now with the incorporation of Java into the Oracle database, this debate has been resolved. PL/SQL is the premier database programming language (specific to Oracle but superior to the others, such as Informix's 4GL and Sybase/ Microsoft's Transact-SQL), as demonstrated by the adoption of many PL/SQL features and syntax into the ANSI standards. Oracle will focus its energies on maintaining that position.

What we see in Oracle 8.1 and what we will continue to see in future releases is a permanent revolution in the PL/SQL language, with the goals of making it ever easier to use, more efficient, and more functional. Hey, they are even exploring the possibility of compiling PL/SQL programs! Now that would be a turbo-charged PL/SQL. Of course, the proof is in the programming. What have they done for us lately? What can we do with PL/SQL in 8.1 that we couldn't do before? Join me on a journey into the depths of Oracle8*i* Release 8.1 to answer these questions.

New PL/SQL Features Roundup

Even if I stick to the narrow course of exploring only those PL/SQL-related new features of Oracle8*i*, I can still find *lots* to talk about. This section previews the chapters of the book and introduces you to the main PL/SQL enhancements in this release of Oracle.

Autonomous Transactions (Chapter 2)

One long-standing request from PL/SQL developers has been to have the ability to execute and then save or cancel certain Data Manipulation Language (DML) statements (INSERT, UPDATE, DELETE) without affecting the overall session's transaction. You can now do this with *autonomous transactions*.

Where would you find autonomous transactions useful in your applications? Here are some ideas:

Logging mechanism
> This is the classic example of the need for an autonomous transaction. You need to log error information in a database table, but don't want that log entry to be a part of the logical transaction.

Commits or rollbacks in your database triggers
> Finally! If you define a trigger as an autonomous transaction, then you can commit and/or roll back in that code.

Retry counter
> Autonomous transactions can help you keep track of how many times a user tries to connect to a database or get access to a resource (you'll reject access after a certain number of attempts).

Software usage meter
> A similar type of situation is when you want to track how often a program is called during an application session. In fact, autonomous transactions are helpful in meeting any application requirement that calls for persistently storing a state (how many times did Joe try to update the salary column?).

Reusable application components
> You are building an Internet application. You want to combine components from many different vendors and layers. They need to interact in certain well-defined ways. If when one component commits, it affects all other aspects of your application, it will not function well in this environment.

When you define a PL/SQL block (anonymous block, procedure, function, packaged procedure, packaged function, database trigger) as an autonomous transaction, you isolate the DML in that block from the rest of your session. That block becomes an independent transaction that is started by another transaction, referred to as the *main transaction*. Within the autonomous transaction block, the main transaction is suspended. You perform your SQL operations, commit or roll back those operations, and then resume the main transaction.

There isn't much involved in defining a PL/SQL block as an autonomous transaction. You simply include the following statement in your declaration section:

```
PRAGMA AUTONOMOUS_TRANSACTION;
```

Here is a very simple logging mechanism relying on the autonomous transaction feature to save changes to the log without affecting the rest of the session's transaction:

```
PROCEDURE write_log (
   code IN INTEGER, text IN VARCHAR2)
```

```
IS
    PRAGMA AUTONOMOUS_TRANSACTION;
BEGIN
    INSERT INTO log VALUES (
        code, text,
        USER, SYSDATE
        );
    COMMIT:
END;
```

Of course, there are all sorts of rules and some restrictions to be aware of; see Chapter 2, *Choose Your Transaction!*, for all the details.

Invoker Rights (Chapter 3)

Back in the "old days" of Oracle7 and Oracle 8.0, whenever you executed a stored program, it executed under the authority of the owner of that program. This was not a big deal if your entire application—code, data, and users—worked out of the same Oracle account. That scenario probably fit about 0.5% of all Oracle shops. It proved to be a real pain in the neck for the other 99.5%, though, because usually code was stored in one schema and then shared through GRANT EXECUTE statements with other users (directly or through roles).

For one thing, that centralized, stored code would not automatically apply the privileges of a user (also known as an *invoker*) to the code's objects. The user might not have had DELETE privileges on a table, but the stored code did, so delete away! Now, in some circumstances, that is just how you wanted it to work. In others, particularly when you were executing programs relying on the DBMS_SQL (dynamic SQL) package, awesome complications could ensue.

In Oracle 8.1, PL/SQL has now been enhanced so that at the time of compilation, you can decide whether a program (or all programs in a package) should run under the authority of the definer (the only choice in Oracle 8.0 and below) or of the invoker of that program.

The syntax to support this feature is simple enough. Here is a generic "run DDL" engine that relies on the new native dynamic SQL statement EXECUTE IMMEDIATE:

```
CREATE OR REPLACE PROCEDURE runddl (ddl_in in VARCHAR2)
    AUTHID CURRENT_USER
IS
BEGIN
    EXECUTE IMMEDIATE ddl_in;
END;
/
```

The AUTHID CURRENT_USER clause before the IS keyword indicates that when runddl executes, it should run under the authority of the invoker, or "current user," not the authority of the definer.

Native Dynamic SQL (Chapter 4)

Ever since Oracle 7.1, we PL/SQL developers have been able to use the built-in DBMS_SQL package to execute dynamic SQL and PL/SQL. This means that at run-time you can construct the query, a DELETE or CREATE TABLE, or even a PL/SQL block, as a string—and then execute it. Dynamic SQL comes in extremely handy when you are building ad hoc query systems, when you need to execute Data Definition Language (DDL) inside PL/SQL, and just generally when you don't know in advance exactly what you need to do or what the user will want to do. Dynamic SQL is a frequent requirement in Web-based applications.

But there are some problems with DBMS_SQL:

- It is a very complicated package.

- It has a number of restrictions (such as not recognizing and being able to work with new Oracle8 datatypes).

- It is relatively slow.

So our dear friends at PL/SQL Central in Redwood Shores took pity on us all and reimplemented dynamic SQL directly in the PL/SQL language itself. This is called *native dynamic SQL* (NDS).

In my latest book on PL/SQL, *Oracle Built-in Packages* (O'Reilly & Associates, coauthored with John Beresniewicz and Charles Dye), I spent about 100 pages explaining dynamic SQL and the DBMS_SQL package. While NDS makes it much easier to get your dynamic job done, there is still a whole lot to say on this subject. Let's just compare a DBMS_SQL and NDS implementation of a program that displays all the employees for the specified and dynamic WHERE clause.

The DBMS_SQL implementation:

```
CREATE OR REPLACE PROCEDURE showemps (
   where_in IN VARCHAR2 := NULL)
IS
   cur INTEGER := DBMS_SQL.OPEN_CURSOR;
   rec employee%ROWTYPE;
   fdbk INTEGER;
BEGIN
   DBMS_SQL.PARSE
     (cur,
      'SELECT employee_id, last_name
         FROM employee
        WHERE ' || NVL (where_in, '1=1'),
      DBMS_SQL.NATIVE);
   DBMS_SQL.DEFINE_COLUMN (cur, 1, 1);
   DBMS_SQL.DEFINE_COLUMN (cur, 2, user, 30);
   fdbk := DBMS_SQL.EXECUTE (cur);
   LOOP
      /* Fetch next row. Exit when done. */
```

```
            EXIT WHEN DBMS_SQL.FETCH_ROWS (cur) = 0;
            DBMS_SQL.COLUMN_VALUE (cur, 1, rec.employee_id);
            DBMS_SQL.COLUMN_VALUE (cur, 2, rec.last_name);
            DBMS_OUTPUT.PUT_LINE (
               TO_CHAR (rec.employee_id) || '=' ||
               rec.last_name);
         END LOOP;
         DBMS_SQL.CLOSE_CURSOR (cur);
      END;
      /
```

And now the NDS implementation:

```
CREATE OR REPLACE PROCEDURE showemps (
   where_in IN VARCHAR2 := NULL)
IS
   TYPE cv_typ IS REF CURSOR;
   cv cv_typ;
   v_id employee.employee_id%TYPE;
   v_nm employee.last_name%TYPE;
BEGIN
   OPEN cv FOR
      'SELECT employee_id, last_name
        FROM employee
        WHERE ' || NVL (where_in, '1=1');
   LOOP
      FETCH cv INTO v_id, v_nm;
      EXIT WHEN cv%NOTFOUND;
      DBMS_OUTPUT.PUT_LINE (TO_CHAR (v_id) || '=' || v_nm);
   END LOOP;
   CLOSE cv;
END;
/
```

I know which one I would prefer. I'll be looking at native dynamic SQL in much more detail in Chapter 4, *Native Dynamic SQL in Oracle8i*. And if you are an expert at DBMS_SQL and feel tears coming to your eyes about all that wasted intellectual property, take heart in these factoids:

- No one has invested more time and typed words in DBMS_SQL than yours truly.

- DBMS_SQL is not completely obsolete. There are still times when you will want to use it instead of NDS, and there are things you can do with DBMS_SQL that are not yet possible with NDS.

Bulk Binds and Collects (Chapter 5)

One of the major priorities of the PL/SQL development team is to speed up the performance of their language. This effort cannot come a moment too soon. We developers have been complaining about runtime performance for years, and finally the developers are responding (though, to be brutally honest, it seems to me that the intensive tuning steps taken in Oracle 8.0 were motivated at least partly by the need to make PL/SQL fast enough to support object types).

One area of improvement concerns the execution of "bulk" DML inside PL/SQL. Consider, for example, the following code that deletes each employee identified by the employee number found in the nested table list:

```
CREATE TYPE empnos_list_t IS VARRARY(100) OF NUMBER;
CREATE OR REPLACE del_emps (list_in IN empnos_list_t)
IS
BEGIN
   FOR listnum IN list_in.FIRST.. list_in.LAST
   LOOP
      DELETE FROM emp WHERE empno = list_in (listnum);
   END LOOP;
END;
```

Easy to write, easy to read. But what about performance? Whenever this program issues its DELETE, a *context switch* takes place from PL/SQL to SQL to execute that command. If there are 100 elements in the list, there are 100 switches, with corresponding performance degradation.

Recognizing this common requirement and its overhead, Oracle now offers a *bulk bind* variation on the FOR loop—the FORALL statement. With this statement, you can recode the del_emps procedure as follows:

```
CREATE OR REPLACE del_emps (list_in IN empnos_list_t)
IS
BEGIN
   FORALL listnum IN list_in.FIRST.. list_in.LAST
   LOOP
      DELETE FROM emp WHERE empno = list_in (listnum);
 END;
```

Now there will be just *one* context switch: all of the DELETE operations will be bundled into a single bulk operation and passed to the SQL layer together.

In addition to the FORALL bulk DML operator, Oracle 8.1 also offers the BULK COLLECT variation on the INTO clause of an implicit query. This operation allows you to retrieve multiple rows in a single context switch.

New Trigger Capabilities (Chapter 6)

Oracle8*i* expands significantly the use of triggers to administer a database and "publish" information about events taking place within the database. By employing database triggers on the newly defined system events and using Oracle Advanced Queuing within those triggers, you can take advantage of the publish/subscribe capabilities of Oracle8*i*.

The database event publication feature allows applications to subscribe to database events just as they subscribe to messages from other applications. The trigger syntax is extended to support system and other data events on database or schema. Trigger syntax also supports a CALL to a procedure as the trigger body.

You can now enable the publication of (i.e., define a programmatic trigger on) the following actions:

- DML statements (DELETE, INSERT, and UPDATE)

- DDL events (e.g., CREATE, DROP, and ALTER)

- Database events (SERVERERROR, LOGON, LOGOFF, STARTUP, and SHUT-DOWN)

These are the new trigger features available in Oracle8*i*:

Triggers on nested table columns
> The CAST. . .MULTISET operation allows you to trigger activity when only an attribute in a nested table column is modified.

Database-level event triggers
> You can now define triggers to respond to such system events as LOGON, DATABASE SHUTDOWN, and even SERVERERROR.

Schema-level event triggers
> You can now define triggers to respond to such user- or schema-level events as CREATE, DROP, and ALTER.

New and Enhanced Built-in Packages (Chapter 7)

Oracle has added a number of new built-in packages in Oracle8*i*. Many of them are for fairly specialized purposes, such as the replication facility or online analytical processing (OLAP)/data warehouse optimization, but a number of the packages, including those listed here, will come in very handy for database administrators (DBAs) and PL/SQL developers:

DBMS_JAVA
> Gives you the ability to modify the behavior of the Aurora Java Virtual Machine (JVM) in Oracle. You can enable output (meaning that System.out. println will act like DBMS_OUTPUT.PUT_LINE), set compiler and debugger options, and more.

DBMS_PROFILER
> Accesses performance and code coverage analysis of your PL/SQL application.

DBMS_RLS
> Offers an interface to the fine-grained access control administrative features of Oracle8*i*; it is only available with the Enterprise Edition.

DBMS_TRACE

Allows PL/SQL developers to trace the execution of stored PL/SQL functions, procedures, and exceptions.

UTL_COLL

Allows PL/SQL programs to use collection locators in order to perform queries and updates.

Oracle has also enhanced a number of packages, including DBMS_UTILITY, DBMS_AQ, and DBMS_LOB.

Chapter 7, *New and Enhanced Built-in Packages in Oracle8i,* introduces you to a subset of the capabilities of these packages. Comprehensive, reference-oriented coverage of these packages will be included in the second edition of *Oracle Built-in Packages* (O'Reilly & Associates, expected in 2000).

Fine-Grained Access Control (Chapter 8)

Fine-grained access control (FGAC) is a new feature in Oracle8*i* that allows you to implement security policies with functions and then use those security policies to implement row-level security on tables or views. The database server automatically enforces security policies, no matter how the data is accessed—through SQL*Plus or the Internet, as an ad hoc query, or as an update processed through an Oracle Forms application.

What, you might ask, is a security policy? Consider the following very simple scenario (I'll expand upon this scenario in Chapter 8, *Deploying Fine-Grained Access Control*). Suppose that I have tables of hospital patients and their doctors defined as follows:

```
CREATE TABLE patient (
    patient_id NUMBER,
    name VARCHAR2(100),
    dob DATE,
    doctor_id INTEGER
    );

CREATE TABLE doctor (
    doctor_id NUMBER,
    name VARCHAR2(100)
    );
```

Now suppose that I want to let a doctor see only her patients when she issues a query against the table. More than that, I don't want to let doctors modify patient records unless they are that doctor's patients. You could achieve much of what is needed through the creation of a set of views, but wouldn't it be grand if you could just let any doctor connect to her schema in Oracle and say:

```
SELECT * FROM patient;
```

and see only her patients? In other words, hide all the rules needed to enforce the appropriate privacy and security rules (the *policy*) so that the policy is transparent to users of the data structures. That's what the fine-grained access control feature does for you!

With Oracle8*i*'s fine-grained access control, also known as *row-level security*, you can apply different policies to SELECT, INSERT, UPDATE, and DELETE, and use security policies only where you need them (for example, on salary information). You can also design and enforce more than one policy for a table, and can even construct layers of policies (one policy building on top of an existing policy) to handle complex situations.

Calling Java from PL/SQL (Chapter 9)

Java is a very powerful language, much more robust in many ways than PL/SQL. Java also offers hundreds of classes that provide clean, easy-to-use application programming interfaces (APIs) to a wide range of functionality.

In Oracle8*i*, Oracle includes a new product called JServer. JServer consists of the following elements:

- Oracle's Java Virtual Machine, called Aurora, the supporting runtime environment, and Java class libraries

- Tight integration with PL/SQL and Oracle relational database management system (RDBMS) functionality

- An Object Request Broker (the Aurora/ORB) and Enterprise JavaBeans™ (EJB)

- The JServer Accelerator (native compiler); available in the 8.1.6 Enterprise Edition only

The Aurora JVM executes Java methods (also known as Java stored procedures, or JSPs) and classes if they are stored in the database itself. This means that even if you are a full-time Oracle PL/SQL developer, you can take advantage of the wonderful world of Java to build your applications.

Java in the Oracle database is a big topic; Java programming all by itself is an even bigger topic. Complete treatment of either is outside the scope of this book. Chapter 9, *Calling Java from PL/SQL*, focuses on the exciting new feature of Oracle8*i* that allows a developer to call Java stored procedures from within PL/SQL.

Miscellaneous New Features and Performance Improvements (Chapter 10)

By the time you get to Chapter 10, *More Goodies for Oracle8i PL/SQL Developers*, you will have learned about a wide range of significant new capabilities in PL/SQL.

Yet there is still more! This chapter covers some other features that improve either the performance or usability of PL/SQL in Oracle8*i*. I'll also review transparent improvements, that is, changes to the language that improve the performance or behavior of your PL/SQL-based applications without necessitating any modifications to your code.

Major topics include the following:

The NOCOPY compiler hint
> You can avoid the overhead of copying IN OUT parameter values with this enhancement. When you are working with large collections and records, NOCOPY can have a noticeable impact on program performance.

Calling PL/SQL functions from SQL
> Oracle8*i* offers some big relief for PL/SQL developers when it comes to calling their own functions: you no longer have to use the RESTRICT_REFERENCES pragma! Oracle8*i* also offers two new keywords, DETERMINISTIC and PARALLEL_ENABLE, to help you integrate your PL/SQL, C, and Java code into all aspects of your database.

SQL99 compliance
> Oracle8*i* adds or expands the TRIM and CAST operators to better support the SQL99 standard.

SQL operations on collections
> Oracle8*i* makes it even easier to integrate PL/SQL (transient) collections into SQL statements.

2

Choose Your Transaction!

One of the more exciting new features of Oracle8*i* Release 8.1's version of PL/SQL is a capability called *autonomous transactions*. In this chapter, I'll discuss several ways you can put this feature to use in your application development environment.

Transaction Management in PL/SQL

PL/SQL is tightly integrated with the Oracle RDBMS; that is, after all, why it is called "PL/SQL"—procedural language extensions to SQL. When you perform operations in the database, you do so within the context of a *transaction*, a series of one or more SQL statements that perform a logical unit of work. A transaction can have associated with it a variety of locks on resources (rows of data, program units, etc.). These locks define the *context* of the transaction; the context also contains the actual data.

To appreciate transactions in Oracle, consider the "ACID" principle: a transaction has atomicity, consistency, isolation, and durability, which are defined as follows:

Atomic
> A transaction's changes to a state are atomic: either they all happen or none happens.

Consistent
> A transaction is a correct transformation of state. The actions taken as a group do not violate any integrity constraints associated with that state.

Isolated

Even though many transactions may be executing concurrently, from any given transaction's point of view, other transactions appear to have executed before or after its execution.

Durable

Once a transaction completes successfully, the changes to the state are made permanent, and they survive any subsequent failures.

A transaction can either be saved by performing a COMMIT or erased by requesting a ROLLBACK. In either case, the affected locks on resources are released (a ROLLBACK TO might only release some of the locks). The session can then start a new transaction.

Before the release of PL/SQL 8.1, each Oracle session could have at most one active transaction at a given time. In other words, any and all changes made in your session had to be either saved or erased in their entirety. This restriction has long been considered a drawback in the PL/SQL world. Developers have requested the ability to execute and save or cancel certain DML statements (INSERT, UPDATE, DELETE) without affecting the overall session's transaction.

You can now accomplish this goal with the autonomous transaction feature of PL/SQL 8.1. When you define a PL/SQL block (anonymous block, procedure, function, packaged procedure, packaged function, database trigger) as an autonomous transaction, you isolate the DML in that block from the caller's transaction context. That block becomes an independent transaction that is started by another transaction, referred to as the *main transaction.*

Within the autonomous transaction block, the main transaction is suspended. You perform your SQL operations, commit or roll back those operations, and then resume the main transaction. This flow of transaction control is illustrated in Figure 2-1.

Defining Autonomous Transactions

There isn't much involved in defining a PL/SQL block as an autonomous transaction. You simply include the following statement in your declaration section:

```
PRAGMA AUTONOMOUS_TRANSACTION;
```

The pragma instructs the PL/SQL compiler to establish a PL/SQL block as autonomous or independent. For the purposes of the autonomous transaction, a PL/SQL block can be any of the following:

- Top-level (but not nested) anonymous PL/SQL blocks

- Functions and procedures, defined either in a package or as standalone programs

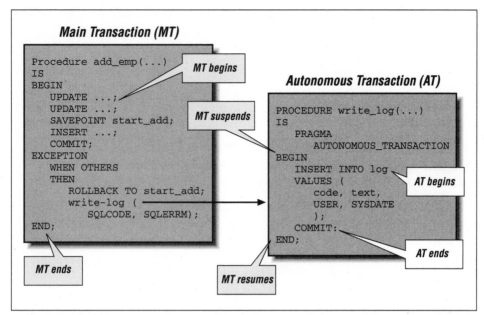

Figure 2-1. Flow of transaction control between main, nested, and autonomous transactions

- Methods (functions and procedures) of a SQL object type
- Database triggers

You can put the autonomous transaction pragma anywhere in the declaration section of your PL/SQL block. You would probably be best off, however, placing it before any data structure declarations. That way, anyone reading your code will immediately identify the program as an autonomous transaction.

This pragma is the only syntax change made to PL/SQL to support autonomous transactions. COMMIT, ROLLBACK, the DML statements—all the rest is as it was before. However, these statements have a different scope of impact and visibility (discussed later in this chapter) when executed within an autonomous transaction, and you will *have* to include a COMMIT or ROLLBACK in your program.

Let's look at a simple example. Suppose you are responsible for building a database to keep track of war criminals for the International Court of Justice. You create a package called wcpkg to keep track of alleged war criminals. One of the programs in the package registers a new criminal. You always want that register program to save its changes, even if the calling program hasn't yet issued a COMMIT. These characters are, after all, fairly slippery and you don't want them to get away.

The package specification holds no surprises; the transaction type is not evident here:

```
CREATE PACKAGE wcpkg AS
   ...
   PROCEDURE register (
      culprit IN VARCHAR2, event IN VARCHAR2);
END wcpkg;
/
```

The package body, however, contains that new and wonderful pragma:

```
CREATE PACKAGE BODY wcpkg AS
   ...
   PROCEDURE register (
      culprit IN VARCHAR2, event IN VARCHAR2)
   IS
      PRAGMA AUTONOMOUS_TRANSACTION;
   BEGIN
      INSERT INTO war_criminal (name, activity)
         VALUES (culprit, event);
      COMMIT;
   END;
END wcpkg;
/
```

Now when I call wcpkg.register, I am assured that my changes have been duly recorded:

```
BEGIN
   wcpkg.register ('Kissinger', 'Secret Bombing of Cambodia');
```

When to Use Autonomous Transactions

Where would you find autonomous transactions useful in your applications? First, let's reinforce the general principle: you will want to define your program module as an autonomous transaction whenever you want to *isolate* the changes made in that module from the caller's transaction context.

Here are some specific ideas:

Logging mechanism
   On the one hand, you need to log an error to your database log table. On the other hand, you need to roll back your core transaction because of the error. And you don't want to roll back over other log entries. What's a person to do? Go autonomous!

Commits and rollbacks in your database triggers
   If you define a trigger as an autonomous transaction, then you can commit and/or roll back in that code. Developers have been asking for this capability for a long time.

Retry counter

> Suppose that you want to let a user try to get access to a resource N times before an outright rejection; you also want to keep track of attempts between connections to the database. This persistence requires a COMMIT, but one that should remain independent of the transaction.

Software usage meter

> You want to keep track of how often a program is called during an application session. This information is not dependent on, and cannot affect, the transaction being processed in the application.

Reusable application components

> This usage goes to the heart of the value of autonomous transactions. As we move more thoroughly into the dispersed, multilayered world of the Internet, it becomes ever more important to be able to offer standalone units of work (also known as *cartridges*) that get their job done without any side effects on the calling environment. Autonomous transactions will play a crucial role in this area.

Before we take a look at how you might use autonomous transactions for these scenarios, let's get a clearer picture about what you can and cannot do with autonomous transactions.

Another Tool in the Toolbox

As Oracle database technology matures and broadens, we can sometimes (often?) feel overwhelmed by all of its features, its opportunities, and its increasing sophistication and complexity. How can we keep up with it all? Well, perhaps we don't *have* to keep up with it all. Perhaps we can take a different approach: develop a basic familiarity with the latest and greatest stuff.

Recognize this feature or that as just another potential tool you can use to implement your applications. Learn to distill out from the technobabble of daily life the core advantages of a feature. Then, when you encounter a particular requirement, you can evaluate which of all these tools can best be applied to come up with an optimal solution.

Autonomous transactions are not going to be useful or applicable in every one (or even very many) of your programs. The autonomous transaction feature is, however, a very handy new tool in the PL/SQL developer's toolbox. Keep it in mind, and pull it out as needed.

Rules and Restrictions

While it is certainly very easy to add the autonomous transaction pragma to your code, there are some rules and restrictions on the use of this feature. You can only make a top-level anonymous block an autonomous transaction. This will work:

```
DECLARE
    PRAGMA AUTONOMOUS_TRANSACTION;
    myempno NUMBER;
BEGIN
    INSERT INTO emp VALUES (myempno, ...);
    COMMIT;
END;
/
```

whereas this construction:

```
DECLARE
    myempno NUMBER;
BEGIN
    DECLARE
        PRAGMA AUTONOMOUS_TRANSACTION;
    BEGIN
        INSERT INTO emp VALUES (myempno, ...);
        COMMIT;
    END;
END;
/
```

results in this error:

```
PLS-00710: PRAGMA AUTONOMOUS_TRANSACTION cannot be declared here
```

Just to expand your vision of what is possible, you can now use COMMIT and ROLLBACK inside your database triggers. These actions will *not* affect the transaction that caused the database trigger to fire, of course. See the section "Using Autonomous Transactions in a Database Trigger," later in this chapter, for more details on what you can accomplish.

If an autonomous transaction attempts to access a resource held by the main transaction (which has been suspended until the autonomous routine exits), you can cause a deadlock to occur in your program. Here is a simple example to demonstrate the problem. I create a procedure to perform an update, and then call it after having already updated all rows:

```
/* Filename on companion disk: autondlock.sql*/
CREATE OR REPLACE PROCEDURE
    update_salary (dept_in IN NUMBER)
IS
    PRAGMA AUTONOMOUS_TRANSACTION;

    CURSOR myemps IS
```

```
        SELECT empno FROM emp
         WHERE deptno = dept_in
            FOR UPDATE NOWAIT;
BEGIN
   FOR rec IN myemps
   LOOP
      UPDATE emp SET sal = sal * 2
       WHERE empno = rec.empno;
   END LOOP;
   COMMIT;
END;
/

BEGIN
   UPDATE emp SET sal = sal * 2;
   update_salary (10);
END;
/
```

The results are not pretty:

```
ERROR at line 1:
ORA-00054: resource busy and acquire with NOWAIT specified
```

You cannot mark all subprograms in a package (or all methods in an object type) as autonomous with a single PRAGMA declaration. You must indicate autonomous transactions explicitly in each program. For example, the following package specification is invalid:

```
CREATE PACKAGE warcrimes_pkg
AS
   PRAGMA AUTONOMOUS_TRANSACTION;

   PROCEDURE register (
      culprit IN VARCHAR2, event IN VARCHAR2);
END warcrimes_pkg;
/
```

One consequence of this rule is that you cannot tell by looking at the package specification which, if any, programs will run as autonomous transactions.

To exit without errors from an autonomous transaction program, you must perform an explicit commit or rollback. If the program (or any program called by it) has transactions pending, the runtime engine will raise an exception—and then it will roll back those uncommitted transactions.

Suppose, for example, that my job in life is to take over failing companies and make them profitable by firing lots of employees. I would then want to carry around this handy procedure in my software toolbox:

```
CREATE OR REPLACE PROCEDURE fire_em_all
IS
   PRAGMA AUTONOMOUS_TRANSACTION;
```

```
BEGIN
    DELETE FROM emp;
END;
/
```

I want to make the program an autonomous transaction because I don't want any-one to back out the changes when I am not looking. Unfortunately, I forget to explicitly commit. As a result, when I run this procedure, I get the following error:

```
SQL> exec fire_em_all
*
ERROR at line 1
ORA-06519: active autonomous transaction detected and rolled back
```

The COMMIT and ROLLBACK statements end the active autonomous transaction; they do not, however, force the termination of the autonomous routine. You can, in fact, have multiple COMMIT and/or ROLLBACK statements inside your autono-mous block.

An autonomous block is one in which autonomous transactions are expected. Zero, one, or more autonomous transactions can be exe-cuted within an autonomous block.

You can roll back only to savepoints marked in the current transaction. When you are in an autonomous transaction, therefore, you cannot roll back to a savepoint set in the main transaction. If you try to do so, the runtime engine will raise this exception:

```
ORA-01086: savepoint 'your savepoint' never established
```

The TRANSACTIONS parameter in the Oracle initialization file (*INIT.ORA*) specifies the maximum number of transactions allowed concurrently in a session. If you use autonomous transactions (which run concurrently with the main transaction), you might exceed this number—and raise an exception—unless you raise the TRANS-ACTIONS value. This is the error you will get if you encounter this problem:

```
ORA-01574: maximum number of concurrent transactions exceeded
```

The default value for TRANSACTIONS in Oracle8*i* is 75.

Using Autonomous Transactions from Within SQL

Ever since Oracle 7.3, you have been able to call your own functions from within SQL—provided that you follow a variety of rules. The main one is this: you are not allowed to update the database. And you certainly can't save or cancel changes from within the function.

With the autonomous transaction feature, however, the picture changes a good deal. An autonomous transaction program *never* violates the two database-related purity levels, RNDS (reads no database state) and WNDS (writes no database state), even if that program actually does read from or write to the database. How can this be? Because those purity levels or constraints apply to the SQL statement (which, in this case, is the main transaction), yet an autonomous transaction's DML actions never affect the main transaction.

So as long as you define a program to be an autonomous transaction, you can also call it directly or indirectly in a SQL statement. Of course, if your program cannot assert another purity level, such as WNPS (writes no package state), you may be restricted from calling that program in certain parts of the SQL statement, such as the WHERE clause.

As an example, suppose that I want to keep a trace of all the rows that have been touched by a query. I create this table:

```
/* Filename on companion disk: trcfunc.sf */
CREATE TABLE query_trace (
    table_name VARCHAR2(30),
    rowid_info ROWID,
    queried_by VARCHAR2(30),
    queried_at DATE
    );
```

I then create this simple function to perform the audit:

```
CREATE OR REPLACE FUNCTION traceit (
    tab IN VARCHAR2,
    rowid_in IN ROWID)
    RETURN INTEGER
IS
BEGIN
    INSERT INTO query_trace VALUES (tab, rowid_in, USER, SYSDATE);
    RETURN 0;
END;
/
```

When I try to use this function inside a query, I get the expected error:

```
SQL> select ename, traceit ('emp', rowid) from emp;
                    *
ERROR at line 1:
ORA-14551: cannot perform a DML operation inside a query
```

However, if I now transform traceit into an autonomous transaction by adding the pragma (and committing my results *before* the RETURN statement!), the results are very different. My query works, and the query_trace table is filled:

```
SQL> SELECT ename, traceit ('emp', ROWID)
  2    FROM emp;
```

```
ENAME        TRACEIT('EMP',ROWID)
----------   --------------------
KING                      0
...
MILLER                    0
14 rows selected.
SQL>
SQL> SELECT table_name, rowid_info, queried_by,
  2          TO_CHAR (queried_at, 'HH:MI:SS') queried_at
  3       FROM query_trace;
TABLE_NAME ROWID_INFO          QUERIED_BY QUERIED_AT
---------- ------------------- ---------- ----------
emp        AAADEPAACAAAAg0AAA  SCOTT       05:32:54
...
emp        AAADEPAACAAAAg0AAN  SCOTT       05:36:50
```

You have other options when it comes to tracing queries: you can write to the
screen with the DBMS_OUTPUT built-in package or send information to a pipe
with DBMS_PIPE. Now that autonomous transactions are available, if you do want
to send information to a database table (or delete rows or update data, etc.), you
can take that route instead, but be sure to analyze carefully the overhead of this
approach.

Transaction Visibility

The default behavior of autonomous transactions is that once a COMMIT or ROLL-
BACK occurs in the autonomous transaction, those changes are visible immediately in the main transaction. But what if you want to *hide* those changes from the
main transaction? You want them saved or erased—no question about that—but
that information should not be available to the main transaction.

Oracle offers a SET TRANSACTION statement option to achieve this effect.

```
SET TRANSACTION ISOLATION LEVEL SERIALIZABLE;
```

The default isolation level is READ COMMITTED, which means that as soon as
changes are committed, they are visible to the main transaction.

As is usually the case with the SET TRANSACTION statement, you must call it
before you initiate your transactions (i.e., issue any SQL statements); in addition,
the setting affects your entire session, not just the current program. The following
script demonstrates the SERIALIZABLE isolation level at work (the *autonserial.sql*
file will let you run these steps yourself).

First, I create my autonomous transaction procedure:

```
/* Filename on companion disk: autonserial.sql */
CREATE OR REPLACE PROCEDURE fire_em_all
IS
   PRAGMA AUTONOMOUS_TRANSACTION;
BEGIN
   DELETE FROM emp2;
```

```
        COMMIT;
    END;
    /
```

I run a script that sets the isolation level to SERIALIZABLE, then display the number of rows that appear in the emp2 table at the following times:

- Before I call fire_em_all

- After I call fire_em_all but before the main transaction is committed or rolled back

- After I commit in the main transaction, here is the script I run:

```
DECLARE
    PROCEDURE showcount (str VARCHAR2) IS
        num INTEGER;
    BEGIN
        SELECT COUNT(*) INTO num FROM emp2;
        DBMS_OUTPUT.PUT_LINE (str || ' ' || num);
    END;
BEGIN
    SET TRANSACTION ISOLATION LEVEL SERIALIZABLE;
    showcount ('Before isolated AT delete');
    fire_em_all;
    showcount ('After isolated AT delete');
    COMMIT;
    showcount ('After MT commit');
END;
/
```

Here is the output from running the script:

```
Before isolated AT delete 14
After isolated AT delete 14
After MT commit 0
```

Examples

This section provides some complete examples of where you might use autonomous transactions in your applications.

Building an Autonomous Logging Mechanism

A very common requirement in applications is to keep a log of errors that occur during transaction processing. The most convenient repository for this log is a database table; with a table, all the information is retained in the database and you can use SQL to retrieve and analyze the log.

One problem with a database table log, however, is that entries in the log become a part of your transaction. If you perform (or have performed to you) a ROLLBACK, you can easily erase your log. How frustrating! Now, it is true that you can get fancy and use savepoints to preserve your log entries while cleaning up your transaction, but that approach is not only fancy, it is complicated. With autonomous transactions, however, logging becomes simpler, more manageable, and less error prone.

Suppose I have a log table defined as follows:

```
/* Filename on companion disk: log81.pkg */
CREATE TABLE log81tab (
    code INTEGER,
    text VARCHAR2(4000),
    created_on DATE,
    created_by VARCHAR2(100),
    changed_on DATE,
    changed_by VARCHAR2(100),
    machine VARCHAR2(100),
    program VARCHAR2(100)
    );
```

I can use it to store errors (SQLCODE and SQLERRM) that have occurred, or even use it for non-error-related logging. The machine and program columns record information available from the virtual V$SESSION table, as you will see.

So I have my table. Now, how should I write to my log? Here's what you should *not* do:

```
EXCEPTION
    WHEN OTHERS
    THEN
        v_code := SQLCODE;
        v_msg := SQLERRM;
        INSERT INTO log81tab VALUES (
            v_code, v_msg, SYSDATE, USER, SYSDATE, USER, NULL, NULL);
END;
```

In other words, never expose your underlying logging mechanism by explicitly inserting into it in your exception sections and other locations. Instead, you should build a layer of code around the table (this is known as *encapsulation*). Why do this? Two reasons:

- If you ever change your table's structure, all those uses of the log table will not be disrupted.

- People will be able to use the log table in a much easier, more consistent manner.

So here is my very simple logging package. It consists of two procedures:

```
CREATE OR REPLACE PACKAGE log81
IS
    PROCEDURE putline (
        code_in IN INTEGER,
```

```
        text_in IN VARCHAR2
        );

    PROCEDURE saveline (
        code_in IN INTEGER,
        text_in IN VARCHAR2
        );
END;
/
```

What is the difference between putline and saveline? The log81.saveline procedure (as you will see in the package body) is an autonomous transaction routine,
whereas log81.putline simply performs the insert. Here is the package body:

```
/* Filename on companion disk: log81.pkg */
CREATE OR REPLACE PACKAGE BODY log81
IS
    CURSOR sess IS
        SELECT MACHINE, PROGRAM
          FROM V$SESSION
         WHERE AUDSID = USERENV('SESSIONID');
    rec sess%ROWTYPE;

    PROCEDURE putline (
        code_in IN INTEGER,
        text_in IN VARCHAR2
        )
    IS
    BEGIN
        INSERT INTO log81tab
            VALUES (
                code_in,
                text_in,
                SYSDATE,
                USER,
                SYSDATE,
                USER,
                rec.machine,
                rec.program
            );
    END;

    PROCEDURE saveline (
        code_in IN INTEGER,
        text_in IN VARCHAR2
        )
    IS
        PRAGMA AUTONOMOUS_TRANSACTION;
    BEGIN
        putline (code_in, text_in);
        COMMIT;
    EXCEPTION WHEN OTHERS THEN ROLLBACK;
    END;
BEGIN
```

```
     OPEN sess; FETCH sess INTO rec; CLOSE sess;
END;
/
```

Here are some comments on this implementation that you might find helpful:

- I obtain some useful information from V$SESSION when the package is initialized (the values are not going to change during my session, so I should only query it once) and incorporate that into the log.

- The putline procedure performs the straight insert. You would probably want to add some exception handling to this program if you applied this idea in your production application.

- The saveline procedure calls the putline procedure (I don't want any redundant code), but does so from within the context of an autonomous transaction.

With this package in place, my error handler shown earlier can be as simple as this:

```
EXCEPTION
   WHEN OTHERS
   THEN
      log81.saveline (SQLCODE, SQLERRM);
END;
```

No muss, no fuss; developers don't have to concern themselves with the structure of the log table. They don't even have to know they are writing to a database table. And because I have used an autonomous transaction, they can rest assured that no matter what happens in their application, the log entry has been saved.

Using Autonomous Transactions in a Database Trigger

The grand new benefit of autonomous transactions for database triggers is that inside those triggers you can now issue COMMITs and ROLLBACKs, statements that are otherwise not allowed in database triggers. The changes you commit and roll back will not, however, affect the main transaction that caused the database trigger to fire. They will only apply to DML activity taking place inside the trigger itself (or through stored program units called within the trigger).

Why would this be of value to you? You may want to take an action in the database trigger that is not affected by the ultimate disposition of the transaction that caused the trigger to fire. For example, suppose that you want to keep track of each action against a table, whether or not the action completed. You might even want to be able to detect which actions failed. Let's see how you can use autonomous transactions to do this.

First, let's construct a simple autonomous transaction trigger on the ceo_compensation table that writes a simple message to the following ceo_comp_history table. Here are the two table definitions:

```
/* Filename on companion disk: autontrigger.sql */
CREATE TABLE ceo_compensation (
    company VARCHAR2(100),
    name VARCHAR2(100),
    compensation NUMBER,
    layoffs NUMBER);
CREATE TABLE ceo_comp_history (
    name VARCHAR2(100),
    description VARCHAR2(255),
    occurred_on DATE);
```

Here is the before-insert trigger to run all the elements in the script:

```
CREATE OR REPLACE TRIGGER bef_ins_ceo_comp
BEFORE INSERT ON ceo_compensation FOR EACH ROW
DECLARE
    PRAGMA AUTONOMOUS_TRANSACTION;
BEGIN
    INSERT INTO ceo_comp_history VALUES (
        :new.name, 'BEFORE INSERT', SYSDATE);
    COMMIT;
END;
/
```

With this trigger in place, I can now be certain to track every insert *attempt*, as shown in the steps below:

```
BEGIN
    INSERT INTO ceo_compensation VALUES (
        'Mattel', 'Jill Barad', 9100000, 2700);

    INSERT INTO ceo_compensation VALUES (
        'American Express Company',
        'Harvey Golub', 33200000, 3300);

    INSERT INTO ceo_compensation VALUES (
        'Eastman Kodak', 'George Fisher', 10700000, 20100);

    ROLLBACK; --I wish!
END;
/
SELECT name,
       description,
       TO_CHAR (occurred_on,
          'MM/DD/YYYY HH:MI:SS') occurred_on
  FROM ceo_comp_history;
NAME                    DESCRIPTION           OCCURRED_ON
--------------------    -------------------   -------------------
Jill Barad              BEFORE INSERT         03/17/1999 04:00:56
Harvey Golub            BEFORE INSERT         03/17/1999 04:00:56
George Fisher           BEFORE INSERT         03/17/1999 04:00:56
```

You will find in the *autontrigger.sql* script all the statements needed to create these objects and run your own test. You can even add your CEO's name to the series of INSERTs if he or she fits the bill.

Fine-tuning the database trigger

But there is something of a problem with the trigger I just defined. I defined the trigger as an autonomous transaction because I performed the alert in the body of the trigger. But what if I want to perform some additional DML for the main transaction here in the trigger? It won't be rolled back with the rest of the transaction (if a rollback occurs). That won't do at all, from the perspective of data integrity.

Generally, I would recommend that you not make a database trigger itself the autonomous transaction. Instead, push all of the independent DML activity (such as writing to the audit or history table) into its own procedure. Make *that* procedure the autonomous transaction. Have the trigger call the procedure.

The *autontrigger2.sql* script contains the following reworking of the database trigger. First, I create the audit procedure:

```
/* Filename on companion disk: autontrigger2.sql */
CREATE OR REPLACE PROCEDURE audit_ceo_comp (
    name IN VARCHAR2,
    description IN VARCHAR2,
    occurred_on IN DATE
    )
IS
    PRAGMA AUTONOMOUS_TRANSACTION;
BEGIN
    INSERT INTO ceo_comp_history VALUES (
        audit_ceo_comp.name,
        audit_ceo_comp.description,
        audit_ceo_comp.occurred_on
        );
    COMMIT;
END;
/
```

Then I change the trigger to the following.

```
CREATE OR REPLACE TRIGGER aft_ins_ceo_comp
AFTER INSERT ON ceo_compensation FOR EACH ROW
DECLARE
    ok BOOLEAN := is_valid_comp_info (:NEW.name);
BEGIN
    IF ok
    THEN
        audit_ceo_comp (
            :new.name, 'AFTER INSERT', SYSDATE);
    ELSE
        RAISE VALUE_ERROR;
```

```
        END IF;
    END;
    /
```

Note the following differences:

- The trigger is now an after-insert trigger, rather than a before-insert trigger. I want to wait until after the INSERT to the compensation table takes place. Then I will perform my audit.

- When the is_valid_comp_info function returns FALSE, I will not even perform an audit. Instead, I will stop the transaction by raising an error. This demonstrates the other reason you don't want the trigger itself to be autonomous. In some situations, I always want to perform my audit. Under other circumstances, however, I may want to *stop* my main transaction by raising an exception. I can't have both of those events happen if the exception is raised in the same block and transaction as the audit DML.

As you take advantage of the new autonomous transaction pragma, plan out how you will be using these new code elements. You will almost always be better off hiding the details of your new, independent transactions behind a procedural interface.

Building a Retry Counter

Suppose that you want to let a user try to get access to a resource (a file, a row of data, etc.) *N* times before an outright rejection. You also want to keep track of attempts between connections to the database. The autonomous transaction is a perfect fit, due to the COMMITs required.

You will find a simple prototype of a retry mechanism in the *retry.pkg* file on the companion disk. This mechanism allows you to specify the "item" on which you are placing a limit and keeping track of attempts. These limits are maintained for each unique username. Here is the specification of this package:

```
/* Filename on companion disk: retry.pkg */
CREATE OR REPLACE PACKAGE retry
IS
    PROCEDURE incr_attempts (item IN VARCHAR2);

    PROCEDURE set_limit (item IN VARCHAR2, limit IN INTEGER);

    FUNCTION limit (item IN VARCHAR2) RETURN INTEGER;

    FUNCTION limit_reached (item IN VARCHAR2) RETURN BOOLEAN;

    PROCEDURE clear_attempts (item IN VARCHAR2);

    FUNCTION attempts (item IN VARCHAR2) RETURN INTEGER;
```

```
    FUNCTION attempts_left (item IN VARCHAR2) RETURN INTEGER;

    FUNCTION attempted_at (item IN VARCHAR2) RETURN DATE;

    PROCEDURE show_retries (item IN VARCHAR2 := '%');
END retry;
/
```

The programs are self-explanatory; the implementations are also very straightforward. Here, for example, is the implementation of the procedure that lets you increment the number of attempts. Notice the COMMITs and ROLLBACKs; these are required, since I have used the autonomous transaction pragma.

```
PROCEDURE incr_attempts (item IN VARCHAR2)
IS
    PRAGMA AUTONOMOUS_TRANSACTION;
BEGIN
    INSERT INTO retry_counter VALUES (
        USER, incr_attempts.item, SYSDATE, 1);
    COMMIT;
EXCEPTION
    WHEN DUP_VAL_ON_INDEX
    THEN
        UPDATE retry_counter
            SET last_attempt = SYSDATE,
                tries = tries + 1
        WHERE username = USER
            AND item = incr_attempts.item;
        COMMIT;

    WHEN OTHERS THEN ROLLBACK; RAISE;
END;
```

Here is a script based on the "three strikes" law in California that exercises the package:

```
/* Filename on companion disk: retry.tst */
DECLARE
    law_and_order VARCHAR2(20) := 'law_and_order';
    TYPE string_t IS TABLE OF VARCHAR2(50);
    crime string_t := string_t (
        'Steal car at age 14',
        'Caught with a joint at 17',
        'Steal pack of cigarettes at age 42'
        );

BEGIN
    retry.set_limit (law_and_order, 2);

    FOR indx IN crime.FIRST .. crime.LAST
    LOOP
        DBMS_OUTPUT.PUT_LINE (crime(indx));
        IF retry.limit_reached (law_and_order)
```

```
          THEN
             DBMS_OUTPUT.PUT_LINE (
                '...Spend rest of life in prison');
          ELSE
             DBMS_OUTPUT.PUT_LINE (
                 '...Receive punishment that fits the crime');
             retry.incr_attempts (law_and_order);
          END IF;
      END LOOP;
   END;
   /
```

Here is the output in SQL*Plus:

```
SQL> @retry.tst
Steal car at age 14
...Receive punishment that fits the crime
Caught with a joint at 17
...Receive punishment that fits the crime
Steal pack of cigarettes at age 42
...Spend rest of life in prison
```

3

Invoker Rights: Your Schema or Mine?

Invoker rights refers to a new model for resolving references to database elements (tables, views, objects, programs) in a PL/SQL program unit.

Back in the "old days" of Oracle7 and Oracle 8.0 (those days, of course, in which most of us still spend our time), whenever you executed a stored program, it executed under the authority of the owner of that program. This was not a big deal if your entire application—code, data, and users—worked out of the same Oracle account, a scenario that probably covers about 0.5% of all Oracle shops. It proved to be a real pain in the neck for the other 99.5%, though, because code was usually stored in one schema and then shared through GRANT EXECUTE statements with other users (directly or through roles).

For one thing, that centralized, stored code would not automatically apply the privileges of a user (also known as an *invoker*) to the code's objects. The user might not have had DELETE privileges on a table, but the stored code did, so delete away! Now, in some circumstances, that is just how you wanted it to work. In other situations, particularly when you were executing programs relying on the DBMS_SQL (dynamic SQL) package, awesome complications could ensue.

In Oracle 8.1, PL/SQL has now been enhanced so that at the time of compilation, you can decide whether a program (or all programs in a package) should run under the authority of the definer (the only choice in Oracle 8.0 and earlier) or of the invoker of that program.

A Look at the Definer Rights Model

Before exploring the new invoker rights feature of PL/SQL, let's review the definer rights model. You need to understand the nuances of both models, because most PL/SQL applications will very likely rely on a *combination* of those models.

Before a PL/SQL program can be executed from within a database instance, it must be compiled and stored in the database itself. Thus, program units are always stored within a specific schema or Oracle account. A program can reference other PL/SQL programs, database tables, and so on. These are called *external references*, since these database elements are not defined within the current program unit.

With the definer rights model, you should keep the following rules in mind:

- Any external reference in a program unit is resolved at compile time using the directly granted privileges of the schema in which the program unit is compiled.

- Database roles are ignored completely at compile time.

- Whenever you run a program compiled with the definer rights model (the default), it executes under the authority of the schema that owns the program.

- Although direct grants are needed to compile a program, you can rely on grants of EXECUTE authority to give other schemas the ability to run your program.

Figure 3-1 shows how you can use the definer rights model to control access to underlying data objects. All the order entry data is stored in the OEData schema. All the order entry code is defined in the OECode schema. OECode has been granted the direct privileges necessary to compile the Order_Mgt package, which allows you to both place and cancel orders.

To make sure that the orders table is updated properly, no direct access (either via roles or privileges) is allowed to that table through any schema other than OECode. Suppose, for example, that the Sam_Sales schema needs to run through all the outstanding orders and close out old ones. Sam will *not* be able to issue a DELETE statement from the Close_Old_Orders procedure. Instead, Sam will have to call Order_Mgt.cancel to get the job done.

The Advantages of Definer Rights

There are certainly situations that cry out for (and are handled well by) the definer rights model. With definer rights:

- You are better able to control access to underlying data structures. You can guarantee that the only way the contents of a table can be changed is by going through a specific programmatic interface (usually a package).

- Application performance improves, because the PL/SQL engine does not have to perform checks at runtime to determine if you have the appropriate privileges or—just as important—which object you should actually be manipulating (my accounts table may be quite different from yours!).

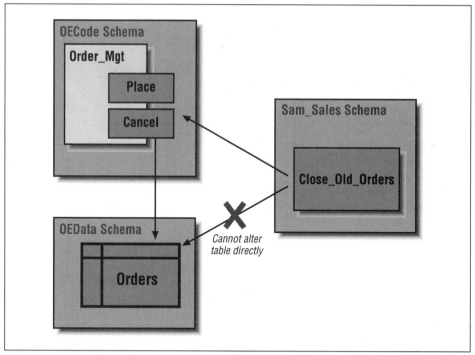

Figure 3-1. Controlling access to data with the definer rights model

- You don't have to worry about manipulating the wrong table. With definer rights, your code will work with the same data structure you would be accessing directly in SQL in your SQL*Plus (or other execution) environment. It is simply more intuitive.

But there are problems with the definer rights model as well. These are explored in the next sections.

Where'd My Table Go?

Let's see what all those definer rights rules can mean to a PL/SQL developer on a day-to-day basis. In many database instances, developers write code against tables and views that are owned by other schemas, with public synonyms created for them to hide the schema. Privileges are then granted via database roles.

This very common setup can result in some frustrating experiences. Suppose that my organization relies on roles to grant access to objects. I am working with a table called accounts, and can execute this query without any problem in SQL*Plus:

```
SQL> SELECT account#, name FROM accounts;
```

Yet, when I try to use that same table (same query, even) inside a procedure, I get an error:

```
SQL> CREATE OR REPLACE PROCEDURE show_accounts
  2  IS
  3  BEGIN
  4     FOR rec IN (SELECT account#, name FROM accounts)
  5     LOOP
  6        DBMS_OUTPUT.PUT_LINE (rec.name);
  7     END LOOP;
  8  END;
  9  /

Warning: Procedure created with compilation errors.

SQL> sho err
Errors for PROCEDURE SHOW_ACCOUNTS:

LINE/COL ERROR
-------- ------------------------------------------------------------
4/16     PL/SQL: SQL Statement ignored
4/43     PLS-00201: identifier 'ACCOUNTS' must be declared
```

This doesn't make any sense . . . or does it? The problem is that accounts is actually owned by another schema; I was unknowingly relying on a synonym and roles to get at the data. So if you are ever faced with this seemingly contradictory situation, don't bang your head against the wall in frustration. Instead, obtain the directly granted privileges you require to get the job done.

How Do I Maintain All That Code?

Suppose that my database instance is set up with a separate schema for each of the regional offices in my company. I build a large body of code that each office uses to analyze and maintain its data. Everybody has the same sets of tables, but the data is different.

Now, I would like to install this code so that I spend the absolute minimum amount of time and effort setting up and maintaining the application. The way to do that would be to install the code in one schema and share that code among all the regional office schemas.

With the definer rights model, unfortunately, this goal and architecture would be impossible to achieve. If I install the code in a central schema and grant EXE-CUTE authority to all regional schemas, then all those offices will be working with whatever set of tables is accessible to the central schema (perhaps one particular regional office or, more likely, a dummy set of tables). That's no good. I must instead install this body of code in each separate regional schema, as shown in Figure 3-2.

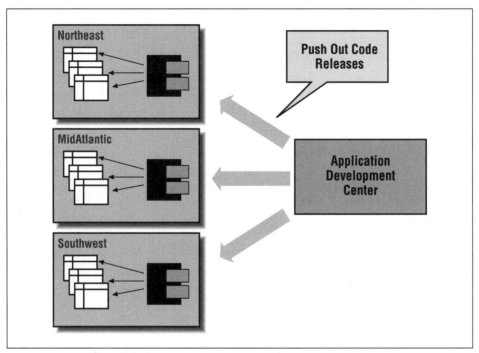

Figure 3-2. Repetitive installations of code needed with definer rights

The result is a maintenance and enhancement nightmare. Perhaps invoker rights will give us new options for a better solution.

Dynamic SQL and Definer Rights

Another common source of confusion with definer rights occurs when using dynamic SQL. Suppose I create a generic "run DDL" program using DBMS_SQL as follows:

```
/* Filename on companion disk: runddl.sp */
CREATE OR REPLACE PROCEDURE runddl (ddl_in in VARCHAR2)
IS
    cur INTEGER:= DBMS_SQL.OPEN_CURSOR;
    fdbk INTEGER;
BEGIN
    DBMS_SQL.PARSE (cur, ddl_in, DBMS_SQL.NATIVE);
    fdbk := DBMS_SQL.EXECUTE (cur);
    DBMS_SQL.CLOSE_CURSOR (cur);
EXCEPTION
    WHEN OTHERS
    THEN
        DBMS_OUTPUT.PUT_LINE (
            'RunDDL Failure on ' || ddl_in);
        DBMS_OUTPUT.PUT_LINE (SQLERRM);
```

```
          DBMS_SQL.CLOSE_CURSOR (cur);
   END;
   /
```

Now, dynamic SQL can be tricky stuff (notice the exception handler that closes the cursor instead of leaving it hanging open—we often forget housekeeping like this). So I decide to share this neat utility (after testing it in my schema with outstanding results) with everyone else in my development organization. I compile it into the COMMON schema, where all reusable code is managed, grant EXECUTE to public, and create a public synonym. Then I send out an email announcing its availability.

A few weeks later, I start getting calls from my coworkers. "Steven, I asked it to create a table and it ran without any errors, but I don't have the table." "Steven, I asked it to drop my table, and runddl said that there is no such table. But I can do a DESCRIBE on it." "Steven. . . ." Well, you get the idea. I begin to have serious doubts about sharing my code with other people. Sheesh, if they can't use something as simple as runddl without screwing things up . . . but I decide to withhold judgment and do some research.

I log into the COMMON schema and find that, sure enough, all of the objects people were trying to create or drop or alter were sitting here in COMMON. And then it dawns on me: unless a user of runddl specifies his own schema when he asks to create a table, the results will be most unexpected.

In other words, this call to runddl:

```
SQL> exec runddl ('create table newone (rightnow DATE)');
```

would create the newone table in the COMMON schema. And this call to runddl:

```
SQL> exec runddl ('create table scott.newone (rightnow DATE)');
```

might solve the problem, but would *fail* with the following error:

```
ORA-01031: insufficient privileges
```

unless I grant CREATE ANY TABLE to the COMMON schema. Yikes . . . my attempt to share a useful piece of code got very complicated very fast! It sure would be nice to let people run the runddl procedure under their own authority and not that of COMMON, without having to install multiple copies of the code.

The Invoker Rights Model

To help developers get around the obstacles raised by the definer rights model, Oracle 8.1 offers an alternative: the invoker rights model. With this approach, all external references in a PL/SQL program unit are resolved according to the privileges and roles of the *invoking* schema, not the owning or defining schema.

Figure 3-3 demonstrates the fundamental difference between the definer and the invoker rights models. Recall that in Figure 3-2, it was necessary for me to push out copies of my application to each regional office so that the code would manipulate the correct tables.

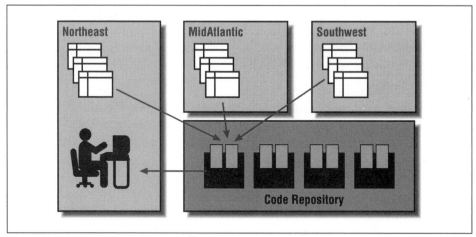

Figure 3-3. Use of invoker rights model to allow a "pass through" to user data

With invoker rights, this step is no longer necessary. Now I can compile the code into a single code repository. When a user from the Northeast region executes the centralized program (probably via a synonym), it will automatically work with tables in the Northeast schema.

So that's the idea behind invoker rights. Let's see what is involved codewise, and then explore how best to exploit the feature.

Invoker Rights Syntax

The syntax to support this feature is simple enough. You add the following clause before your IS or AS keyword in the program header:

```
AUTHID CURRENT_USER
```

Here, for example, is a generic "run DDL" engine that relies on the new Oracle 8.1 native dynamic SQL statement EXECUTE IMMEDIATE (described in Chapter 4, *Native Dynamic SQL in Oracle8i*) *and* the invoker rights model:

```
CREATE OR REPLACE PROCEDURE runddl (ddl_in in VARCHAR2)
   AUTHID CURRENT_USER
IS
BEGIN
   EXECUTE IMMEDIATE ddl_in;
END;
/
```

That's certainly lots simpler than the earlier implementation, isn't it?

The AUTHID CURRENT_USER clause before the IS keyword indicates that when runddl executes, it should run under the authority of the invoker or "current user," not the authority of the definer. And that's all you have to do. If you do not include the AUTHID clause or if you include it and explicitly request definer rights as shown:

```
AUTHID DEFINER
```

then all references in your program will be resolved according to the directly granted privileges of the owning schema.

Some Rules and Restrictions

There are a number of rules and restrictions to keep in mind when you are taking advantage of the invoker rights model:

- AUTHID DEFINER is the default option.

- The invoker rights model checks the roles assigned to the invoker at the time of program execution to resolve any external references. This means that with invoker rights, you can now take advantage of all the work you put into setting up roles in your database.

- The AUTHID clause is allowed only in the header of a standalone subprogram (procedure or function), a package specification, or an object type specification. You cannot apply the AUTHID clause to individual programs or methods within a package or object type.

- Invoker rights resolution of external references will work for the following kinds of statements:

  — SELECT, INSERT, UPDATE, and DELETE data manipulation statements

  — LOCK TABLE transaction control statement

  — OPEN and OPEN-FOR cursor control statements

  — EXECUTE IMMEDIATE and OPEN-FOR-USING dynamic SQL statements

  — SQL statements parsed using DBMS_SQL.PARSE

- Definer rights will always be used to resolve at compile time all external references to PL/SQL programs and object type methods. To verify and understand this behavior, consider the following script:

```
/* Filename on companion disk: authid2.sql */
CONNECT demo/demo
CREATE PROCEDURE dummy1 IS
BEGIN
    DBMS_OUTPUT.put_line ('Dummy1 owned by demo');
END;
```

```
/
GRANT execute on dummy1 to public;
CONNECT scott/tiger
CREATE PROCEDURE dummy1 IS
BEGIN
    DBMS_OUTPUT.put_line ('Dummy1 owned by scott');
END;
/
GRANT execute on dummy1 to public;
CREATE PROCEDURE dummy2 AUTHID CURRENT_USER
IS
BEGIN
    dummy1;
END;
/
GRANT execute on dummy2 to public;

EXEC scott.dummy2

CONNECT demo/demo
SET serveroutput on
EXEC scott.dummy2
```

When you run this script (needing both the DEMO and SCOTT accounts to be defined), you will see the following output:

```
SQL> @authid2
Connected.
Procedure created.
Grant succeeded.
Connected.
Procedure created.
Grant succeeded.
Procedure created.
Grant succeeded.
Connected.
Dummy1 owned by scott
```

As you can see, DEMO called SCOTT's dummy2 procedure, which was set up as an invoker rights procedure. But SCOTT.dummy2 did *not* call DEMO's dummy1 procedure. Instead it called its own version. Contrast the behavior of *authid2.sql* with that found in *authid3.sql* (you'll find it on the companion disk); there you will see that table access is redirected to the DEMO schema.

So just remember this: you can use invoker rights to change the resolution of external data element references (tables and views) but not that of program elements.

One Program, Multiple Schemas

You have the syntax down and we've covered some rules. Let's try out the new AUTHID clause in a more elaborate example.

A couple of years ago, a group of people started the Stolen Lives Project. The objective of this project is to document the lives "stolen" from families and communities when people are killed by law enforcement officers. I will use this project as the basis for my example in this section.

Neither the Stolen Lives Project nor I believe that all law enforcement officers commit acts of brutality. I also recognize that some killings by officers are justifiable, and that many, if not the vast majority of, officers are committed to improving the lives and guaranteeing the safety of *all* the citizens in their jurisdiction.

You can get lots more information about the Stolen Lives Project (hereafter referred to as SLP) at the following URL:

http://www.unstoppable.com/22/english/stolenlivesPROJECT

Suppose then that there is a national headquarters for the SLP, and that Headquarters maintains an Oracle database with a separate schema for each city and town in which information is being collected by local law enforcement brutality activists. Each schema has its own stolen_life table, but all schemas perform the same analyses on this information.

The DBA/developer for SLP, Salinda, has upgraded recently to 8.1 and sees an immediate opportunity for the AUTHID feature. She would like to maintain all the code in one place, but when activists in a given city run that code for their locale, they see their data and analyses. Figure 3-4 shows the architecture Salinda wants to implement.

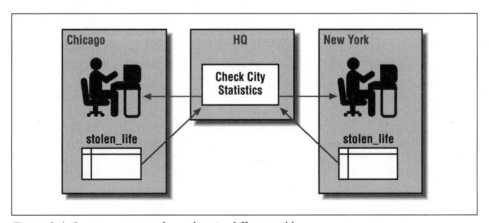

Figure 3-4. One program analyzes data in different tables

I do not show all the statements needed to set up the various schemas in Oracle; you will find them, however, in the *authid.ins* file on the companion disk.

Salinda connects to the HQ schema and creates the following objects. First, a stolen_life table that contains just one row, indicating that you shouldn't look here for data:

```
/* Filename on companion disk: authid.hql */
CREATE TABLE stolen_life (
    dod DATE,
    ethnicity VARCHAR2(100),
    victim VARCHAR2(100),
    age NUMBER,
    description VARCHAR2(2000)
    );

INSERT INTO stolen_life (dod, ethnicity, victim, age, description) VALUES (
    SYSDATE, 'N/A', 'HQ Table', 0,
    'All information is stored in city tables.');
```

As you will see, Salinda needs to have this table in the schema so that she can compile the stored program units that will be shared throughout all the local schemas.

Next, she creates two programs, only the second of which specifies invoker rights. First, a program to display information about a life stolen:

```
/* Create a display program, run as DEFINER. */
CREATE OR REPLACE PROCEDURE show_victim (
    stolen_life IN stolen_life%ROWTYPE
    )
AS
BEGIN
    DBMS_OUTPUT.PUT_LINE (stolen_life.victim);
    DBMS_OUTPUT.PUT_LINE ('');
    DBMS_OUTPUT.PUT_LINE (stolen_life.description);
    DBMS_OUTPUT.PUT_LINE ('');
END;
/
```

And then the analysis program (which, in this case, simply displays the victims for a location):

```
CREATE OR REPLACE PROCEDURE show_descriptions
    AUTHID CURRENT_USER
AS
BEGIN
    FOR lifestolen IN (SELECT * FROM stolen_life)
    LOOP
        show_victim (lifestolen);
```

```
    END LOOP;
END;
/
```

Both of these programs compile by resolving the reference to stolen_life against the all-but-empty HQ table. Since these programs are to be used by all, Salinda then performs the necessary grants:

```
GRANT EXECUTE ON show_descriptions TO PUBLIC;
DROP PUBLIC SYNONYM show_descriptions;
CREATE PUBLIC SYNONYM show_descriptions FOR show_descriptions;
```

All of the above statements can be found, by the way, in the *authid.hq1* file.

Once the centralized objects are in place, Salinda can now get everything defined in the local (city/town) schemas. Remember that the objective in this architecture is to store all of the code in one schema; the only step Salinda should have to take in her local schemas, therefore, is to create the stolen_life table specific to that locale. Here are the steps for Chicago. For these steps see *authid.chi*—and note that all data shown is taken from the web site and reflects real-world tragedy:

```
/* Filename on companion disk: authid.chi */
DROP TABLE stolen_life;

CREATE TABLE stolen_life (
    dod DATE,
    ethnicity VARCHAR2(100),
    victim VARCHAR2(100),
    age NUMBER,
    description VARCHAR2(2000),
    moreinfoat VARCHAR(200) DEFAULT
        'http://www.unstoppable.com/22/english/stolenlivesPROJECT'
    );
```

Now that the table is created, Salinda populates it with just a tiny fragment of all the broken lives you will find on the web site. I will show just a single entry in the text:

```
INSERT INTO stolen_life (dod, ethnicity, victim, age, description) VALUES (
    '23-OCT-96', 'Puerto Rican', 'Angel Castro, Jr.', 15,
    'After being beaten, abused with racial epithets and told by police
that he would be killed if he did not move, Angel Castro's family moved.
Angel returned to the neighborhood for a friend's birthday party. After
leaving the party, a police car rammed him as he rode his bike. As Angel
tried to get on his knees, the police shot and killed him');
```

Salinda also performs the same steps for New York City; see the *authid.ny* file for all the details. Now let's see how well it all works.

I connect to the NY schema and show the stolen lives:

```
SQL> CONNECT newyork/newyork
SQL> set serveroutput on size 1000000 format wrapped
```

```
SQL> exec show_descriptions
Amadou Diallo

Shot 19 times by four police officers outside his Bronx apartment. Diallo
was a devout Muslim working 12 hour days selling CDs and tapes to earn
money to finish his bachelor's degree. He was unarmed.
...
```

And when I connect to CHICAGO, I see different information:

```
SQL> CONNECT chicago/chicago
SQL> set serveroutput on size 1000000 format wrapped
SQL> exec show_descriptions
Angel Castro, Jr.

After being beaten, abused with racial epithets and told by police that he
would be killed if he did not move, Angel Castro's family moved. Angel
returned to the neighborhood for a friend's birthday party. After leaving the
party, a police car rammed him as he rode his bike. As Angel tried to get on
his knees, the police shot and killed him.
...
```

Perfectly abominable behavior, but perfect implementation of shared code and nonshared data!

Let's just verify that Salinda did need the AUTHID clause to get things to work right. Suppose she goes back to the HQ account and recompiles the show_ descriptions procedure, this time with the default rights model:

```
CREATE OR REPLACE PROCEDURE show_descriptions
   AUTHID DEFINER -- The default
AS
BEGIN
   FOR lifestolen IN (SELECT * FROM stolen_life)
   LOOP
      show_victim (lifestolen);
   END LOOP;
END;
/
```

Then when activists connect to the CHICAGO and NY schemas to see their data, this is all they see:

```
SQL> exec show_descriptions
HQ Table

All information is stored in city tables.
```

Clearly, without the help of the invoker rights model, Salinda could not achieve her design objectives. With AUTHID CURRENT_USER, though, it will be easier for the Stolen Lives Project to inform the American public about this issue.

Invoker Rights for Dynamic SQL

I have written hundreds of programs using dynamic SQL, and prior to Oracle 8.1, I always had to worry about schema issues: where is the program running? Who is running the program? What will happen when someone runs the program? These are scary questions to ask about your own code!

Now with the invoker rights model, those issues fall away. You should as a rule always include the AUTHID CURRENT_USER clause for any stored program unit that uses either the built-in package DBMS_SQL for dynamic SQL or the new 8.1 native dynamic SQL implementation (described in Chapter 4).

Once you take this step, you can rest assured that no matter where the program is compiled and no matter which schema runs the program, it will always act on the currently connected schema.

Combining the Definer and Invoker Rights Models

Invoker rights programs allow central code to reflect back to the calling schema. Definer rights programs allow remote schemas to access local data (i.e., data in the same schema as the program). Many applications require a combination of these flavors.

Suppose, for example, that the national Stolen Lives Project also maintains a table of "perpetrators," law enforcement officers who have killed one or more people in the United States. Due to the sensitivity of the information, the SLP has decided to maintain a single headquarters table that cannot be accessed directly by the city/town schemas. Yet both the location-specific stolen_life table and the systemwide perpetrators table need to be accessed by the check_city_statistics procedure.

What's a code architect to do? One thought might be to create a public synonym for the perpetrators table and make sure that no city schema has its own perpetrators table. When the city schema runs the central code under invoker rights, the reference to perpetrators would, in fact, be to that central source of data.

That works fine for the check_city_statistics procedure, but what about the rest of the application? With this approach, any city schema can directly access the perpetrators table, a violation of security. So the synonyms solution is no solution at all.

With Oracle 8.1, however, you don't need to do anything more than introduce a layer of code around the shared data structure. You need to do at least that, however, so that you can *change* the model used for resolving external references.

If the perpetrators table is accessed directly by the check_city_statistics procedure, the reference can only be resolved by the city schema's having direct access (via a synonym) to the table, which is a no-no. The check_city_statistics procedure cannot, therefore, query the perpetrators table directly. Instead, as shown in Figure 3-5, it will call another procedure, compiled under the definer rights model, which, in turn, works with the perpetrators table.

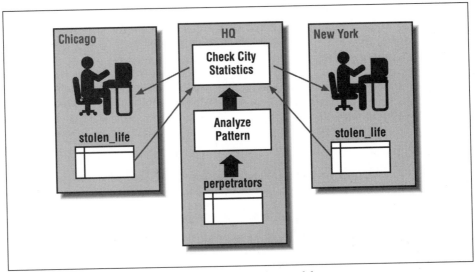

Figure 3-5. Combination of definer and invoker rights model

The *authid4.sql* file provides an implementation that reflects this blended approach. It creates a separate procedure, show_perps, to access the perpetrators table:

```
/* Filename on companion disk: authid4.sql */
CREATE OR REPLACE PROCEDURE show_perps (loc IN VARCHAR2)
   AUTHID DEFINER
AS
BEGIN
   FOR rec IN (SELECT * FROM perpetrator WHERE location = loc)
   LOOP
      pl (loc || ' perpetrator is ' || rec.rank || ' ' || rec.name);
   END LOOP;
END;
/
```

After granting PUBLIC access to this procedure (but not to the table), I modify show_descriptions to include this information:

```
CREATE OR REPLACE PROCEDURE show_descriptions
   AUTHID CURRENT_USER
AS
BEGIN
```

```
   HQ.show_perps (USER);

   pl ('');

   FOR lifestolen IN (SELECT * FROM stolen_life)
   LOOP
      show_victim (lifestolen);
   END LOOP;
END;
/
```

The Chicago group can then access a full array of information:

```
SQL> exec show_descriptions
CHICAGO perpetrator is Sergeant Tim "BigBoy" Cop
CHICAGO perpetrator is Commander John Burge


Bernard Solomon

After years of police harassment, Solomon was told by police that they
would kill him. A few days later he was arrested. He was found hung in
his cell at the 2259 S. Damen police station. Although police claim he
hung himself with his shirt, when his body was examined by family
members, he was found still wearing his shirt on one arm.
```

even though Chicago cannot directly access this table:

```
SQL> connect chicago/chicago
Connected.
SQL> select * from hq.perpetrators;
select * from hq.perpetrators
                    *
ERROR at line 1:
ORA-00942: table or view does not exist
```

The *authid5.sql* file on the disk offers a somewhat simpler example of this same basic technique.

By offering both the definer and invoker rights models in Oracle8*i*, Oracle demonstrates its continuing commitment to the PL/SQL language. As we move to the more distributed model of the Internet (and not just distributed data—distributed *everything*), PL/SQL needs to become more flexible in the way that it lets us build and execute our code.

The invoker rights model gives all of us another tool to use as we construct our applications. By coming up with a simple syntax for applying this model, Oracle makes it easier for us to learn and implement this new approach.

4

Native Dynamic SQL in Oracle8i

Ever since Oracle 7.1, we PL/SQL developers have been able to use the built-in DBMS_SQL package to execute dynamic SQL and PL/SQL. This means, for example, that at runtime you can construct a query, a DELETE statement, a CREATE TABLE statement, or even a PL/SQL block as a string—and then execute it. Dynamic SQL comes in extremely handy when you are building ad hoc query systems, when you need to execute DDL inside PL/SQL, and just generally when you don't know in advance exactly what you need to do or what the user will want to do. Dynamic SQL is a frequent requirement in Web-based applications.

But there are some problems with DBMS_SQL:

- It is a very complicated package.

- It has a number of restrictions (such as not recognizing and being able to work with new Oracle8 datatypes).

- It is relatively slow.

So our dear friends at PL/SQL Central in Redwood Shores took pity on us all and reimplemented dynamic SQL directly in the PL/SQL language itself. This new facility is called *native dynamic SQL*. I will refer to it as NDS in this chapter.

Here's the free advertisement for Oracle Corporation: NDS is faster and easier than DBMS_SQL. Truth in advertising? Absolutely, although my tests indicate that with the performance enhancements already in place for DBMS_SQL, NDS is on average just slightly faster. There is no doubt, however, that NDS is much easier to use—when you can use it.

Before diving into the syntax and details of NDS, let's take a look at a comparison between the two approaches to dynamic SQL.

DBMS_SQL Versus NDS

Let's compare the DBMS_SQL and NDS implementations of a program that displays all the employees for the specified and very dynamic WHERE clause.

The DBMS_SQL implementation:

```
CREATE OR REPLACE PROCEDURE showemps (
   where_in IN VARCHAR2 := NULL)
IS
   cur INTEGER := DBMS_SQL.OPEN_CURSOR;
   rec employee%ROWTYPE;
   fdbk INTEGER;
BEGIN
   DBMS_SQL.PARSE
     (cur,
      'SELECT employee_id, last_name
         FROM employee
        WHERE ' || NVL (where_in, '1=1'),
      DBMS_SQL.NATIVE);

   DBMS_SQL.DEFINE_COLUMN (cur, 1, 1);
   DBMS_SQL.DEFINE_COLUMN (cur, 2, user, 30);

   fdbk := DBMS_SQL.EXECUTE (cur);
   LOOP
      /* Fetch next row. Exit when done. */
      EXIT WHEN DBMS_SQL.FETCH_ROWS (cur) = 0;
      DBMS_SQL.COLUMN_VALUE (cur, 1, rec.employee_id);
      DBMS_SQL.COLUMN_VALUE (cur, 2, rec.last_name);
      DBMS_OUTPUT.PUT_LINE (
         TO_CHAR (rec.employee_id) || '=' ||
         rec.last_name);
   END LOOP;

   DBMS_SQL.CLOSE_CURSOR (cur);
END;
/
```

The NDS implementation:

```
CREATE OR REPLACE PROCEDURE showemps (
   where_in IN VARCHAR2 := NULL)
IS
   TYPE cv_typ IS REF CURSOR;
   cv cv_typ;
   v_id employee.employee_id%TYPE;
   v_nm employee.last_name%TYPE;
BEGIN
   OPEN cv FOR
```

```
            'SELECT employee_id, last_name
               FROM employee
              WHERE ' || NVL (where_in, '1=1');
    LOOP
       FETCH cv INTO v_id, v_nm;
       EXIT WHEN cv%NOTFOUND;
       DBMS_OUTPUT.PUT_LINE (
          TO_CHAR (v_id) || '=' || v_nm);
    END LOOP;
    CLOSE cv;
END;
/
```

As you can see (and this is true in general), you can write dramatically less code using NDS. And since the code you write relies less on built-in packaged programs and more on native, standard elements of PL/SQL, that code is easier to build, read, and maintain.

Given this situation, why would anyone use DBMS_SQL ever again? Because NDS cannot do everything and anything you might want to do. The following lists show the operations that can be performed exclusively by each of these dynamic SQL implementations.

Exclusive NDS capabilities:

- Works with all SQL datatypes, including user-defined objects and collection types (variable arrays, nested tables, and index-by tables). DBMS_SQL only works with Oracle7-compatible datatypes.

- Allows you to fetch multiple columns of information directly into a PL/SQL record. With DBMS_SQL, you must fetch into individual variables.

Exclusive DBMS_SQL capabilities:

- Supports Method 4 dynamic SQL, which means that at compile time, you don't know how many columns you will be querying and/or how many bind variables will need to be set. Method 4 is the most complex form of dynamic SQL, and NDS doesn't support it (except under certain restricted circumstances).

- As of Oracle8, allows you to describe the columns of your dynamic cursor, obtaining column information in an index-by table of records.

- Supports SQL statements that are more than 32KB in length.

- Supports the use of the RETURNING clause into an array of values; NDS only allows the use of RETURNING for a single statement.

- Allows you to reuse your dynamic SQL cursors, which can improve performance.

- Can be executed from client-side (Oracle Developer) applications.

For more information about DBMS_SQL and the listed capabilities of this code, please see Chapter 3 of *Oracle Built-in Packages* (O'Reilly & Associates, 1998).

What can we conclude from these lists? The NDS implementation will be able to handle something like 80 to 90% of the dynamic SQL requirements you are likely to face. It is good to know, however, that there is still a place for DBMS_SQL (especially since I wrote a 100-page chapter on that package in *Oracle Built-in Packages*).

NDS Statement Summary

One of the nicest things about NDS is its simplicity. Unlike DBMS_SQL, which has dozens of programs and lots of rules to follow, NDS has been integrated into the PL/SQL language by adding one new statement, EXECUTE IMMEDIATE, and by enhancing the existing OPEN FOR statement:

EXECUTE IMMEDIATE
> Executes a specified SQL statement immediately

OPEN FOR
> Allows you to perform multiple-row dynamic queries

The EXECUTE IMMEDIATE Statement

Use EXECUTE IMMEDIATE to execute (immediately!) the specified SQL statement. Here is the syntax of this statement:

```
EXECUTE IMMEDIATE SQL_string
   [INTO {define_variable[, define_variable]... | record}]
   [USING [IN | OUT | IN OUT] bind_argument
      [, [IN | OUT | IN OUT] bind_argument]...];
```

SQL_string
> A string expression containing the SQL statement or PL/SQL block

define_variable
> A variable that receives a column value returned by a query

record
> A record based on a user-defined TYPE or %ROWTYPE that receives an entire row returned by a query

bind_argument
> An expression whose value is passed to the SQL statement or PL/SQL block

INTO clause
> Use for single-row queries; for each column value returned by the query, you must supply an individual variable or field in a record of compatible type.

USING clause

   Allows you to supply bind arguments for the SQL string. This clause is used
   for both dynamic SQL and PL/SQL, which is why you can specify a parameter
   mode. This usage is only relevant for PL/SQL, however; the default is IN,
   which is the only kind of bind argument you would have for SQL statements.

You can use EXECUTE IMMEDIATE for any SQL statement or PL/SQL block,
except for multiple-row queries. If *SQL_string* ends with a semicolon, it will be
treated as a PL/SQL block; otherwise, it will be treated as either DML (Data Manipulation Language—SELECT, INSERT, UPDATE, or DELETE) or DDL (Data Definition Language, such as CREATE TABLE). The string may contain placeholders for
bind arguments, but you cannot use bind values to pass in the names of schema
objects, such as table names or column names.

When the statement is executed, the runtime engine replaces each placeholder (an
identifier with a colon in front of it, such as :salary_value) in the SQL string with
its corresponding bind argument (by position). You can pass numeric, date, and
string expressions. You cannot, however, pass a Boolean, because it is a PL/SQL
datatype. Nor can you pass a NULL literal value. Instead, you must pass a variable
of the correct type that has a value of NULL.

NDS supports all SQL datatypes available in Oracle8*i*. So, for example, define variables and bind arguments can be collections, large objects (LOBs), instances of an
object type, and REFs. On the other hand, NDS does not support datatypes that
are specific to PL/SQL, such as Booleans, index-by tables, and user-defined record
types. The INTO clause may, however, contain a PL/SQL record.

Let's take a look at a few examples:

   1. Create an index:

      ```
      EXECUTE IMMEDIATE 'CREATE INDEX emp_u_1 ON employee (last_name)';
      ```

      It can't get much easier than that, can it?

   2. Create a stored procedure that will execute any DDL statement:

      ```
      CREATE OR REPLACE PROCEDURE execDDL (ddl_string IN VARCHAR2)
      IS
      BEGIN
         EXECUTE IMMEDIATE ddl_string;
      END;
      /
      ```

      With execDDL in place, I can create that same index as follows:

      ```
      execDDL ('CREATE INDEX emp_u_1 ON employee (last_name)');
      ```

   3. Obtain the count of rows in any table, in any schema, for the specified
      WHERE clause:

      ```
      /* Filename on companion disk: tabcount.sf */
      CREATE OR REPLACE FUNCTION tabCount (
      ```

```
        tab IN VARCHAR2,
        whr IN VARCHAR2 := NULL,
        sch IN VARCHAR2 := NULL)
        RETURN INTEGER
IS
    retval INTEGER;
BEGIN
    EXECUTE IMMEDIATE
        'SELECT COUNT(*)
            FROM ' || NVL (sch, USER) || '.' || tab ||
        ' WHERE ' || NVL (whr, '1=1')
        INTO retval;
    RETURN retval;
END;
/
```

So now I never again have to write SELECT COUNT(*), whether in SQL*Plus or within a PL/SQL program, as in the following:

```
BEGIN
    IF tabCount ('emp', 'deptno = ' || v_dept) > 100
    THEN
        DBMS_OUTPUT.PUT_LINE ('Growing fast!');
    END IF;
```

4. Here's a function that lets you update the value of any numeric column in any table. It's a function because it returns the number of rows that have been updated.

```
/* Filename on companion disk: updnval.sf */
CREATE OR REPLACE FUNCTION updNVal (
        tab IN VARCHAR2,
        col IN VARCHAR2,
        val IN NUMBER,
        whr IN VARCHAR2 := NULL,
        sch IN VARCHAR2 := NULL)
        RETURN INTEGER
IS
BEGIN
    EXECUTE IMMEDIATE
        'UPDATE ' || NVL (sch, USER) || '.' || tab ||
        '    SET ' || col || ' = :the_value
          WHERE ' || NVL (whr, '1=1')
        USING val;
    RETURN SQL%ROWCOUNT;
END;
/
```

Where I come from, that is a very small amount of code to achieve all of that flexibility! This example introduces the bind argument: after the UPDATE statement is parsed, the PL/SQL engine replaces the :the_value placeholder with the value in the val variable. Notice also that I am able to rely on the SQL%ROWCOUNT cursor attribute that I have already been using for static DML statements.

5. Suppose that I need to run a different stored procedure at 9 a.m. each day of the week. Each program's name has this structure: DAYNAME_set_schedule. Each procedure has the same four arguments: you pass in employee_id and hour for the first meeting of the day; it returns the name of the employee and the number of appointments for the day. I can use dynamic PL/SQL to handle this situation:

```
/* Filename on companion disk: run9am.sp */
CREATE OR REPLACE PROCEDURE run_9am_procedure (
    id_in IN employee.employee_id%TYPE,
    hour_in IN INTEGER)
IS
    v_apptCount INTEGER;
    v_name VARCHAR2(100);
BEGIN
    EXECUTE IMMEDIATE
        'BEGIN ' || TO_CHAR (SYSDATE, 'DAY') ||
            '_set_schedule (:id, :hour, :name, :appts); END;'
        USING IN
            id_in, IN hour_in, OUT v_name, OUT v_apptCount;

    DBMS_OUTPUT.PUT_LINE (
        'Employee ' || v_name || ' has ' || v_apptCount ||
        ' appointments on ' || TO_CHAR (SYSDATE));
END;
/
```

This is a very easy and accessible syntax!

The OPEN FOR Statement

The OPEN FOR statement is not brand-new to PL/SQL in Oracle8*i*; it was first offered in Oracle7 to support cursor variables. Now it is deployed in an especially elegant fashion to implement multiple-row dynamic queries. With DBMS_SQL, you go through a particularly painful series of steps to implement multirow queries: parse, bind, define each column individually, execute, fetch, extract each column value individually. My gosh, what a lot of code to write!

For native dynamic SQL, Oracle took an existing feature and syntax—that of cursor variables—and extended it in a very natural way to support dynamic SQL. The next section explores multirow queries in detail; let's take a look now specifically at the syntax of the OPEN FOR statement:

```
OPEN {cursor_variable | :host_cursor_variable} FOR SQL_string
    [USING bind_argument[, bind_argument]...];
```

cursor_variable

 A weakly typed cursor variable

:host_cursor_variable

A cursor variable declared in a PL/SQL host environment such as an Oracle Call Interface (OCI) program

SQL_string

Contains the SELECT statement to be executed dynamically

USING clause

Follows the same rules as it does in the EXECUTE IMMEDIATE statement

Many PL/SQL developers are not very familiar with cursor variables, so a quick review is in order (for lots more details, check out Chapter 6 of *Oracle PL/SQL Programming,* second edition).

A *cursor variable* is a variable of type REF CURSOR, or referenced cursor. Here is an example of a declaration of a cursor variable based on a "weak" REF CURSOR (the sort you will use for NDS):

```
DECLARE
    TYPE cv_type IS REF CURSOR;
    cv cv_type;
```

A cursor variable *points to* a cursor object; it is, however, a variable. You can have more than one variable pointing to the same cursor object, you can assign one cursor variable to another, and so on. Once you have declared a cursor variable, you can assign a value to it by referencing it in an OPEN FOR statement:

```
DECLARE
    TYPE cv_type IS REF CURSOR;
    cv cv_type;
BEGIN
    OPEN cv FOR SELECT COUNT(guns) FROM charlton_heston_home;
```

In this example, the query is static—it is not contained in single quotes, and it is frozen at compilation time. That is the only way we have been able to work with cursor variables until Oracle8*i.* Now we can use the same syntax as before, but the query can be a literal or an expression, as in the following:

```
OPEN dyncur FOR SQL_string;
```

or, to show the use of a bind argument:

```
OPEN dyncur FOR
    'SELECT none_of_the_above FROM senate_candidates
      WHERE state = :your_state_here'
    USING state_in;
```

Once you have opened the query with the OPEN FOR statement, the syntax used to fetch rows, close the cursor variable and check the attributes of the cursor are all the same as for static cursor variables—and hardcoded explicit cursors, for that matter. The next section demonstrates all of this syntax through examples.

To summarize, there are two differences between the OPEN FOR statement for static and dynamic SQL:

- The static version does not support the USING clause of NDS.

- The static version requires a static SQL statement after the FOR keyword, whereas with NDS, the SQL string is always either a literal string or an expression that evaluates to a string.

Multirow Queries with Cursor Variables

Now that you have seen the syntax of OPEN FOR and been introduced to cursor variables, let's explore the nuances involved in multirow queries with NDS.

When you execute an OPEN FOR statement, the PL/SQL runtime engine does the following:

1. Associates a cursor variable with the query found in the query string

2. Evaluates any bind arguments and substitutes those values for the placeholders found in the query string

3. Executes the query

4. Identifies the result set

5. Positions the cursor on the first row in the result set

6. Zeros out the rows-processed count returned by %ROWCOUNT

Note that any bind arguments (provided in the USING clause) in the query are evaluated only when the cursor variable is opened. This means that if you want to use a different set of bind arguments for the same dynamic query, you must issue a new OPEN FOR statement with those arguments.

 This approach is actually less efficient than the DBMS_SQL approach, which will allow you to simply rebind and then execute without having to reparse.

To perform a multirow query, you take these steps:

1. Declare a REF CURSOR type (if one is not already available, as it could be if defined in a package specification).

2. Declare a cursor variable based on the REF CURSOR.

3. OPEN the cursor variable FOR your query string.

4. Use the FETCH statement to fetch one row at a time from the query.

5. Check cursor attributes (%FOUND, %NOTFOUND, %ROWCOUNT, %ISOPEN) as necessary.

6. Close the cursor variable using the normal CLOSE statement.

Here is a simple program to display the specified column of any table for the rows indicated by the WHERE clause (it will work for number, date, and string columns):

```
/* Filename on companion disk: showcol.sp */
CREATE OR REPLACE PROCEDURE showcol (
    tab IN VARCHAR2,
    col IN VARCHAR2,
    whr IN VARCHAR2 := NULL)
IS
    TYPE cv_type IS REF CURSOR;
    cv cv_type;
    val VARCHAR2(32767);
BEGIN
    /* Construct the very dynamic query and open the cursor. */
    OPEN cv FOR
        'SELECT ' || col ||
        '  FROM ' || tab ||
        ' WHERE ' || NVL (whr, '1 = 1');

    LOOP
        /* Fetch the next row, and stop if no more rows. */
        FETCH cv INTO val;
        EXIT WHEN cv%NOTFOUND;

        /* Display the data, with a header before the first row. */
        IF cv%ROWCOUNT = 1
        THEN
            DBMS_OUTPUT.PUT_LINE (RPAD ('-', 60, '-'));
            DBMS_OUTPUT.PUT_LINE (
                'Contents of ' ||
                UPPER (tab) || '.' || UPPER (col));
            DBMS_OUTPUT.PUT_LINE (RPAD ('-', 60, '-'));
        END IF;
        DBMS_OUTPUT.PUT_LINE (val);
    END LOOP;

    CLOSE cv; --All done, so clean up!
END;
/
```

Here are some examples of output from this procedure:

```
SQL> exec showcol ('emp', 'ename', 'deptno=10')
--------------------------------------------------
Contents of EMP.ENAME
--------------------------------------------------
CLARK
KING
MILLER
```

I can even combine columns:

```
BEGIN
   showcol (
      'emp',
      'ename || ''-$'' || sal',
      'comm IS NOT NULL');
END;
/
--------------------------------------------------
Contents of EMP.ENAME || '-$' || SAL
--------------------------------------------------
ALLEN-$1600
WARD-$1250
MARTIN-$1250
TURNER-$1500
```

FETCH into Variables or Records

The FETCH statement in the showcol procedure shown in the previous section fetches into an individual variable. You could also FETCH into a sequence of variables, as shown here:

```
DECLARE
   TYPE cv_type IS REF CURSOR;
   cv cv_type;
   mega_bucks company.ceo_compensation%TYPE;
   achieved_by company.layoff_count%TYPE;
BEGIN
   OPEN cv FOR
      'SELECT ceo_compensation, layoff_count
         FROM company
        WHERE ' || NVL (whr, '1 = 1');

   LOOP
      FETCH cv INTO mega_bucks, achieved_by;
```

Working with a long list of variables in the FETCH list gets cumbersome and inflexible: you have to declare the variables, keep that set of values synchronized with the FETCH statement, and so on. To ease our troubles, NDS allows us to fetch into a record, as shown here:

```
DECLARE
   TYPE cv_type IS REF CURSOR;
   cv cv_type;
   ceo_info company%ROWTYPE;
BEGIN
   OPEN cv FOR
      'SELECT *
         FROM company
        WHERE ' || NVL (whr, '1 = 1');

   LOOP
      FETCH cv INTO ceo_info;
```

Of course, in many situations you will not want to do a SELECT *; this statement can be very inefficient if your table has hundreds of columns and you only need to work with three of those hundreds. A better approach is to create record TYPEs that correspond to different requirements. The best place to put these structures is in a package specification, so they can be used throughout your application. Here's one such package:

```
CREATE OR REPLACE PACKAGE company_struc
IS
    TYPE dynsql_curtype IS REF CURSOR;

    TYPE ceo_info_rt IS RECORD (
        mega_bucks company.ceo_compensation%TYPE,
        achieved_by company.layoff_count%TYPE);

END company_struc;
```

With this package in place, I can rewrite my CEO-related code as follows:

```
DECLARE
    cur company_struc.dynsql_curtype;
    rec company_struc.ceo_info_rt;
BEGIN
    OPEN cv FOR
        'SELECT ceo_compensation, layoff_count
          FROM company
        WHERE ' || NVL (whr, '1 = 1');

    LOOP
        FETCH cv INTO rec;
```

The USING Clause in OPEN FOR

As with the EXECUTE IMMEDIATE statement, you can pass in bind arguments when you open a cursor. You can only provide IN arguments for a query. By using bind arguments you can improve the performance of your SQL also, and also make it easier to write and maintain that code. (See the "Binding Variables" section later in this chapter for information about this technique.)

Let's revisit the showcol procedure. That procedure accepted a completely generic WHERE clause. Suppose that I have a more specialized requirement: I want to display (or in some other way process) all column information for rows that contain a date column with a value within a certain range. In other words, I want to be able to satisfy this query:

```
SELECT ename
  FROM emp
 WHERE hiredate BETWEEN x AND y;
```

as well as this query:

```
SELECT name
  FROM war_criminal
 WHERE killing_date BETWEEN x AND y;
```

I also want to make sure that the time component of the date column does not play a role in the WHERE condition.

Here is the header for the procedure:

```
/* Filename on companion disk: showcol2.sp */
PROCEDURE showcol (
    tab IN VARCHAR2,
    col IN VARCHAR2,
    dtcol IN VARCHAR2,
    dt1 IN DATE,
    dt2 IN DATE := NULL)
```

The OPEN FOR statement now contains two placeholders and a USING clause to match:

```
OPEN cv FOR
      'SELECT ' || col ||
      '  FROM ' || tab ||
      ' WHERE ' || dtcol ||
         ' BETWEEN TRUNC (:startdt)
               AND TRUNC (:enddt)'
    USING dt1, NVL (dt2, dt1+1);
```

I have crafted this statement so that if the user does not supply an end date, the WHERE clause returns rows whose date column is the same day as the dt1 provided. The rest of the showcol procedure remains the same, except for some cosmetic changes in the display of the header.

The following call to this new version of showcol asks to see the names of all employees hired in 1982:

```
BEGIN
   showcol ('emp',
      'ename', 'hiredate',
      '01-jan-82', '31-dec-82');
END;
/
----------------------------------------------------------------------
Contents of EMP.ENAME for HIREDATE between 01-JAN-82 and 31-DEC-82
----------------------------------------------------------------------
MILLER
```

Generic GROUP BY Procedure

How many times have you written a query along these lines:

```
SELECT some-columns, COUNT(*)
  FROM your-table
GROUP BY some-columns;
```

And then there is the variation involving the HAVING clause (you don't want to see *all* the counts, you just want to see those groupings where there is more than one identical value, and so on). These are very common requirements, but with NDS, you can easily build a program that does all the work for you, for any table, and for any single column (and this is extensible to multiple columns as well).

Here is the header of such a procedure:

```
/* Filename on companion disk: countby.sp */
PROCEDURE countBy (
    tab IN VARCHAR2,
    col IN VARCHAR2,
    atleast IN INTEGER := NULL,
    sch IN VARCHAR2 := NULL,
    maxlen IN INTEGER := 30)
```

tab

> The name of the table.

col

> The name of the column.

sch

> The name of the schema (default of NULL = USER).

atleast

> If you supply a non-NULL value for atleast, then the SELECT statement includes a HAVING COUNT(*) greater than that value.

maxlen

> Used for formatting of the output.

You can look at the *countby.sp* file on the companion disk to see the full implementation; here is all the code except that used to do the formatting (header string and so on):

```
IS
    TYPE cv_type IS REF CURSOR;
    cv cv_type;

    SQL_string VARCHAR2(32767) :=
        'SELECT ' || col || ', COUNT(*)
            FROM ' || NVL (sch, USER) || '.' || tab ||
        ' GROUP BY ' || col;

    v_val VARCHAR2(32767);
    v_count INTEGER;
BEGIN
    IF atleast IS NOT NULL
```

```
        THEN
            SQL_string := SQL_string || ' HAVING COUNT(*) >= ' || atleast;
        END IF;

        OPEN cv FOR SQL_String;

        LOOP
            FETCH cv INTO v_val, v_count;
            EXIT WHEN cv%NOTFOUND;
            DBMS_OUTPUT.PUT_LINE (RPAD (v_val, maxlen) || ' ' || v_count);
        END LOOP;

        CLOSE cv;
    END;
    /
```

As you start to build more and more of these generic utilities, you will find that it doesn't take very much code or effort—you just have to think through the steps of the SQL string construction carefully.

Generic GROUP BY Package

Displaying information is useful for test purposes, but in many cases you want to work with the queried information further, not simply show it. Let's build on the countby procedure shown in the previous section to provide an implementation in which the results of the dynamic query are stored in an index-by table for subsequent analysis.

Here is the specification of the package:

```
/* Filename on companion disk: countby.pkg */
CREATE OR REPLACE PACKAGE grp
IS
    TYPE results_rt IS RECORD (
        val VARCHAR2(4000),
        countby INTEGER);

    TYPE results_tt IS TABLE OF results_rt
        INDEX BY BINARY_INTEGER;

    FUNCTION countBy (
        tab IN VARCHAR2,
        col IN VARCHAR2,
        atleast IN INTEGER := NULL,
        sch IN VARCHAR2 := NULL,
        maxlen IN INTEGER := 30)
        RETURN results_tt;
END grp;
/
```

The implementation of the countby function is virtually the same as the procedure. The main difference is that I now have a record structure to fetch into, and an index-by table to fill. You can see both these changes in the loop that fetches the rows:

```
LOOP
   FETCH cv INTO rec;
   EXIT WHEN cv%NOTFOUND;
   retval(cv%ROWCOUNT) := rec;
END LOOP;
```

With this package in place, I can very easily build programs that access this analytical information. Here is one example:

```
/* Filename on companion disk: countby.tst */
DECLARE
   results grp.results_tt;
   indx PLS_INTEGER;
   minrow PLS_INTEGER;
   maxrow PLS_INTEGER;
BEGIN
   results := grp.countby ('employee', 'department_id');

   /* Find min and max counts. */
   indx := results.FIRST;
   LOOP
      EXIT WHEN indx IS NULL;

      IF minrow IS NULL OR
         minrow > results(indx).countby
      THEN
         minrow := indx;
      END IF;

      IF maxrow IS NULL OR
         maxrow < results(indx).countby
      THEN
         maxrow := indx;
      END IF;

      /* Perform other processing as well... */

      /* Move to next group count. */
      indx := results.NEXT(indx);
   END LOOP;
END;
/
```

Binding Variables

You have seen several examples of the use of bind variables or arguments with NDS. Let's now go over the various rules and special situations you may encounter when binding.

Binding Versus Concatenation

In most situations, you will be able to take two different paths to insert program values into your SQL string: binding and concatenation. The following table contrasts these approaches for a dynamic UPDATE statement.

Concatenation	Binding

```EXECUTE IMMEDIATE```
   `'UPDATE ' || tab`
      `'SET sal = ' || v_sal;`
	```EXECUTE IMMEDIATE```
	   `'UPDATE ' || tab`
	      `'SET sal = :new_sal'`
	   `USING v_sal;`

Binding involves the use of placeholders and the USING clause; concatenation shortcuts that process by adding the values directly to the SQL string. Two different approaches—which should you use and when?

I recommend that you bind arguments whenever possible (see the next section for limitations on binding) rather than rely on concatenation. There are two reasons for taking this approach:

Binding is faster

   When you bind in a value, the SQL string itself does not contain the value, just the placeholder name. Therefore, you can bind different values to the same SQL statement without changing that statement. Since it is the same SQL statement, your application is more likely to be able to take advantage of the pre-parsed cursors that are cached in the System Global Area (SGA) of the database.

Binding is easier to write and maintain

   When you bind, you don't have to worry about datatype conversion. It is all handled for you by the NDS engine. Binding, in fact, minimizes datatype conversion, since it works with the native datatypes. If you use concatenation, you will often need to write very complex, error-prone string expressions involving multiple single quotes, TO_DATE and TO_CHAR function calls, and so on. For example, consider the following comparison of concatenation and binding for a more complex statement:

```
/* Binding */
EXECUTE IMMEDIATE
   'UPDATE employee SET salary = :val
     WHERE hire_date BETWEEN :lodate AND :hidate'
   USING v_start, v_end;

/* Concatenation */
EXECUTE IMMEDIATE
  'UPDATE employee SET salary = ' || val_in ||
  ' WHERE hire_date BETWEEN ' ||
     ' TO_DATE (''' || TO_CHAR (v_start) || ''')' ||
```

```
    ' AND ' ||
    ' TO_DATE ('''' || TO_CHAR (v_end)  || '''')';
```

So bind whenever possible . . . which leads to the question: when is binding not an option?

Limitations on Binding

You can only bind into your SQL statement expressions (literals, variables, complex expressions) that replace placeholders for data values inside the dynamic string. You cannot bind in the names of schema elements (tables, columns, etc.) or entire chunks of the SQL statement (such as the WHERE clause). For those parts of your string, you must use concatenation.

For example, suppose you want to create a procedure that will truncate the specified view or table. Your first attempt might look something like this:

```
CREATE OR REPLACE PROCEDURE truncobj (
   nm IN VARCHAR2,
   tp IN VARCHAR2 := 'TABLE',
   sch IN VARCHAR2 := NULL)
IS
BEGIN
   EXECUTE IMMEDIATE
       'TRUNCATE :trunc_type :obj_name'
       USING tp, NVL (sch, USER) || '.' || nm;
END;
/
```

This code seems perfectly reasonable. But when you try to run the procedure you'll get this error:

```
ORA-03290: Invalid truncate command - missing CLUSTER or TABLE keyword
```

And if you rewrite the procedure to simply truncate tables, as follows:

```
EXECUTE IMMEDIATE 'TRUNCATE TABLE :obj_name' USING nm;
```

Then the error becomes:

```
ORA-00903: invalid table name
```

Why does NDS (and DBMS_SQL) have this restriction? When you pass a string to EXECUTE IMMEDIATE, the runtime engine must first parse the statement. The parse phase guarantees that the SQL statement is properly defined. PL/SQL can tell that the following statement is valid:

```
'UPDATE emp SET sal = :xyz'
```

without having to know the value of :xyz. But how can PL/SQL know if the following statement is well formed?

```
'UPDATE emp SET :col_name = :xyz'
```

Even if you don't pass in nonsense for col_name, it won't work. For that reason, you must use concatenation:

```
CREATE OR REPLACE PROCEDURE truncobj (
    nm IN VARCHAR2,
    tp IN VARCHAR2 := 'TABLE',
    sch IN VARCHAR2 := NULL)
IS
BEGIN
    EXECUTE IMMEDIATE
        'TRUNCATE ' || tp || ' ' || NVL (sch, USER) || '.' || nm;
END;
/
```

Argument Modes

Bind arguments can have one of three modes:

IN

> Read-only value (the default mode)

OUT

> Write-only variable

IN OUT

> Can read the value coming in and write the value going out

When you are executing a dynamic query, all bind arguments must be IN mode, except when you are taking advantage of the RETURNING clause, as shown here:

```
CREATE OR REPLACE PROCEDURE wrong_incentive (
    company_in IN INTEGER,
    new_layoffs IN NUMBER
    )
IS
    sql_string VARCHAR2(2000);
    sal_after_layoffs NUMBER;
BEGIN
    sql_string :=
        'UPDATE ceo_compensation
            SET salary = salary + 10 * :layoffs
          WHERE company_id = :company
          RETURNING salary INTO :newsal';

    EXECUTE IMMEDIATE sql_string
        USING new_layoffs, company_in, OUT sal_after_layoffs;

    DBMS_OUTPUT.PUT_LINE (
        'Benefiting from the misery of others at $' || sal_after_layoffs);
END;
```

Besides being used with the RETURNING clause, OUT and IN OUT bind arguments come into play mostly when you are executing dynamic PL/SQL. In this

case, the modes of the bind arguments must match the modes of any PL/SQL program parameters, as well as the usage of variables in the dynamic PL/SQL block.

Let's take a look at how this works with a few examples. Suppose that I have created the following stored procedure (I am writing this text in May 1999, as Kosovar Albanians are being pushed from their homes by Milosevic, and NATO bombs ravage Yugoslavia):

```
/* Filename on companion disk: natotarg.sql */
PROCEDURE pick_nato_targets (
    media_outlet_ok IN BOOLEAN,
    electric_grid_ok IN BOOLEAN,
    maternity_ward_ok IN BOOLEAN,
    cumulative_regrets IN OUT NUMBER,
    civilian_casualities OUT NUMBER
    )
```

Now I will just wander kind of naively into the territory of dynamic PL/SQL and execute the procedure, as follows:

```
BEGIN
    EXECUTE IMMEDIATE
        'BEGIN
            pick_nato_targets (TRUE, TRUE, TRUE, 10, 100);
        END;';
END;
/
```

Since cumulative_regrets is an IN OUT argument, however, I get these errors:

```
PLS-00363: expression '10' cannot be used as an assignment target
PLS-00363: expression '100' cannot be used as an assignment target
```

The procedure wants to pass *back* a value through the last two arguments. I need to provide a data structure to hold those values. Literals will not do, so I change it to this:

```
DECLARE
    next_to_old_defense_building BOOLEAN := TRUE;
    we_all_make_mistakes NUMBER;
    others_die_for_them NUMBER;
BEGIN
    EXECUTE IMMEDIATE
        'BEGIN
            pick_nato_targets (
                TRUE, TRUE, :baby_place, :whoops, :it_happens);
        END;'
        USING next_to_old_defense_building,
                we_all_make_mistakes,
                others_die_for_them;
END;
/
```

And now I get the following error:

```
PLS-00457: in USING clause, expressions have to be of SQL types
```

which reminds me that even though I am running dynamic PL/SQL, I have to conform to the rules and restrictions of NDS: only SQL datatypes are allowed, and Boolean is *still* not one of them, though I sure don't understand why.

But, fine, I will *not* pass in the Boolean value; I'll stick to numeric bind values:

```
EXECUTE IMMEDIATE
   'BEGIN
       pick_nato_targets (
           TRUE, TRUE, TRUE, :whoops, :it_happens);
   END;'
   USING we_all_make_mistakes,
       others_die_for_them;
```

But then I get this error:

```
ORA-06536: IN bind variable bound to an OUT position
```

I have left both bind arguments with the default IN mode, and that does not match the arguments. And if I change them both to OUT:

```
USING OUT we_all_make_mistakes,
    OUT others_die_for_them;
```

I get this error:

```
ORA-06537: OUT bind variable bound to an IN position
```

That would seem to be darn confusing, but the reality is that when you have an IN OUT argument, the error message treats it as if it's an IN argument.

And so we find that the only way to call this procedure successfully in NDS is with the following statement:

```
EXECUTE IMMEDIATE
   'BEGIN
       pick_nato_targets (
           TRUE, TRUE, FALSE, :whoops, :it_happens);
   END;'
   USING IN OUT we_all_make_mistakes,
       OUT others_die_for_them;
```

Duplicate Placeholders

In a dynamically constructed and executed SQL string, NDS associates placeholders with USING clause bind arguments by *position*, rather than by name. The treatment of multiple placeholders with the same name varies, however, according to whether you are using dynamic SQL or dynamic PL/SQL. You need to follow these rules:

- When you are executing a dynamic SQL string (DML or DDL; in other words, the string does *not* end in a semicolon), you must supply an argument for each placeholder, even if there are duplicates.

- When you are executing a dynamic PL/SQL block (the string ends in a semico-lon), you supply an argument for each unique placeholder.

Passing NULL Values

We will all encounter special moments when we want to pass a NULL value as a bind argument, as follows:

```
EXECUTE IMMEDIATE
   'UPDATE employee SET salary = :newsal
    WHERE hire_date IS NULL'
   USING NULL;
```

You will, however, get this error:

```
PLS-00457: in USING clause, expressions have to be of SQL types
```

Basically, what this is saying is that NULL has no datatype, and "no datatype" is not a valid SQL datatype.

So what are you supposed to do if you need to pass in a NULL value? You can do one of two things:

1. Hide it behind a variable façade, most easily done with an uninitialized vari-able, as shown here:

```
DECLARE
   /* Default initial value is NULL */
   no_salary_when_fired NUMBER;
BEGIN
   EXECUTE IMMEDIATE
      'UPDATE employee SET salary = :newsal
       WHERE hire_date IS NULL'
      USING no_salary_when_fired;
END;
```

2. Use a conversion function to convert the NULL value to a typed value explicitly:

```
BEGIN
   EXECUTE IMMEDIATE
      'UPDATE employee SET salary = :newsal
       WHERE hire_date IS NULL'
      USING TO_NUMBER (NULL);
END;
```

Working with Objects and Collections

One of the most important advantages of NDS over DBMS_SQL is its support for new Oracle8 datatypes: objects and collections. You don't need to change the structure of the code you write in NDS to use it with objects and collections.

Suppose that I am building an internal administrative system for the national health management corporation Health$.Com. To reduce costs, the system will work in a distributed manner, creating and maintaining separate tables of customer information for each for-profit hospital owned by Health$.Com.

I'll start by defining an object type (person) and VARRAY type (preexisting_conditions), as follows:

```
CREATE TYPE person AS OBJECT (
   name VARCHAR2(50), dob DATE, income NUMBER);
/

CREATE TYPE preexisting_conditions IS TABLE OF VARCHAR2(25);
/
```

Once these types are defined, I can build a package to manage my most critical health-related information—data needed to maximize profits at Health$.Com. Here is the specification:

```
/* Filename on companion disk: health$.pkg */
CREATE OR REPLACE PACKAGE health$
AS
   PROCEDURE setup_new_hospital (hosp_name IN VARCHAR2);

   PROCEDURE add_profit_source (
      hosp_name IN VARCHAR2,
      pers IN Person,
      cond IN preexisting_conditions);

   PROCEDURE weed_out_poor_and_sick (
      hosp_name VARCHAR2,
      min_income IN NUMBER := 100000,
      max_preexist_cond IN INTEGER := 0);

   PROCEDURE show_profit_centers (hosp_name VARCHAR2);
  END health$;
/
```

With this package, I can do the following:

1. Set up a new hospital, which means create a new table to hold information about that hospital. Here's the implementation from the body:

```
FUNCTION tabname (hosp_name IN VARCHAR2) IS
BEGIN
   RETURN hosp_name || '_profit_center';
END;

PROCEDURE setup_new_hospital (hosp_name IN VARCHAR2) IS
BEGIN
   EXECUTE IMMEDIATE
      'CREATE TABLE ' || tabname (hosp_name) || ' (
         pers Person,
         cond preexisting_conditions)
```

```
        NESTED TABLE cond STORE AS cond_st';
END;
```

 Since preexisting_conditions is a nested table, I must specify the
"store table" that will hold it.

2. Add a "profit source" (formerly known as a "patient") to the hospital, including his or her preexisting conditions. Here's the implementation from the
   body:

```
PROCEDURE add_profit_source (
    hosp_name IN VARCHAR2,
    pers IN Person,
    cond IN preexisting_conditions)
IS
BEGIN
    EXECUTE IMMEDIATE
        'INSERT INTO ' || tabname (hosp_name) ||
            ' VALUES (:revenue_generator, :revenue_inhibitors)'
        USING pers, cond;
END;
```

The use of objects and collections is transparent. I could be inserting scalars
like numbers and dates, and the syntax and code would be the same.

3. Remove from the hospital all the really poor and sick people, those individu-
   als who are not contributing to the profit margins of my corporation (hey,
   maybe we shouldn't mix profit margins and health care!). This is the most
   complex of the programs; here is the implementation:

```
PROCEDURE weed_out_poor_and_sick (
    hosp_name VARCHAR2,
    min_income IN NUMBER := 100000,
    max_preexist_cond IN INTEGER := 1)
IS
    cv RefCurTyp;
    human Person;
    known_bugs preexisting_conditions;

    v_table VARCHAR2(30) := tabname (hosp_name);
    v_rowid ROWID;
BEGIN
    /* Find all rows with more than the specified number
       of preconditions and deny them coverage. */
    OPEN cv FOR
        'SELECT ROWID, pers, cond
           FROM ' || v_table || ' alias
          WHERE (SELECT COUNT(*) FROM TABLE (alias.cond))
                > ' ||
                max_preexist_cond ||
            ' OR
```

```
                        alias.pers.income < ' || min_income;
        LOOP
           FETCH cv INTO v_rowid, human, known_bugs;
           EXIT WHEN cv%NOTFOUND;
           EXECUTE IMMEDIATE
               'DELETE FROM ' || v_table ||
               ' WHERE ROWID = :rid'
               USING v_rowid;
        END LOOP;
        CLOSE cv;
     END;
```

 I decided to retrieve the ROWID of each profit source so that when I do the DELETE it would be easy to identify the row. It would be awfully convenient to make the query FOR UPDATE, and then use WHERE CURRENT OF cv in the DELETE statement, but that is not possible, for two reasons: (1) The cursor variable would have to be globally accessible to be referenced inside a dynamic SQL statement, and (2) You cannot declare cursor variable in packages, because they don't have persistent state. See the later section called "Dynamic PL/SQL" for more details.

Building Applications with NDS

By now, you should have a solid understanding of how native dynamic SQL works in PL/SQL. This section covers some topics that you should be aware of as you start to build production applications with this new PL/SQL feature.

Sharing NDS Programs with Invoker Rights

I have created a number of useful generic programs in my presentation on NDS, including functions and procedures that do the following:

- Execute any DDL statement

- Return the count of rows in any table

- Return the count for each grouping by specified column

These are pretty darn useful utilities and I want to let everyone on my development team use them. So I compile them into the COMMON schema and grant EXECUTE authority on the programs to PUBLIC.

However, there is a problem with this strategy. When Sandra connects to her SANDRA schema and executes this command:

```
SQL> exec COMMON.execDDL ('create table temp (x date)');
```

she will inadvertently create a table in the COMMON schema—unless I take advantage of the invoker rights model described in Chapter 3, *Invoker Rights: Your Schema or Mine?*

The invoker rights model means that you define your stored programs so they execute under the authority, and with the privileges, of the invoking schema rather than the defining schema (which is the default in Oracle 8.1 and the only option prior to Oracle 8.1).

Fortunately, there isn't much you have to do to take advantage of this new feature. Here is a version of execDDL that executes any DDL statement—but always having an impact in the calling or invoking schema:

```
CREATE OR REPLACE PROCEDURE execDDL (ddl_string IN VARCHAR2)
   AUTHID CURRENT_USER
IS
BEGIN
   EXECUTE IMMEDIATE ddl_string;
END;
/
```

I recommend that you use the AUTHID CURRENT_USER clause in *all* of your dynamic SQL programs, particularly in those that you plan to share among a group of developers. The package discussed at the end of this chapter in "NDS Utility Package" follows this standard.

Error Handling

Any robust application needs to anticipate and handle errors. Error detection and correction with dynamic SQL can be especially challenging.

Sometimes the most challenging aspect to building and executing dynamic SQL programs is getting the string of dynamic SQL correct. You might be combining a list of columns in a query with a list of tables and then a WHERE clause that changes with each execution. You have to concatenate that stuff, getting the commas right, the ANDs and ORs right, and so on. What happens if you get it wrong?

Well, Oracle raises an error. And this error usually tells you exactly what is wrong with the SQL string, but that information can still leave lots to be desired and figured out. Consider the following nightmare scenario: I am building the most complicated PL/SQL application ever. It uses dynamic SQL left and right, but that's OK. I am a pro at the new NDS. I can, in a flash, type EXECUTE IMMEDIATE, OPEN FOR, and all the other statements I need. I blast through the development phase. I also rely on some standard exception-handling programs I have built that display an error message when an exception is encountered.

Then the time comes to test my application. I build a test script that runs through a lot of my code; I place it in a file named *testall.sql* (you'll find it on the companion disk). With trembling fingers, I start my test:

```
SQL> @testall
```

And, to my severe disappointment, here is what shows up on my screen:

```
ORA-00942: table or view does not exist
ORA-00904: invalid column name
ORA-00921: unexpected end of SQL command
ORA-00936: missing expression
```

Now, what am I supposed to make of all these error messages? Which error message goes with which SQL statement? Bottom line: when you do lots of dynamic SQL, it is very easy to get very confused and waste lots of time debugging your code—unless you take precautions *as* you write your dynamic SQL.

Here are my recommendations:

- Always include an error handling section in code that calls EXECUTE IMMEDIATE and OPEN FOR.

- In each handler, record and/or display the error message *and* the SQL statement when an error occurs.

How do these recommendations translate into changes in your code? First, let's apply these changes to the execDDL routine, and then generalize from there. Here is the starting point:

```
CREATE OR REPLACE PROCEDURE execDDL (ddl_string IN VARCHAR2)
   AUTHID CURRENT_USER IS
BEGIN
   EXECUTE IMMEDIATE ddl_string;
END;
```

Now let's add an error handling section to show us problems when they occur:

```
/* Filename on companion disk: execddl.sp */
CREATE OR REPLACE PROCEDURE execDDL (ddl_string IN VARCHAR2)
   AUTHID CURRENT_USER IS
BEGIN
   EXECUTE IMMEDIATE ddl_string;
EXCEPTION
   WHEN OTHERS
   THEN
      DBMS_OUTPUT.PUT_LINE (
         'Dynamic SQL Failure: ' || SQLERRM);
      DBMS_OUTPUT.PUT_LINE (
         '   on statement: "' || ddl_string || '"');
      RAISE;
END;
```

When I use this version to attempt to create a table using really bad syntax, this is what I see:

```
SQL> exec execddl ('create table x')
Dynamic SQL Failure: ORA-00906: missing left parenthesis
    on statement: "create table x"
```

Of course, in your production version, you might want to consider something a bit more sophisticated than the DBMS_OUTPUT built-in package.

 With DBMS_SQL, if your parse request fails and you do not explicitly close your cursor in the error section, that cursor remains open (and uncloseable), leading to possible "maximum open cursors exceeded" errors. This will not happen with NDS; cursor variables declared in a local scope are automatically closed—and memory released—when the block terminates.

Now let's broaden our view a bit: when you think about it, the execDDL procedure is not really specific to DDL statements. It can be used to execute *any* SQL string that does not require either USING or INTO clauses. From that perspective, we now have a single program that can and should be used in place of a direct call to EXECUTE IMMEDIATE—it has all that error handling built in. I supply such a procedure in the ndsutil package (see the later "NDS Utility Package" section).

We could even create a similar program for OPEN FOR—again, only for situations that do not require a USING clause. Since OPEN FOR sets a cursor value, we would probably want to implement it as a function, which would return a type of weak REF CURSOR. This leads right to a packaged implementation along these lines:

```
PACKAGE ndsutil
IS
    TYPE cv_type IS REF CURSOR;

    FUNCTION openFor (sql_string IN VARCHAR2) RETURN cv_type;
END;
```

The NDS utility package (available on the companion disk in *ndsutil.pkg*) contains the complete implementation of this function; the body is quite similar to the execDDL procedure shown earlier.

Dynamic PL/SQL

I think I can safely say that some of the most enjoyable moments I have had with PL/SQL (and, believe me, given all the time I spend with the language, I keep a sharp eye out for those moments!) occurred when I was constructing and executing PL/SQL blocks of code dynamically.

Think of it: while a user is running your application, it can do any of the following:

- Create a program, including a package that contains globally accessible data structures

- Obtain (and modify) by name the value of global variables

- Call functions and procedures whose names are not known at compile time

I have used this technique to build very flexible code generators, softcoded calculation engines for users, and much more. Dynamic PL/SQL allows you to work at a higher level of generality, which can be both challenging and exhilarating.

There are some rules and tips you need to keep in mind when working with dynamic PL/SQL blocks and NDS:

- The dynamic string must be a valid PL/SQL block. It must start with the DECLARE or BEGIN keywords, and end with an END statement and a semicolon. The string will not be considered PL/SQL code unless it ends with a semicolon.

- In your dynamic block, you can only access PL/SQL code elements that have global scope (standalone functions and procedures, and elements defined in the specification of a package). Dynamic PL/SQL blocks execute outside the scope of the local enclosing block.

- Errors raised within a dynamic PL/SQL block can be trapped and handled by the local block in which the string was run with the EXECUTE IMMEDIATE statement.

Let's explore these rules so as to avoid any confusion. First of all, I will build a little utility to execute dynamic PL/SQL:

```
/* Filename on companion disk: dynplsql.sp */
CREATE OR REPLACE PROCEDURE dynPLSQL (blk IN VARCHAR2)
IS
BEGIN
   EXECUTE IMMEDIATE
      'BEGIN ' || RTRIM (blk, ';') || '; END;';
END;
/
```

This one program encapsulates many of the rules mentioned previously for PL/SQL execution. By enclosing the string within a BEGIN-END pairing, I guarantee that whatever I pass in is executed as a valid PL/SQL block. For instance, I can execute the calc_ totals procedure dynamically as simply as this:

```
SQL> exec dynPLSQL ('calc_totals');
```

Now let's use this program to examine what kind of data structures you can reference within a dynamic PL/SQL block. In the following anonymous block, I want to use DBMS_SQL to assign a value of 5 to the local variable num:

```
<<dynamic>>
DECLARE
   num NUMBER;
BEGIN
   dynPLSQL ('num := 5');
END;
/
```

This string is executed within its own BEGIN-END block, which would *appear* to be a nested block within the anonymous block named "dynamic" with the label. Yet when I execute this script I receive the following error:

```
PLS-00302: component 'NUM' must be declared
ORA-06512: at "SYS.DBMS_SYS_SQL", line 239
```

The PL/SQL engine is unable to resolve the reference to the variable named num. I get the same error even if I qualify the variable name with its block name:

```
<<dynamic>>
DECLARE
   num NUMBER;
BEGIN
   /* Also causes a PLS-00302 error! */
   dynPLSQL ('dynamic.num := 5');
END;
/
```

Now suppose that I define the num variable inside a package called dynamic:

```
CREATE OR REPLACE PACKAGE dynamic
IS
   num NUMBER;
END;
/
```

I am now able to execute the dynamic assignment to this newly defined variable successfully:

```
BEGIN
   dynPLSQL ('dynamic.num := 5');
END;
/
```

What's the difference between these two pieces of data? In my first attempt, the variable num is defined locally in the anonymous PL/SQL block. In my second attempt, num is a public global variable defined in the dynamic package. This distinction makes all the difference with dynamic PL/SQL.

It turns out that a dynamically constructed and executed PL/SQL block is not treated as a *nested* block; instead, it is handled as if it were a procedure or function called from within the current block. So any variables local to the current or enclosing blocks are not recognized in the dynamic PL/SQL block. You can only make references to globally defined programs and data structures. These PL/SQL elements include standalone functions and procedures and any elements defined in the specification of a package.

Fortunately, the dynamic block *is* executed within the context of the calling block. If you have an exception section within the calling block, it will trap exceptions raised in the dynamic block. So if I execute this anonymous block in SQL*Plus:

```
BEGIN
    dynPLSQL ('undefined.packagevar := ''abc''');
EXCEPTION
    WHEN OTHERS THEN DBMS_OUTPUT.PUT_LINE (SQLCODE);
END;
/
```

I will not get an unhandled exception.

The assignment performed in this anonymous block is an example of *indirect referencing*. I don't reference the variable directly, but instead do so by specifying the *name* of the variable. Oracle Developer's FormsBuilder product (formerly known as SQL*Forms and Oracle Forms) offers an implementation of indirect referencing with the NAME_IN and COPY programs. This feature allows developers to build logic that can be shared across all forms in the application. PL/SQL does not support indirect referencing, but you can implement it with dynamic PL/SQL. See the *dynvar.pkg* file on the disk for an example of such an implementation.

In the following sections, I offer several examples of dynamic PL/SQL to spark your interest and, perhaps, inspire your creativity.

Dramatic code reduction

Here is a true story, I kid you not. I once spent some time at an insurance company here in Chicago. Now, top management at insurance companies is notorious for burying any sense of compassion under a mountain of red tape—and that inclination gets pushed down into the software we have to write. So, for example, a policy might have hundreds of lines of fine print, each of which has a number associated with it, and each of which applies or does not apply to a given claim.

For each line number, the developers had written a "process line" procedure. So if they needed to process line 1, they would call:

```
process_line1
```

If line 514 applied to the claim, then it was time to call:

```
process_line514
```

The remarkable thing about this situation is that the developers ended up with a program like this:

```
CREATE OR REPLACE PROCEDURE process_line (line IN INTEGER)
IS
BEGIN
   IF line = 1 THEN process_line1;
   ELSIF line = 2 THEN process_line2;
   ...
   ELSIF line = 514 THEN process_line514;
   ...
   END IF;
END;
```

and it was so long that it often would fail to compile, and when it did manage to compile, it took a long time to execute. Nasty!

Dynamic SQL is, of course, suited perfectly to this scenario, and I was able to fix their problem in no time at all (well, to be honest, at the time I fixed it using DBMS_SQL, but here's the NDS implementation):

```
CREATE OR REPLACE PROCEDURE process_line (line IN INTEGER)
IS
BEGIN
   EXECUTE IMMEDIATE
       'BEGIN process_line' || line || '; END;';
END;
```

From thousands of lines of code down to one executable statement. I like it!

Generic calculator function

Here's the scenario for which I wrote the dyncalc function shown in this section: suppose I have to build a GUI application that allows users to select their calculation of choice, enter the arguments, and then display the results. There are a dozen different calculations, accepting from one to five arguments, all returning a single value.

I could write a separate screen for each calculation. However, that approach is not only labor-intensive, but also high-maintenance. Every time a new calculation is added to the mix, I have to go in and write another screen. Yuck! Wouldn't it be nice if I could "soft code" my application, so that (ideally) when users need access to another calculation, they can essentially add it themselves?

So I build a set of database tables to store header-level information about the calculation, including a description, the name of the calculation function, the number of arguments, descriptions of each argument, and so forth. But now I need a utility that will run any of the calculations I send to it. This is where dynamic PL/ SQL comes into play.

Here is the header of a function that accepts up to five arguments and runs whatever function is requested:

```
/* Filename on companion disk: dyncalc.sf */
CREATE OR REPLACE FUNCTION dyncalc (
    oper_in IN VARCHAR2,
    nargs_in IN INTEGER := 0,
    arg1_in IN VARCHAR2 := NULL,
    arg2_in IN VARCHAR2 := NULL,
    arg3_in IN VARCHAR2 := NULL,
    arg4_in IN VARCHAR2 := NULL,
    arg5_in IN VARCHAR2 := NULL
    )
    RETURN VARCHAR2
```

The implementation uses the EXECUTE IMMEDIATE statement in a cascading IF statement. Here is a portion of the function body:

```
ELSIF nargs_in = 2
THEN
    EXECUTE IMMEDIATE v_code || '(:1, :2); END;'
        USING OUT retval, arg1_in, arg2_in;
ELSIF nargs_in = 3
THEN
    EXECUTE IMMEDIATE v_code || '(:1, :2, :3); END;'
        USING OUT retval, arg1_in, arg2_in, arg3_in;
```

No rocket science here . . . but it gets the job done, as shown in the SQL*Plus session below:

```
SQL> BEGIN
  2     DBMS_OUTPUT.PUT_LINE (dyncalc('sysdate'));
  3     DBMS_OUTPUT.PUT_LINE (dyncalc('power', 2, 2, 44));
  4     DBMS_OUTPUT.PUT_LINE (
  5         dyncalc ('greatest', 5, 66, 5, 88, 1020, -4));
  6  END;
  7  /
05-MAY-99
17592186044416
1020
```

NDS Utility Package

To make it easier for my readers to take advantage of the various generic utilities discussed in this chapter, I have created a single package called ndsutil. This package, available on the companion disk in *ndsutil.pkg,* contains the programs listed in Table 4-1.

Table 4-1. Contents of the NDS Utility Package

Name	Description
execImmed	Substitute for EXECUTE IMMEDIATE that does not need a USING or INTO clause; includes error handling.
openFor	Substitute for OPEN FOR that does not need a USING clause; includes error handling.
showCol	Shows the contents of a single column in the specified table.
tabCount	Returns the number of rows in the specified table, with an optional WHERE clause.
countBy	Returns the number of rows in the specified table for a particular GROUP BY expression, with an optional HAVING clause.
dynPLSQL	Executes a dynamic PL/SQL string, automatically making sure that it is a valid block and that it ends in a semicolon. The USING clause is not allowed.

The package is defined using the invoker rights mode (AUTHID CURRENT_USER). This means that no matter who owns the package, any external references in the dynamic SQL you execute via ndsutil are resolved according to the authority of the invoking schema, not the owner.

All programs contain exception sections that display the error and the offending SQL. Procedures then reraise the error, whereas functions generally return NULL or a NULL/empty structure.

I am sure there are many programs you can add to this package. Please post any additions to the PL/SQL Pipeline at *http://www. revealnet.com/plsql-pipeline*, in the Pipetalk area. Then we can all gain from your experience and creativity!

5

Bulking Up with PL/SQL 8.1

We all know that PL/SQL is tightly integrated with the underlying SQL engine in the Oracle database. PL/SQL is *the* database programming language of choice for Oracle—even if you now can at least theoretically use Java inside the database as well.

But this tight integration does not necessarily mean that there isn't any overhead associated with running SQL from a PL/SQL program. When the PL/SQL runtime engine processes a block of code, it executes the procedural statements within its own engine, but it passes the SQL statements on to the SQL engine. The SQL layer executes the SQL statements and then returns information to the PL/SQL engine, if necessary.

This transfer of control (shown in Figure 5-1) between the PL/SQL and SQL engines is called a *context switch*. Each time a switch occurs, there is additional overhead. There are a number of scenarios in which many switches occur and performance degrades. Oracle 8.1 now offers two enhancements to PL/SQL that allow you to bulk together multiple context switches into a single switch, thereby improving the performance of your applications.

These new features are as follows:

FORALL

A variation on the FOR loop that bundles together multiple DML statements based on data in a collection

BULK COLLECT

An enhancement to implicit and explicit query cursor syntax that allows the transfer of multiple rows of data in a single round-trip between the PL/SQL and SQL engines

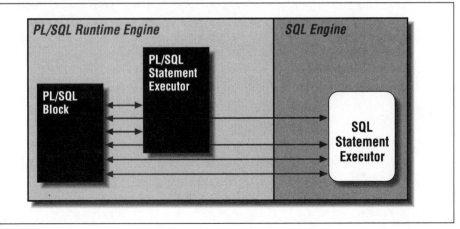

Figure 5-1. Context switching between PL/SQL and SQL

Make Collections a Part of Your PL/SQL Diet

With each new release, PL/SQL gets more robust, faster, and easier to use. The "bulk bind" features discussed in this chapter, FORALL and BULK COLLECT, are clear reflections of this trend.

As you will soon see, you won't be able to take advantage of FORALL and BULK COLLECT unless you work with collections (variable arrays, nested tables, or index-by tables). Sadly, many PL/SQL developers have not yet become conversant in these relatively new structures (variable arrays and nested tables are new with Oracle8; index-by tables were first available in PL/SQL 2.3 as "PL/SQL tables"). If you are one of those developers, perhaps these bulk bind capabilities will offer the required incentive for you to dig in to your books and knowledge bases.

If you don't use collections and you don't use bulk bind operations, then the applications you write will run more slowly and be more complicated than you—and your manager—would like.

Context-Switching Problem Scenarios

Before we take a look at the details of FORALL and BULK COLLECT, let's examine the scenarios where excessive context switches are likely to cause problems. These are likely to happen when you are processing multiple rows of information stored (or to be deposited) in a collection (a VARRAY, nested table, index-by table, or host array).

Suppose, for example, that I have filled two variable arrays with war criminals' ID numbers and the latest count of their victims. I then want to update the war criminals table with this information. Here's the solution I would have written prior to Oracle 8.1 (referencing a couple of already defined variable arrays):

```
CREATE OR REPLACE PROCEDURE update_tragedies (
    warcrim_ids IN name_varray,
    num_victims IN number_varray
    )
IS
BEGIN
    FOR indx IN warcrim_ids.FIRST .. warcrim_ids.LAST
    LOOP
        UPDATE war_criminal
            SET victim_count = num_victims (indx)
            WHERE war_criminal_id = warcrim_ids (indx);
    END LOOP;
END;
```

If I needed to update 100 rows, then I would be performing 100 context switches, since each update is processed in a separate trip to the SQL engine. Figure 5-2 illustrates this excessive (but previously unavoidable) switching.

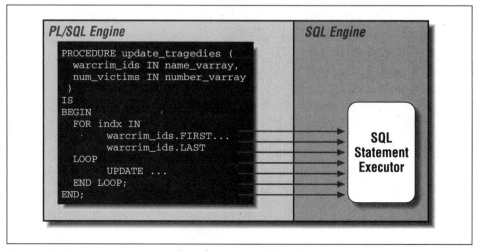

Figure 5-2. Excessive context switching for multiple UPDATEs

You can also run into lots of switching when you fetch multiple rows of information from a cursor into a collection. Here is an example of the kind of code that cries out for the Oracle 8.1 bulk collection feature:

```
DECLARE
    CURSOR major_polluters IS
        SELECT name, mileage
            FROM cars_and_trucks
            WHERE vehicle_type IN ('SUV', 'PICKUP');
```

```
      names name_varray := name_varray();
      mileages number_varray := number_varray();
   BEGIN
      FOR bad_car IN major_polluters
      LOOP
         names.EXTEND;
         names (major_polluters%ROWCOUNT) := bad_car.name;
         mileages.EXTEND;
         mileages (major_polluters%ROWCOUNT) := bad_car.mileage;
      END LOOP;

      ... now work with data in the arrays ...
   END;
```

If you find yourself writing code like either of the previous examples, you will be much better off switching to one of the bulk operations explored in the following sections. In particular, you should keep an eye out for these cues in your code:

- A recurring SQL statement inside a PL/SQL loop (it doesn't have to be a FOR loop, but that is the most likely candidate).

- Some parameter that can be made a bind variable. You need to be able to load those values into a collection to then have it processed by FORALL.

Bulk DML with the FORALL Statement

PL/SQL has a new keyword: FORALL. This keyword tells the PL/SQL runtime engine to bulk bind into the SQL statement all the elements of one or more collections *before* sending anything to the SQL engine.

Although the FORALL statement contains an iteration scheme (it iterates through all the rows of a collection), it is not a FOR loop. It does not, consequently, have either a LOOP or an END LOOP statement. Its syntax is as follows:

```
FORALL index_row IN lower_bound ... upper_bound
   sql_statement;
```

index_row

The specified collection; the FORALL will iterate through the rows of this collection

lower_bound

The starting index number (row or collection element) for the operation

upper_bound

The ending index number (row or collection element) for the operation

sql_statement

The SQL statement to be performed on each collection element

You must follow these rules when using FORALL:

- The body of the FORALL statement is a single DML statement—an INSERT, UPDATE, or DELETE.

- The DML must reference collection elements, indexed by the *index_row* variable in the FORALL statement. The scope of the *index_row* variable is the FORALL statement only; you may not reference it outside of that statement.

- Do not declare an INTEGER variable for *index_row*. It is declared implicitly by the PL/SQL engine.

- The lower and upper bounds must specify a valid range of consecutive index numbers for the collection(s) referenced in the SQL statement. The following script, for example:

```
DECLARE
    TYPE NumList IS TABLE OF NUMBER;
    ceo_payoffs NumList :=
        NumList(1000000, 42000000, 20000000, 17900000);
BEGIN
    ceo_payoffs.DELETE(3);  -- delete third element
    FORALL indx IN ceo_payoffs.FIRST..ceo_payoffs.LAST
        UPDATE excessive_comp
            SET salary = ceo_payoffs(indx)
            WHERE layoffs > 10000;
END;
```

will cause the following error:

```
ORA-22160: element at index [3] does not exist
```

This error occurs because the DELETE method has removed an element from the collection; the FORALL statement requires a densely filled collection. See the *diffcount.sql* file on the companion disk for an example (and resulting behavior) of this scenario.

- The collection subscript referenced in the DML statement cannot be an expression. For example, the following script:

```
DECLARE
    names name_varray := name_varray();
BEGIN
    FORALL indx IN names.FIRST .. names.LAST
        DELETE FROM emp WHERE ename = names(indx+10);
END;
/
```

will cause the following error:

```
PLS-00430: FORALL iteration variable INDX is not allowed in this context
```

The DML statement can reference more than one collection. The upper and lower bounds do not have to span the entire contents of the collection(s). When this statement is bulk bound and passed to SQL, the SQL engine executes the statement once for each index number in the range. In other words, the same SQL statements will be executed, but they will all be run in the same round-trip to the SQL layer, minimizing the context switches, as shown in Figure 5-3.

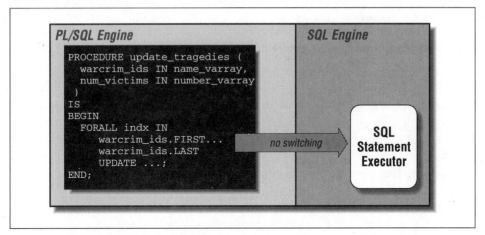

Figure 5-3. One context switch with FORALL

FORALL Examples

Here are some examples of the use of the FORALL statement:

1. Let's rewrite the update_tragedies procedure to use FORALL:

```
CREATE OR REPLACE PROCEDURE update_tragedies (
    warcrim_ids IN name_varray,
    num_victims IN number_varray
    )
IS
BEGIN
    FORALL indx IN warcrim_ids.FIRST .. warcrim_ids.LAST
        UPDATE war_criminal
            SET victim_count = num_victims (indx)
        WHERE war_criminal_id = warcrim_ids (indx);
END;
```

Notice that the only changes in this example are to change FOR to FORALL, and to remove the LOOP and END LOOP keywords. This use of FORALL accesses and passes to SQL each of the rows defined in the war criminals array (and the corresponding values for the number of victims).

2. In the following call to FORALL, I am passing a subset of the collection's full range of values to the SQL statement:

```
DECLARE
    TYPE not_enough_names IS VARRAY(2000) OF VARCHAR2(100);
    usda_inspectors not_enough_names := not_enough_names ();
BEGIN
    -- Fill varray with the names of the US Department of Agriculture
```

```
-- inspectors who are supposed to inspect over 7,000,000 businesses
-- in the United States.
...

-- Make government smaller: DELETE all but 100 inspectors
-- and then wait for the E. coli to attack.
FORALL indx IN 101 .. usda_inspectors.LAST
   DELETE FROM federal_employee
      WHERE name = usda_inspectors(indx);
END;
```

3. The previous example shows how the DML statement can reference more than
   one collection. In this next case, I have three: denial, patient_name, and illnesses. Only the first two are subscripted. Since the PL/SQL engine bulk binds
   only subscripted collections, the same illnesses collection is inserted as a
   whole into the hmo_coverage table for each of the rows inserted:

```
FORALL indx IN denial.FIRST .. denial.LAST
   INSERT INTO hmo_coverage
      VALUES (denial(indx), patient_name(indx), illnesses);
```

ROLLBACK Behavior with FORALL

The FORALL statement allows you to pass multiple SQL statements all together (in
bulk) to the SQL engine. This means that as far as context switching is concerned,
you have one SQL "block," but these blocks are still treated as individual DML
operations.

What happens when one of those DML statements fails? The following rules apply:

- The FORALL statement stops executing. It isn't possible to request that the
  FORALL skip over the offending statement and continue on to the next row in
  the collection.

- The DML statement being executed is rolled back to an implicit savepoint
  marked by the PL/SQL engine before execution of the statement.

- Any previous DML operations in that FORALL statement that already executed
  without error are *not* rolled back.

The following script demonstrates this behavior; it's available in the *forallerr.sql*
file on the companion disk.

First, I create a table for lobbyists of the National Rifle Association (if they are not
"gun happy," then I don't know who is) and fill it with some gun information:

```
/* Filename on companion disk: forallerr.sql */
CREATE TABLE gun_happy (
   name VARCHAR2(15), country VARCHAR2(100), killed INTEGER);
INSERT INTO gun_happy VALUES('AK-47', 'Russia', 100000);
INSERT INTO gun_happy VALUES('Uzi', 'Israel', 50000);
INSERT INTO gun_happy VALUES('Colt-45', 'USA', 25000000);
```

Then I use FORALL to update the names of the guns to include the number of people killed by those guns. (Whoops! Guns don't kill people. People kill people.)

```
DECLARE
    TYPE StgList IS TABLE OF VARCHAR2(100);
    countries StgList := StgList ('Israel', 'Russia', 'USA');
BEGIN
    FORALL indx IN countries.FIRST..countries.LAST
        UPDATE gun_happy SET name = name || '-' || killed
            WHERE country = countries(indx);

    DBMS_OUTPUT.PUT_LINE ('Update performed!');
EXCEPTION
    WHEN OTHERS THEN
        DBMS_OUTPUT.PUT_LINE ('Update did not complete!');
        COMMIT;
END;
/
```

Take note of two things:

- I place the countries in the nested table named "countries" in alphabetical order; thus, the update for the Colt .45 will be the last one processed.

- When I concatenate the name and killed tables for the Colt .45, the length of this string exceeds 15 characters. This will raise a VALUE_ERROR exception.

To see the impact of this block, I run my script with queries to show the contents of the gun_happy table:

```
SQL> @forallerr

Gun Names
---------------
AK-47
Uzi
Colt-45

Use FORALL for update...
Update did not complete!

Gun Names
---------------
AK-47-100000
Uzi-50000
Colt-45
```

As you can see, the first two changes stuck, whereas the last attempt to change the name failed, causing a rollback, but only to the beginning of that third UPDATE statement.

How do you know how many of your DML statements succeeded? You can check the SQL%BULK_ROWCOUNT cursor attribute; this new attribute, used exclusively with bulk binds, is discussed in the later section, "Using Cursor Attributes."

Bulk Querying with the BULK COLLECT Clause

So now you know how to perform bulk DML with FORALL. What about bulk querying? I showed an example earlier of the kind of code that cries out for a bulk transfer. Here is the executable section of that example:

```
BEGIN
    FOR bad_car IN major_polluters
    LOOP
        names.EXTEND;
        names (major_polluters%ROWCOUNT) := bad_car.name;
        mileages.EXTEND;
        mileages (major_polluters%ROWCOUNT) := bad_car.mileage;
    END LOOP;

    ... now work with data in the arrays ...
END;
```

Not only do I have to write a bunch of code, but it is also much slower than I would like, because of the context switches.

To help out in this scenario, PL/SQL now offers the BULK COLLECT keywords. This clause in your cursor (explicit or implicit) tells the SQL engine to bulk bind the output from the multiple rows fetched by the query into the specified collections *before* returning control to the PL/SQL engine. The syntax for this clause is:

```
... BULK COLLECT INTO collection_name[, collection_name] ...
```

where *collection_name* identifies a collection.

Here are some rules and restrictions to keep in mind when using BULK COLLECT:

- You can use these keywords in any of the following clauses: SELECT INTO, FETCH INTO, and RETURNING INTO.

- The collections you reference can only store scalar values (string, number, date). In other words, you cannot fetch a row of data into a record structure that is a row in a collection.

- The SQL engine automatically initializes and extends the collections you reference in the BULK COLLECT clause. It starts filling the collections at index 1, inserts elements consecutively (densely), and overwrites the values of any elements that were previously defined.

- You cannot use the SELECT...BULK COLLECT statement in a FORALL statement.

Let's explore these rules and the usefulness of BULK COLLECT through a series of examples.

First, here is a recoding of the "major polluters" example using BULK COLLECT:

```
DECLARE
   names name_varray;
   mileages number_varray;
BEGIN
   SELECT name, mileage
     FROM cars_and_trucks
     BULK COLLECT INTO names, mileages
     WHERE vehicle_type IN ('SUV', 'PICKUP');

   ... now work with data in the arrays ...
END;
```

I am now able to remove the initialization and extension code from the row-by-row fetch implementation.

But I don't have to rely on implicit cursors to get this job done. Here is another reworking of the major polluters example, retaining the explicit cursor:

```
DECLARE
   CURSOR major_polluters IS
       SELECT name, mileage
         FROM cars_and_trucks
         WHERE vehicle_type IN ('SUV', 'PICKUP');
   names name_varray;
   mileages number_varray;
BEGIN
   OPEN major_polluters;
   FETCH major_polluters BULK COLLECT INTO names, mileages;

   ... now work with data in the arrays ...
END;
```

I recommend that you use this second, explicit cursor-based approach—and that you store your cursors in packages, so that they can be reused. In fact, the optimal approach would involve a bundling of these operations into a procedure, as follows:

```
/* Filename on companion disk: polluters.pkg */
CREATE OR REPLACE PACKAGE pollution
IS
   CURSOR major_polluters (typelist IN VARCHAR2)
   IS
       SELECT name, mileage
         FROM cars_and_trucks
         WHERE INSTR (typelist, vehicle_type) > 0;

   PROCEDURE get_major_polluters (
       typelist IN VARCHAR2,
       names OUT name_varray,
       mileages OUT number_varray);
END;
/
```

```
CREATE OR REPLACE PACKAGE BODY pollution
IS
    PROCEDURE get_major_polluters (
        typelist IN VARCHAR2,
        names OUT name_varray,
        mileages OUT number_varray)
    IS
    BEGIN
        IF major_polluters%ISOPEN
        THEN
            CLOSE major_polluters;
        END IF;
        OPEN major_polluters (typelist);
        FETCH major_polluters BULK COLLECT INTO names, mileages;
        CLOSE major_polluters;
    END;
END;
/
```

Then I can populate my arrays with a minimum of fuss and a maximum of reusability (of both code and SQL):

```
DECLARE
    names name_varray;
    mileages number_varray;
BEGIN
    pollution.get_major_polluters ('SUV,PICKUP');

    ... now work with data in the arrays ...
END;
```

Restricting Bulk Collection with ROWNUM

There is no regulator mechanism built into BULK COLLECT. If your SQL statement identifies 100,000 rows of data, then the column values of all 100,000 rows will be loaded into the target collections. This can, of course, cause serious problems in your application—and in system memory. Remember: these collections are allocated for each session. So if you have 100 users all running the same program that bulk collects 100,000 rows of information, then real memory is needed for a total of 10 million rows.

What can you do about this potentially hazardous scenario? First of all (as should be common sense in your application regardless of the use of BULK COLLECT), be careful about the queries you write and those you offer to developers and/or users to run. You shouldn't provide unrestricted access to very large tables.

You can also fall back on ROWNUM to limit the number of rows processed by your query. For example, suppose that my cars_and_trucks table has a *very* large number of rows of vehicles that qualify as major polluters. I could then add a ROWNUM condition to my WHERE clause and another parameter to my packaged cursor as follows:

```
CREATE OR REPLACE PACKAGE pollution
IS
   CURSOR major_polluters (
      typelist IN VARCHAR2, maxrows IN INTEGER := NULL)
   IS
      SELECT name, mileage
        FROM cars_and_trucks
       WHERE INSTR (typelist, vehicle_type) > 0
         AND ROWNUM < LEAST (maxrows, 10000);

   PROCEDURE get_major_polluters (
      typelist IN VARCHAR2,
      names OUT name_varray,
      mileages OUT number_varray);
END;
/
```

Now there is no way that anyone can ever get more than 10,000 rows in a single query—and the user of that cursor (an individual developer) can also add a further regulatory capability by overriding that 10,000 with an even smaller number.

Bulk Fetching of Multiple Columns

As you have seen in previous examples, you certainly can bulk fetch the contents of multiple columns. However, you must fetch them into separate collections, one per column.

You cannot fetch into a collection of records (or objects). The following example demonstrates the error that you will receive if you try to do this:

```
DECLARE
   TYPE VehTab IS TABLE OF cars_and_trucks%ROWTYPE;
   gas_guzzlers VehTab;
   CURSOR low_mileage_cur IS SELECT * FROM cars_and_trucks WHERE mileage < 10;
BEGIN
   OPEN low_mileage_cur;
   FETCH low_mileage_cur BULK COLLECT INTO gas_guzzlers;
END;
/
```

When I run this code, I get the following somewhat obscure error message:

```
PLS-00493: invalid reference to a server-side object or
           function in a local context
```

You will instead have to write this block as follows:

```
DECLARE
   guzzler_type name_varray;
   guzzler_name name_varray;
   guzzler_mileage number_varray;

   CURSOR low_mileage_cur IS
```

```
        SELECT vehicle_type, name, mileage
          FROM cars_and_trucks WHERE mileage < 10;
BEGIN
   OPEN low_mileage_cur;
   FETCH low_mileage_cur BULK COLLECT
     INTO guzzler_type, guzzler_name, guzzler_mileage;
END;
/
```

Using the RETURNING Clause with Bulk Operations

You've now seen BULK COLLECT put to use for both implicit and explicit query cursors. You can also use BULK COLLECT inside a FORALL statement, in order to take advantage of the RETURNING clause.

The RETURNING clause, new to Oracle8, allows you to obtain information (such as a newly updated value for a salary) from a DML statement. RETURNING can help you avoid additional queries to the database to determine the results of DML operations that just completed.

Suppose Congress has passed a law (overriding the almost certain presidential veto) requiring that a company pay its highest-compensated employee no more than 50 times the salary of its lowest-paid employee.* I work in the IT department of the newly merged company Northrop-Ford-Mattel-Yahoo-ATT, which employs a total of 250,000 workers. The word has come down from on high: the CEO is not taking a pay cut, so we need to increase the salaries of everyone who makes less than 50 times his 2004 total compensation package of $145 million—and decrease the salaries of all upper management except for the CEO. After all, somebody's got to make up for this loss in profit.

Wow! I have lots of updating to do, and I want to use FORALL to get the job done as quickly as possible. However, I also need to perform various kinds of processing on the employee data and then print a report showing the change in salary for each affected employee. That RETURNING clause would come in awfully handy here, so let's give it a try.

See the *onlyfair.sql* file on the companion disk for all of the steps shown here, plus table creation and INSERT statements.

First, I'll create a reusable function to return the compensation for an executive:

```
/* Filename on companion disk: onlyfair.sql */
FUNCTION salforexec (title_in IN VARCHAR2) RETURN NUMBER
IS
   CURSOR ceo_compensation IS
      SELECT salary + bonus + stock_options +
```

---

* Currently in the United States, the average is more like 250 times, a very inequitable situation that almost certainly causes hundreds of thousands of children to go hungry each day in our very rich nation.

```
                   mercedes_benz_allowance + yacht_allowance
           FROM compensation
          WHERE title = title_in;
      big_bucks NUMBER;
BEGIN
      OPEN ceo_compensation;
      FETCH ceo_compensation INTO big_bucks;
      RETURN big_bucks;
END;
/
```

In the main block of the update program, I declare a number of local variables and the following query to identify underpaid employees and overpaid employees who are not lucky enough to be the CEO:

```
DECLARE
    big_bucks NUMBER := salforexec ('CEO');
    min_sal NUMBER := big_bucks / 50;
    names name_varray;
    old_salaries number_varray;
    new_salaries number_varray;

    CURSOR affected_employees (ceosal IN NUMBER)
    IS
        SELECT name, salary + bonus old_salary
          FROM compensation
         WHERE title != 'CEO'
           AND ((salary + bonus < ceosal / 50)
                OR (salary + bonus > ceosal / 10)) ;
```

At the start of my executable section, I load all this data into my collections with a BULK COLLECT query:

```
OPEN affected_employees (big_bucks);
FETCH affected_employees
    BULK COLLECT INTO names, old_salaries;
```

Then I can use the names collection in my FORALL update:

```
FORALL indx IN names.FIRST .. names.LAST
    UPDATE compensation
       SET salary =
           DECODE (
               GREATEST (min_sal, salary),
                   min_sal, min_sal,
               salary / 5)
     WHERE name = names (indx)
     RETURNING salary BULK COLLECT INTO new_salaries;
```

I use DECODE to give an employee either a major boost in yearly income or an 80% cut in pay to keep the CEO comfy. I end it with a RETURNING clause that relies on BULK COLLECT to populate a third collection: the new salaries.

Finally, since I used RETURNING and don't have to write another query against
the compensation table to obtain the new salaries, I can immediately move to
report generation:

```
FOR indx IN names.FIRST .. names.LAST
LOOP
    DBMS_OUTPUT.PUT_LINE (
        RPAD (names(indx), 20) ||
        RPAD (' Old: ' || old_salaries(indx), 15) ||
        ' New: ' || new_salaries(indx)
        );
END LOOP;
```

Here, then, is the report generated from the *onlyfair.sql* script:

```
John DayAndNight      Old: 10500    New: 2900000
Holly Cubicle         Old: 52000    New: 2900000
Sandra Watchthebucks Old: 22000000  New: 4000000
```

Now everyone can afford quality housing and health care; tax revenue at all levels will increase (nobody's a better tax deadbeat than the ultra-rich), so public
schools can get the funding they need. Hey, and rich people are even still rich—
just not *as* rich as before. Now that is what I call a humming economy!

The RETURNING column values or expressions returned by each
execution in FORALL are added to the collection after the values
returned previously. If you use RETURNING inside a non-bulk FOR
loop, previous values are overwritten by the latest DML execution.

Using Cursor Attributes

Whenever you work with explicit and implicit cursors (including cursor variables),
PL/SQL provides a set of cursor attributes that return information about the cursor. PL/SQL 8.1 adds another, composite attribute, SQL%BULK_ROWCOUNT, for
use with or after the FORALL statement. All of the current attributes are summarized in Table 5-1.

Table 5-1. Cursor Attributes

Cursor Attribute	Effect
cur %FOUND	Returns TRUE if the last FETCH found a row
cur %NOTFOUND	Returns FALSE if the last FETCH found a row
cur %ISOPEN	Returns TRUE if the specified cursor is open
cur %ROWCOUNT	Returns the number of rows modified by the DML statement
SQL%BULK_ROWCOUNT	Returns the number of rows processed for each execution of the bulk DML operation

In these attributes, *cur* is the name of an explicit cursor, a cursor variable, or the string "SQL" for implicit cursors (UPDATE, DELETE, and INSERT statements, since none of the attributes can be applied to an implicit query). The %BULK_ROW-COUNT structure has the same semantics as an index-by table. The nth row in this pseudo index-by table stores the number of rows processed by the nth execution of the DML operation in the FORALL statement.

Let's examine the behavior of these cursor attributes in FORALL and BULK COLLECT statements by running the script found in the *showattr.sql* file on the disk. I start out by creating a utility function and general show_attributes procedure:

```
/* Filename on companion disk: showattr.sql */
CREATE OR REPLACE FUNCTION boolstg (bool IN BOOLEAN)
    RETURN VARCHAR2
IS
BEGIN
    IF bool THEN RETURN 'TRUE ';
    ELSIF NOT bool THEN RETURN 'FALSE';
    ELSE RETURN 'NULL ';
    END IF;
END;
/

CREATE OR REPLACE PROCEDURE show_attributes (
    depts IN number_varray)
IS
BEGIN
    FORALL indx IN depts.FIRST .. depts.LAST
        UPDATE emp
          SET sal = sal + depts(indx)
        WHERE deptno = depts(indx);

    DBMS_OUTPUT.PUT_LINE (
        'FOUND-' || boolstg(SQL%FOUND) || ' ' ||
        'NOTFOUND-' || boolstg(SQL%NOTFOUND) || ' ' ||
        'ISOPEN-' || boolstg(SQL%ISOPEN) || ' ' ||
        'ROWCOUNT-' || NVL (TO_CHAR (SQL%ROWCOUNT), 'NULL'));

    FOR indx IN depts.FIRST .. depts.LAST
    LOOP
        DBMS_OUTPUT.PUT_LINE (
            depts(indx) || '-' || SQL%BULK_ROWCOUNT(indx));
    END LOOP;

    ROLLBACK;
END;
/
```

Then I run a query to show some data and show the attributes for two different lists of department numbers, followed by a use of BULK COLLECT:

```
SELECT deptno, COUNT(*) FROM emp GROUP BY deptno;

DECLARE
```

```
        /* No employees in departments 98 and 99 */
        depts1 number_varray := number_varray (10, 20, 98);
        depts2 number_varray := number_varray (99, 98);
BEGIN
        show_attributes (depts1);
        show_attributes (depts2);
END;
/
DECLARE
        CURSOR allsals IS
            SELECT sal FROM emp;
        salaries number_varray;
BEGIN
        OPEN allsals;
        FETCH allsals BULK COLLECT INTO salaries;

        DBMS_OUTPUT.PUT_LINE (
            'FOUND-' || boolstg(SQL%FOUND) || ' ' ||
            'NOTFOUND-' || boolstg(SQL%NOTFOUND) || ' ' ||
            'ISOPEN-' || boolstg(SQL%ISOPEN) || ' ' ||
            'ROWCOUNT-' || NVL (TO_CHAR (SQL%ROWCOUNT), 'NULL'));
END;
/
```

Here is the output from this script:

```
DEPTNO COUNT(*)
------ ---------
    10         3 .
    20         5
    30         6

FOUND-TRUE  NOTFOUND-FALSE ISOPEN-FALSE ROWCOUNT-8
10-3
98-0
20-5
FOUND-FALSE NOTFOUND-TRUE  ISOPEN-FALSE ROWCOUNT-0
99-0
98-0
FOUND-NULL  NOTFOUND-NULL  ISOPEN-FALSE ROWCOUNT-NULL
```

From this output, we can conclude the following:

- For FORALL, %FOUND and %NOTFOUND reflect the overall results, not the results of any individual statement, including the last (this contradicts Oracle documentation). In other words, if any one of the statements executed in the FORALL modified at least one row, %FOUND returns TRUE and %NOT-FOUND returns FALSE.

- For FORALL, %ISOPEN always returns FALSE because the cursor is closed when the FORALL statement terminates.

- For FORALL, %ROWCOUNT returns the total number of rows affected by all the FORALL statements executed, not simply the last statement.

- For BULK COLLECT, %FOUND and %NOTFOUND always return NULL and %ISOPEN returns FALSE because the BULK COLLECT has completed the fetching and closed the cursor. %ROWCOUNT always returns NULL, since this attribute is only relevant for DML statements.

- The *n*th row in this pseudo index-by table stores the number of rows processed by the *n*th execution of the DML operation in the FORALL statement. If no rows are processed, then the value in %BULK_ROWCOUNT is set to 0.

The %BULK_ROWCOUNT attribute is a handy device, but it is also quite limited. Keep the following in mind:

- Even though it looks like an index-by table, you cannot apply any methods to it.

- %BULK_ROWCOUNT cannot be assigned to other collections. Also, it cannot be passed as a parameter to subprograms.

- The only rows defined for this pseudo index-by table are the same rows defined in the collection referenced in the FORALL statement.

- If you reference a row in %BULK_ROWCOUNT that is outside the defined subscripts, you will *not* raise a NO_DATA_FOUND error or subscript error. It will simply return a NULL value.

If I try to execute code like either of these statements:

```
DBMS_OUTPUT.PUT_LINE (SQL%BULK_ROWCOUNT.COUNT);
```

```
IF SQL%BULK_ROWCOUNT.FIRST IS NOT NULL
```

I get this error:

```
PLS-00332: "%BULK_ROWCOUNT" is not a valid prefix for a qualified name
```

All you can really do with %BULK_ROWCOUNT is reference individual rows in this special structure.

Analyzing the Impact of Bulk Operations

Now that you know all about FORALL and BULK COLLECT, let's see if it's really worth the time to learn these new features. These statements are supposed to provide significant performance improvements over the context-switch-heavy, row-by-row processing of earlier versions of PL/SQL.

Let's run some tests to document the gains by running the *bulktiming.sql* script (using the PLVtmr package described in the Preface, in the section "About the Disk").

Leaving out portions of the script not central to the timing, here is the code I used
to compare the performance of a FOR loop and FORALL:

```
/* Filename on companion disk: bulktiming.sql */
BEGIN
   /* Load up the collection. */
   FOR indx IN 1..num LOOP
      pnums(indx) := indx;
      pnames(indx) := 'Part ' || TO_CHAR(indx);
   END LOOP;

   /* Do a bunch of individual inserts. */
   PLVtmr.capture;
   FOR indx IN 1..num LOOP
      INSERT INTO parts VALUES (pnums(indx), pnames(indx));
   END LOOP;
   PLVtmr.show_elapsed ('FOR loop');

   ROLLBACK;

   /* Perform the inserts via FORALL */
   PLVtmr.capture;
   FORALL indx IN 1..num
      INSERT INTO parts VALUES (pnums(indx), pnames(indx));
   PLVtmr.show_elapsed ('FORALL');

   ROLLBACK;
END;
```

And here are the results (drumroll, please!) for the specified number of rows
(1000, 10,000, and 20,000):

```
FOR loop 1000 Elapsed: .39 seconds.
FORALL 1000 Elapsed: .05 seconds.

FOR loop 10000 Elapsed: 5.73 seconds.
FORALL 10000 Elapsed: .79 seconds.

FOR loop 20000 Elapsed: 10.34 seconds.
FORALL 20000 Elapsed: 1.49 seconds.
```

The results indicate that we can expect a single order of magnitude improvement
in performance, always something to appreciate. And the timings increase in a lin-
ear fashion, giving us a comfortable feeling as to the scalability of this feature.

Finally, here is the script (minus various administrative tasks; see *bulktiming.sql* for
all the details) I wrote to compare row-by-row fetching and BULK COLLECT:

```
/* Filename on companion disk: bulktiming.sql */
BEGIN
   /* Fetch the data row by row */
   PLVtmr.capture;
   FOR rec IN (SELECT * FROM parts)
```

```
      LOOP
         pnums(SQL%ROWCOUNT)   := rec.partnum;
         pnames(SQL%ROWCOUNT)  := rec.partname;
      END LOOP;
      PLVtmr.show_elapsed ('Single row fetch '|| num);

      /* Fetch the data row by row */
      PLVtmr.capture;
      SELECT * BULK COLLECT INTO pnums, pnames FROM parts;
      PLVtmr.show_elapsed ('BULK COLLECT '|| num);
   END;
```

The results are as follows for the specified number of rows:

```
Single row fetch 1000 Elapsed: .14 seconds.
BULK COLLECT 1000 Elapsed: .02 seconds.

Single row fetch 10000 Elapsed: 1.56 seconds.
BULK COLLECT 10000 Elapsed: .4 seconds.

Single row fetch 20000 Elapsed: 2.75 seconds.
BULK COLLECT 20000 Elapsed: 1.48 seconds.

Single row fetch 100000 Elapsed: 18.91 seconds.
BULK COLLECT 100000 Elapsed: 85.18 seconds.
```

Again, we see improvements in performance, but notice that the gains through BULK COLLECT diminish with high numbers of rows. In fact, for 100,000 rows, BULK COLLECT was actually much slower than the single-row fetch. I am not sure what might be causing this slowdown.

6

In this chapter:
- *Triggers on Nested Table View Columns*
- *Database-Level Event Triggers*
- *Schema-Level Event Triggers*

New Trigger Features in Oracle8i

Oracle8*i* expands significantly the use of triggers to administer a database and publish information about events taking place within the database. By employing database triggers on the system events defined in Oracle8*i*, and using Oracle Advanced Queuing within those triggers, you can take advantage of the publish/subscribe capabilities of Oracle8*i*.

The database event publication feature allows applications to subscribe to database events just as they subscribe to messages from other applications. Trigger syntax is extended to support system and other data events on the database level or on a particular schema level. Trigger syntax also supports a CALL to a procedure as the trigger body.

You can now enable the publication of (i.e., define a programmatic trigger on) the following actions:

- DML statements (DELETE, INSERT, and UPDATE)

- DDL events (e.g., CREATE, DROP, and ALTER)

- Database events (SERVERERROR, LOGON, LOGOFF, STARTUP, and SHUT-DOWN)

Here are the new trigger features available in Oracle8*i*:

Triggers on nested table columns
> Use of the CAST...MULTISET operation allows you to trigger activity when only an attribute in a nested table column is modified.

Database-level (also known as system-level) event triggers
> You can now define triggers to respond to such database-level events as LOGON, DATABASE SHUTDOWN, and even SERVERERROR.

Schema-level (also known as user-level) event triggers

You can now define triggers to respond to such schema-level events as CRE-ATE, DROP, and ALTER.

Triggers on Nested Table View Columns

Oracle8 Release 8.0 allowed developers to create INSTEAD OF triggers, which could then be applied to any view but were especially handy with object views and any inherently unmodifiable view. Oracle8*i* expands further the usefulness of triggers by allowing you to define a trigger to fire when one or more attributes of a nested table view column are modified. This feature allows you to change an element of a collection synthesized using the CAST...MULTISET operation.

Figure 6-1 illustrates the ability of the nested table trigger to zoom inside the outer table structure and respond to changes made to the nested table.

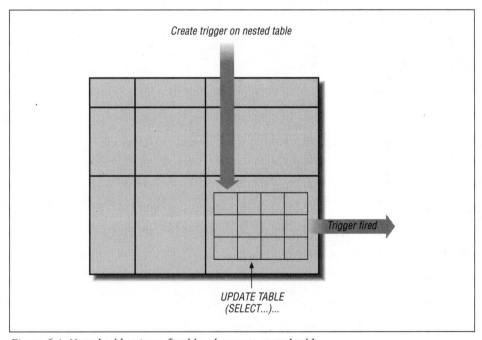

Figure 6-1. Nested table trigger fired by change to nested table

Let's walk through an example illustrating the steps you would take to achieve this effect (use the *nesttrig.sql* file on the companion disk to run all of the following statements in sequence). I'll use membership in the National Rifle Association as an example here. Using the NRA slogan (but not necessarily the belief of all its members) "Guns don't kill people, people kill people" and a little sleight of hand, I've generated the following two relational tables:

```
/* Filename on companion disk: nesttrig.sql */
CREATE TABLE nra_members (
    person_id INTEGER,
    last_name VARCHAR2(100),
    first_name VARCHAR2(20),  );
    age NUMBER);

CREATE TABLE non_killers (
    person_id INTEGER,
    gun_name VARCHAR2(75)
```

I want to build an object view over these two tables that implements the non_killers table as a nested table column. First I must create two object types (a bug in Oracle 8.1.5 requires that I create a table of objects, rather than scalars, for the nested table column to function properly):

```
CREATE OR REPLACE TYPE gun_name_ot AS OBJECT (
    gun_name VARCHAR2(75)
);
/
CREATE OR REPLACE TYPE non_killer_t
    AS TABLE OF gun_name_ot;
/
CREATE OR REPLACE TYPE nra_member_t
AS OBJECT (
    person_id INTEGER,
    last_name VARCHAR2(100),
    first_name VARCHAR2(12),
    age INTEGER,
    gun_names non_killer_t
);
/
```

Now I can create my object view, using CAST...MULTISET to convert my normalized relational table into a nested table column:

```
CREATE OR REPLACE VIEW nra_members_ov
    OF nra_member_t
    WITH OBJECT OID (person_id)
AS
    SELECT luvguns.person_id,
           luvguns.last_name,
           luvguns.first_name,
           luvguns.age,
           CAST (MULTISET (
               SELECT gun_name
                 FROM non_killers bestfriend
                WHERE bestfriend.person_id =
                      bestfriend.person_id)
               AS non_killer_t)
FROM nra_members luvguns;
```

Once I have this view in place, I also need to provide INSTEAD OF triggers to allow a user to update, insert, or delete through the view, making the illusion of my use of objects complete. These capabilities have been present since Oracle 8.0, so I will not repeat the code here (see the *nesttrig.sql* trigger named nra_ members_nest_insert for an example). I will, instead, focus on the new nested table trigger capability.

Here is the trigger definition; notice that the only difference is the line in bold, indicating that the trigger applies only to the specified nested table:

```
/* Filename on companion disk: nesttrig.sql */
CREATE OR REPLACE TRIGGER nra_members_gun_rename
INSTEAD OF INSERT OR UPDATE
ON NESTED TABLE gun_names OF nra_members_ov
BEGIN
   IF INSERTING
   THEN
      INSERT INTO non_killers (person_id, gun_name)
      VALUES (:PARENT.person_id, :NEW.gun_name);
   END IF;

   IF UPDATING
   THEN
      UPDATE non_killers
         SET gun_name = :NEW.gun_name
       WHERE gun_name = :OLD.gun_name
         AND person_id = :PARENT.person_id;
   END IF;
END;
/
```

Let's try it out. I inserted Charlton Heston (national spokesperson of the NRA as of May 1999) and hypothetical information about his guns into the two tables:

```
INSERT INTO nra_members (
   person_id, last_name, first_name, age)
VALUES (100, 'HESTON', 'CHARLTON', 70);

INSERT INTO non_killers (
   person_id, gun_name)
   VALUES (100, 'COLT-45');
INSERT INTO non_killers (
   person_id, gun_name)
   VALUES (100, 'M-16');
INSERT INTO non_killers (
   person_id, gun_name)
   VALUES (100, 'DOUBLE-BARRELED JUSTICE');
```

Suppose then that Charlton Heston undergoes a sea change in philosophy. To demonstrate his new principles, he renames each of his guns, stored in that nested table. Here is the update in a single statement:

```
UPDATE TABLE (SELECT gun_names
              FROM nra_members_ov
```

```
                        WHERE person_id = 100)
         SET gun_name =
                DECODE (gun_name,
                   'COLT-45', 'Pretty Pony',
                   'M-16', 'I Love Mom',
                   'DOUBLE-BARRELED JUSTICE', 'Peace on Earth',
                   gun_name);
```

I use the TABLE...SELECT combination to extract just the nested table column from the object view. The SET clause then applies to the attributes of that nested table.

 Tests indicate that these new nested table triggers will fire only when the DML action occurs on the nested table column, and *not* on any other columns in the table.

Database-Level Event Triggers

Oracle8*i* allows you to define triggers to respond to database-level events (also known as system-level events), including the following:

- Logon to and logoff from a schema

- Startup and shutdown of the database

- Response to a server error

Here is the syntax for these triggers:

```
CREATE [ OR REPLACE ] TRIGGER trigger_name
    { BEFORE | AFTER }
    { SERVERERROR |
      LOGON | LOGOFF |
      STARTUP | SHUTDOWN }
   ON DATABASE
BEGIN
    pl/sql_statements
END;
```

To create a trigger at the database level, you must have the ADMINISTER DATABASE TRIGGER system privilege. You will also need privileges to access any of the external references in the trigger's PL/SQL code.

Table 6-1 lists the different database-level events on which you may define a trigger.

Table 6-1. Database-Level Events for Trigger Definitions

Event	Description
SERVERERROR	Oracle fires the trigger whenever a server error message is logged.
LOGON	Oracle fires the trigger after a client application logs on to the database successfully.

Table 6-1. Database-Level Events for Trigger Definitions (continued)

Event	Description
LOGOFF	Oracle fires the trigger before a client application logs off the database.
STARTUP	Oracle fires the trigger immediately after the database is opened.·
SHUTDOWN	Oracle fires the trigger just before the server starts a shutdown of an instance of the database. Note that a SHUTDOWN trigger will only fire if the database is shut down cleanly using SHUTDOWN or SHUT-DOWN IMMEDIATE. If an instance shuts down abnormally (SHUT-DOWN ABORT), this event will not be fired.

Each database-level event has an associated with it a set of attributes. These attributes are actually functions owned by SYS that return the values of characteristics relevant to the event. Table 6-2 lists the current set of attributes.

Table 6-2. Attributes for Database-Level Events

Name	Datatype	Description
SYSEVENT	VARCHAR2(30)	The database-level event firing the trigger; this value matches the name used in the syntax of the trigger.
LOGIN_USER	VARCHAR2(30)	The login username.
INSTANCE_NUM	NUMBER	The instance number.
DATABASE_NAME	VARCHAR2(50)	The name of the database.
SERVER_ERROR	NUMBER	This function returns the error at the nth position in the stack. You must specify a position (1 equals "top") when you call this function. For example: SERVER_ERROR(1)
IS_SERVERERROR	BOOLEAN	Returns TRUE if the specified error is on the current error stack; FALSE otherwise.

Table 6-3 lists the restrictions and attributes for each database-level event.

Table 6-3. Restrictions and Attributes for Database-Level Events

Event	Conditions/Restrictions	Attributes
SERVERERROR	You can specify a condition that will restrict the trigger to firing only when the specified exception is raised. Otherwise, it will fire for all errors.	SYSEVENT LOGIN_USER INSTANCE_NUM DATABASE_NAME SERVER_ERROR IS_SERVERERROR
LOGON	You can specify a condition using either USERID() or USERNAME().	SYSEVENT LOGIN_USER INSTANCE_NUM DATABASE_NAME

Table 6-3. Restrictions and Attributes for Database-Level Events (continued)

Event	Conditions/Restrictions	Attributes
LOGOFF	You can specify a condition using either USERID( ) or USERNAME( ).	SYSEVENT LOGIN_USER INSTANCE_NUM DATABASE_NAME
STARTUP	No database operations (DML and queries) are allowed. Instead, you might start up listener programs, pin code in memory, etc.	SYSEVENT LOGIN_USER INSTANCE_NUM DATABASE_NAME
SHUTDOWN	No database operations (DML and queries) are allowed. Instead, you might shut down listener programs, run performance collection utilities that write logs to files, etc.	SYSEVENT LOGIN_USER INSTANCE_NUM DATABASE_NAME

Keep in mind the following rules when working with these triggers:

- Whenever a database-level event trigger fires, Oracle opens an autonomous transaction, fires the trigger, and commits any DML in the trigger logic independently of the existing user transaction.

- When defining LOGON, STARTUP, and SERVERERROR triggers, you can only specify the AFTER context. If you specify BEFORE, you will get this error:

  ```
  ORA-30500: database open triggers and server error
            triggers cannot have BEFORE type
  ```

- When defining LOGOFF and SHUTDOWN triggers, you can only specify the BEFORE context. If you specify AFTER, you will get this error:

  ```
  ORA-30509: client logoff triggers cannot have AFTER type
  ```

- You cannot define AFTER STARTUP and BEFORE SHUTDOWN triggers for a schema; these apply only to DATABASE.

- Calls to DBMS_OUTPUT.PUT_LINE do not generate any visible output in the current session. If you want to obtain a record of actions that occurred, you will need to write information to a database table, database pipe, or operating system file. You could also use DBMS_AQ.ENQUEUE to place a message in a queue.

- A SERVERERROR trigger will not fire for any of the following errors:

  ```
  ORA-01403: no data found
  ORA-01422: exact fetch returns more than requested number of rows
  ORA-04030: out of process memory when trying to allocate nnn bytes
  ORA-01034: ORACLE not available
  ORA-01007: variable not in select list
  ```

Examples of Database-Level Event Triggers

There are many different ways you can use database-level event triggers to manage your database. The following examples offer some simple models from which you can build your own, more complex variations.

Pinning packages on database startup

A common requirement for a high-performance database is to pin one or more packages into shared memory. By pinning your code, it is exempted from the least recently used algorithm and will *never* be aged out of the shared pool area.

Before the existence of STARTUP triggers, the DBA would have to set up a script to run after the database was started. Now, I can create a STARTUP trigger like the following:

```
/* Filename on companion disk: startup.trg */
CREATE OR REPLACE TRIGGER pin_code_on_startup
  AFTER STARTUP ON DATABASE
BEGIN
   /* Pin the default packages of PL/SQL to
      improve runtime performance. */
   DBMS_SHARED_POOL.KEEP (
      'SYS.STANDARD', 'P');
   DBMS_SHARED_POOL.KEEP (
      'SYS.DBMS_STANDARD', 'P');
END;
/
```

With this trigger in place, I guarantee that all of my large code elements (including cursors, types, and triggers) and even my sequences are cached in the shared pool until the instance goes down.

If you are going to be pinning objects, you should consider building an infrastructure table to store the names of elements you want pinned. Then instead of hardcoding your pin commands in a trigger (as just shown), you could run a procedure that reads through the table and pins each element found. This approach is explained in detail in Chapter 12 of *Oracle Built-in Packages*.

Tracking logins to the database

Suppose that I want to keep track of logins to my database instance. To make this information available in a structured fashion, I am going to send my login information to a queue using the Oracle Advanced Queuing (AQ) facility.

These steps are illustrated in Figure 6-2. You will find all of the AQ-related steps in the *aq.sql* script on the companion disk; I'll concentrate on the trigger-related components here.

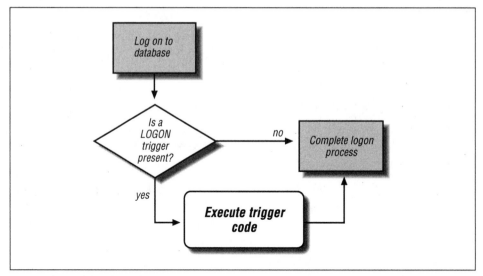

Figure 6-2. Logical flow of LOGON trigger

Let's start in reverse. Here is the LOGON trigger:

```
/* Filename on companion disk: aq.sql */
CREATE OR REPLACE TRIGGER publish_logon
AFTER LOGON ON DATABASE
BEGIN
   oraevent.put ('This is a logon');
END;
/
```

As you can see, there isn't much to it: every time someone logs in to the data-base, we'll put a message in the queue with a call to oraevent.put. So let's take a look at that procedure:

```
PROCEDURE oraevent.put (details_in IN VARCHAR2)
IS
   q_opts DBMS_AQ.ENQUEUE_OPTIONS_T;
   msg_props DBMS_AQ.MESSAGE_PROPERTIES_T;
   msg_handle RAW(16);
   event_l Event_t;
BEGIN
   /* Setting visibility to IMMEDIATE will
   || force the queue to "commit" before the
   || client transaction commits.
   */
   q_opts.visibility := DBMS_AQ.IMMEDIATE;
   event_l := Event_t.make(details_in);

   DBMS_AQ.ENQUEUE(queue_name => 'aqadmin.loginQ',
      enqueue_options => q_opts,
      message_properties => msg_props,
      payload => event_l,
```

```
                msgid => msg_handle);
    END;
```

This procedure calls DMBS_AQ.ENQUEUE to place a message, or *payload*, in the loginQ queue. Each message is an object of type Event_t, defined as follows:

```
CREATE TYPE Event_t AS OBJECT (
    eventname VARCHAR2(64),
    details VARCHAR2(512),
    username VARCHAR2(30),
    timestamp DATE,
    STATIC FUNCTION make (
        details_in IN VARCHAR2) RETURN Event_t
);
/
CREATE OR REPLACE TYPE BODY Event_t
AS
    STATIC FUNCTION make (
        details_in IN VARCHAR2) RETURN Event_t
    IS
    BEGIN
        RETURN Event_t(
            SYSEVENT,
            details_in,
            LOGIN_USER,
            SYSDATE);
    END;
END;
/
```

The RETURN statement relies on two of the event-related functions, SYSEVENT and LOGIN_USER, to record characteristics at the time of login.

Run the *aq.sql* script to create all elements and then test the code by spawning a second SQL*Plus session to watch or dequeue the login messages.

Trapping system errors

The SERVERERROR event will prove to be a very handy mechanism. You can define it at the database level, which means that any error raised in any schema will be interceptable through the trigger. You can also define a trigger for this event at the schema level, limiting the scope of firing of the trigger.

Suppose that you simply want to keep track of errors raised in a particular application running on your instance. When an error occurs, you write a message to a database pipe. Another session (running asynchronously to the application users) can then wake up and dump the contents of the pipe and examine the errors.

To facilitate that process, I have created and included on the disk a package called watch. Stored in *watch.pkg* on the companion disk, this package allows you to watch actions and then direct a message constructed for that action to either the screen via DBMS_OUTPUT or to a pipe via DBMS_PIPE.

If you are comfortable with Oracle Advanced Queuing, you'll find that the AQ facility certainly offers a more robust architecture than the basic database pipes of DBMS_PIPE for intersession communication and logging. DBMS_PIPE, on the other hand, is easier to use and also very handy to know for a variety of development scenarios.

Using the watch package, I first create a utility procedure that I will call in my SERVERERROR triggers:

```
/* Filename on companion disk: serverr.trg */
CREATE OR REPLACE PROCEDURE pipe_error (
   context IN VARCHAR2, msg IN VARCHAR2)
IS
BEGIN
   /* Send the information to a pipe. */
   watch.topipe;

   /* Retrieve all system event attributes. */
   watch.action (context || ' trap_error', msg);
END;
/
```

I can then define a trigger at the database level that displays all of the attributes available from within this trigger:

```
CREATE OR REPLACE TRIGGER trap_error
  AFTER SERVERERROR ON DATABASE
BEGIN
  pipe_error ('DATABASE',
     sysevent || '-' ||
     instance_num || '-' ||
     database_name || '-' ||
     SQLCODE || '-' ||
     server_error (1) || '-' ||
     login_user
     );
END;
/
```

I will also define a SERVERERROR trigger for the SCOTT schema, so we can explore the way multiple triggers of the same type fire:

```
CREATE OR REPLACE TRIGGER scott_trap_error
  AFTER SERVERERROR ON SCOTT.SCHEMA
BEGIN
  pipe_error (login_user,
     sysevent || '-' ||
     instance_num || '-' ||
     database_name || '-' ||
     SQLCODE || '-' ||
     server_error (1) || '-' ||
     login_user
```

```
        );
    END;
    /
```

To test these triggers, I created the following script:

```
/* Filename on companion disk: serverr.tst */
DECLARE
    exc EXCEPTION;
    PRAGMA EXCEPTION_INIT (exc, -&1);
BEGIN
    RAISE exc;
END;
/
```

Now I will connect as SCOTT and run the script emulating a date-related error:

```
SQL> @serverr.tst 1855
*
ERROR at line 1:
ORA-01855: AM/A.M. or PM/P.M. required
```

If the triggers fired, the watch pipe should contain some information. I can dump
the contents of the pipe with a call to watch.show:

```
SQL> exec watch.show
Contents of WATCH Trace:
***WATCHing at: June 1, 1999 12:54:14
    Context: SCOTT trap_error
    Message: SERVERERROR-1-ORACLE-0-1855-SCOTT
***WATCHing at: June 1, 1999 12:54:14
    Context: DATABASE trap_error
    Message: SERVERERROR-1-ORACLE-0-1855-SCOTT
```

We learn a few things from this execution:

- The schema-level trigger fires before the database-level trigger.

Current behavior in the Oracle database is that a schema-level trigger will fire before a database-level trigger. This sequence is not,
however, a documented feature and is subject to change in future
versions of Oracle. You should design your triggers so that the trigger logic does *not* depend on the firing sequence.

- By the time the SERVERERROR trigger fires, the SQLCODE function does not
  return the error that was raised. Instead, it returns 0. You must rely on the
  SERVER_ERROR function to retrieve the error at the top of the error stack.

Now I will connect to the DEMO account in my Oracle 8.1.5 instance and run this
script for a different error:

```
SQL> connect demo/demo.
SQL> @serverr.tst 1652
```

```
*
ERROR at line 1:
ORA-01652: unable to extend temp segment by nnn in tablespace
```

When I take a look at my pipe contents, I have only one entry:

```
SQL> exec watch.show
Contents of WATCH Trace:
***WATCHing at: June 1, 1999 13:01:38
   Context: DATABASE trap_error
   Message: SERVERERROR-1-ORACLE-0-1652-DEMO
```

And that is because I did not create a SERVERERROR trigger in the DEMO schema; only the database-level trigger is fired.

Checking for specific errors

One other useful technique in this type of trigger is to check for a specific error and then take special action in that instance. There are two ways to do this:

- Use the trigger WHEN clause to restrict the execution of the trigger logic for a specific error.

- Use the IS_SERVERERROR function to determine if a specific error has been raised anywhere within the error call stack and then take action.

Let's see how each approach would work. First, suppose that I want to qualify my SERVERERROR trigger at the database level to fire only when the ORA-02292 error occurs ("integrity constraint (*constant name*) violated - child record found").

I can create my trigger as follows:

```
/* Filename on companion disk: serverr2.trg */
CREATE OR REPLACE TRIGGER scott_trap_parent_key
   AFTER SERVERERROR ON DATABASE
WHEN (SYS.SERVER_ERROR(1) = 2292)
BEGIN
   pipe_error (
      'DATABASE trap parent key',
      'Invalid attempt to delete primary key by ' ||
      LOGIN_USER);
END;
/
```

My call to SYS.SERVER_ERROR(1) retrieves the error at the top of the error stack. There are two things to note in this procedure:

- If I do not qualify the call to SERVER_ERROR with its owner, SYS, I get the following error:

```
AFTER SERVERERROR ON DATABASE
                     *
ERROR at line 2:
ORA-00942: table or view does not exist
```

- I must specify the error number as a positive, not negative, integer value. Otherwise, no match will be detected.

Once the trigger is defined, I test it by trying to delete a row from the dept table whose parent key is referenced by an employee:

```
SQL> DELETE FROM dept WHERE deptno=10;
*
ERROR at line 1:
ORA-02292: integrity constraint (SCOTT.FK_DEPTNO) violated -
        child record found
```

I can now see what information was sent to my pipe within the trigger as follows:

```
SQL> exec watch.show
Contents of WATCH Trace:
***WATCHing at: June 2, 1999 16:27:09
   Context: DATABASE trap parent key trap_error
   Message: Invalid attempt to delete primary key by SCOTT
```

Here I will demonstrate the IS_SERVERERROR approach with a modified version of the database-level trigger:

```
/* Filename on companion disk: serverr.trg */
CREATE OR REPLACE TRIGGER trap_error
   AFTER SERVERERROR ON DATABASE
BEGIN
   /* Same tracking as before. */
   pipe_error ('DATABASE', ...);

   IF IS_SERVERERROR (1652) -- POSITIVE NUMBER REQUIRED!
   THEN
      /* Add a file to the tablespace... just a dummy
         entry for the book. */
      pipe_error ('DATABASE', 'Add to tablespace');
   END IF;
END;
/
```

And now if the ORA-01652 error is raised *anywhere* in the error stack from the SCOTT schema, I see three entries in the error pipe:

```
SQL> DECLARE
  2     exc EXCEPTION;
  3     PRAGMA EXCEPTION_INIT (exc, -1652);
  4  BEGIN
  5     RAISE exc;
  6  EXCEPTION
  7     WHEN OTHERS THEN
  8        RAISE VALUE_ERROR;
  9  END;
 10  /
*
ERROR at line 1:
ORA-06502: PL/SQL: numeric or value error
```

```
ORA-01652: unable to extend temp segment by nnn in tablespace

SQL> exec watch.show
Contents of WATCH Trace:
***WATCHing at: June 3, 1999 09:47:05
   Context: SCOTT trap_error
   Message: SERVERERROR-1-ORACLE-0-6502-SCOTT
***WATCHing at: June 3, 1999 09:47:05
   Context: DATABASE trap_error
   Message: SERVERERROR-1-ORACLE-0-6502-SCOTT
***WATCHing at: June 3, 1999 09:47:05
   Context: DATABASE trap_error
   Message: Add to tablespace
```

When you use IS_SERVERERROR, you must pass a *positive* number
for it to find a match on the error. So we must wonder once again:
are Oracle error numbers negative or positive? It looks like the folks
at Oracle have trouble giving a consistent answer to this question.

Schema-Level Event Triggers

Oracle8*i* also allows you to define triggers to respond to schema-level events (also
known as user-level events), including the following:

- Logon to and logoff from a schema

- Response to a server error

- CREATE, DROP, and ALTER DDL commands

Good news! We are finally able to place triggers on this broad set of DDL! We can
keep track of any attempts to drop tables (successful or otherwise), can notify
DBAs of changes to tables or types, and so on.

Here is the syntax for these triggers:

```
CREATE [ OR REPLACE ] TRIGGER trigger_name
   { BEFORE | AFTER }
   { SERVERERROR |
     LOGON | LOGOFF |
      CREATE | DROP | ALTER }
   ON schema_name.SCHEMA
BEGIN
   pl/sql_statements
END;
```
schema_name

The name of the schema in which the trigger will fire

pl/sql_statements

The PL/SQL block

trigger_name

The name of the trigger being created

You must have the CREATE ANY TRIGGER system privilege to create a trigger in any schema, on a table in any schema, or on another user's schema (*schema_name*.SCHEMA in the syntax just given). You will also need privileges to access any of the external references in the trigger's PL/SQL code.

You can define triggers for the same event (such as SERVERERROR) on both the schema and database levels. In this case, the schema-level trigger will fire before the database level, but both will fire.

Table 6-4 describes the different schema-level events on which you may define a trigger.

Table 6-4. Schema-Level Events for Trigger Definitions

Event	Description
SERVERERROR	Oracle fires the trigger whenever a server error message is logged.
LOGON	Oracle fires the trigger after a client application logs on to the database successfully.
LOGOFF	Oracle fires the trigger before a client application logs off the database.
CREATE	Oracle fires the trigger whenever a CREATE statement adds a new database object to the schema.
DROP	Oracle fires the trigger whenever a DROP statement removes an existing database object from the schema.
ALTER	Oracle fires the trigger whenever an ALTER statement modifies an existing database object in the schema.

Each user event has an associated set of attributes. These attributes are actually functions owned by SYS that return the values of characteristics relevant to the event. The current set of available attributes includes those listed in the previous section on database-level events (see Table 6-2), plus those listed in Table 6-5.

Table 6-5. Additional Attributes for Schema-Level Events

Name	Datatype	Description
DICTIONARY_OBJ_ OWNER	VARCHAR2(30)	Owner of the dictionary object on which the DDL operation occurred
DICTIONARY_OBJ_ NAME	VARCHAR2(30)	Name of the dictionary object on which the DDL operation occurred
DICTIONARY_OBJ_ TYPE	VARCHAR2(30)	Type of the dictionary object on which the DDL operation occurred
DES_ENCRYPTED_ PASSWORD	VARCHAR2(30)	DES-encrypted password of the user being created or altered

Table 6-6 lists the restrictions and attributes for each schema-level event.

Table 6-6. Restrictions and Attributes for Schema-Level Events

Event	Conditions/Restrictions	Attributes
LOGON	You can specify a condition using either USERID() or USERNAME().	SYSEVENT LOGIN_USER INSTANCE_NUM DATABASE_NAME
LOGOFF	You can specify a condition using either USERID() or USERNAME().	SYSEVENT LOGIN_USER INSTANCE_NUM DATABASE_NAME
BEFORE CREATE AFTER CREATE	Inside either of these triggers, you cannot drop the object being created. The trigger executes in the current transaction.	SYSEVENT LOGIN_USER INSTANCE_NUM DATABASE_NAME DICTIONARY_OBJ_TYPE DICTIONARY_OBJ_NAME DICTIONARY_OBJ_OWNER
BEFORE ALTER AFTER ALTER	Inside either of these triggers, you cannot drop the object being altered. The trigger executes in the current transaction.	SYSEVENT LOGIN_USER INSTANCE_NUM DATABASE_NAME DICTIONARY_OBJ_TYPE DICTIONARY_OBJ_NAME DICTIONARY_OBJ_OWNER
BEFORE DROP AFTER DROP	Inside either of these triggers, you cannot alter the object being dropped. The trigger executes in the current transaction.	SYSEVENT LOGIN_USER INSTANCE_NUM DATABASE_NAME DICTIONARY_OBJ_TYPE DICTIONARY_OBJ_NAME DICTIONARY_OBJ_OWNER

A Schema-Level Event Trigger Example

Suppose that I want to make sure that even if a user is able to connect to a schema, she or he will not be able to drop tables from that schema. Without these DDL triggers, that would be impossible because, if I can connect, I "own" every-thing and can do with them what I want.

With the DROP trigger, however, I can add this extra level of security. The follow-ing trigger asserts the following rule: you cannot drop any tables starting with "EMP" in the SCOTT schema:

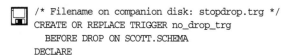

```
/* Filename on companion disk: stopdrop.trg */
CREATE OR REPLACE TRIGGER no_drop_trg
   BEFORE DROP ON SCOTT.SCHEMA
   DECLARE
```

```
      v_msg VARCHAR2(1000) :=
         'No drop allowed on ' ||
         DICTIONARY_OBJ_OWNER || '.' ||
         DICTIONARY_OBJ_NAME || ' from ' ||
         LOGIN_USER;
BEGIN
   IF DICTIONARY_OBJ_OWNER = 'SCOTT' AND
      DICTIONARY_OBJ_NAME LIKE 'EMP%' AND
      DICTIONARY_OBJ_TYPE = 'TABLE'
   THEN
      watch.topipe;
      watch.action (
         'BEFORE DROP trigger',  v_msg);
      RAISE_APPLICATION_ERROR (
         -20905, v_msg);
   END IF;
END;
/
```

I rely on the special attributes available to me in this trigger—namely, the functions returning values for DICTIONARY_OBJ_OWNER, DICTIONARY_OBJ_NAME, and DICTIONARY_OBJ_TABLE, to indicate whether the specified table being dropped is out of bounds. If so, I send a message to my watch pipe and then stop the drop request by raising an exception.

Here's what happens when I attempt to drop a now-undroppable table:

```
SQL> drop table emp2;
drop table emp2
*
ERROR at line 1:
ORA-00604: error occurred at recursive SQL level 1
ORA-20905: No drop allowed on SCOTT.EMP2 from SCOTT
```

7

New and Enhanced Built-in Packages in Oracle8i

Oracle has added a number of new built-in packages in Oracle8*i*. Many of these packages offer very specialized capabilities for replication, database administration, and online analytical processing (OLAP). Other packages will play a more crucial role for PL/SQL developers in the brave new world of Oracle8*i*. We'll introduce you to the capabilities of the packages in this second category (and existing packages, such as DBMS_UTILITY, that have been enhanced) in this chapter. More comprehensive, reference-oriented coverage of the packages will be included in the second edition of *Oracle Built-in Packages* (O'Reilly & Associates, expected in 2000). In addition to the new packages, Oracle8*i* includes a new built-in conversion function, TO_LOB, which is also described in this chapter.

In addition, a number of other new and modified packages are covered throughout the book in their appropriate chapters, as follows:

- The DBMS_JAVA and DBMS_JAVA_TEST packages are described in Chapter 9, *Calling Java from PL/SQL.*

- There are several new programs in DBMS_SESSION, covered in Chapter 8, *Deploying Fine-Grained Access Control.*

Table 7-1 provides a complete list of packages added in Oracle8*i*.

Table 7-1. New Built-in Packages in Oracle8i

Package Name	Description
DBMS_INDEXING	Contains specifications for packages and types used in DBMS extensibility infrastructure (indexing, optimization, etc.).
DBMS_JAVA	Gives you the ability to modify the behavior of the Aurora Java Virtual Machine (JVM) in Oracle. You can enable output (meaning that Java's System.out.println will act like DBMS_OUTPUT.PUT_LINE), set compiler and debugger options, and more.
DBMS_JAVA_TEST	Interface to Aurora JVM to let you easily test methods (functions) defined in classes that you have loaded into Oracle.
DBMS_LOGMNR DBMS_LOGMNR_D	Interact with and support a variety of operations in the new Oracle utility LogMiner, which allows you to read information contained in online and archived redo logs based on selection criteria.
DBMS_PROFILER	Accesses performance and code coverage analysis of your PL/SQL application.
DBMS_REPAIR	Offers a set of procedures to facilitate data corruption repair.
DBMS_REPCAT_FLA DBMS_REPCAT_FLA_MAS DBMS_REPCAT_FLA_UTL	New replication packages.
DBMS_REPCAT_RGT	Offers an API to control the maintenance and definition of refresh group templates.
DBMS_RESOURCE_ MANAGER	An API to the Database Resource Manager that allows you to maintain resource management plans, consumer groups, and plan directives.
DBMS_RESOURCE_ MANAGER_PRIVS	Maintains privileges associated with resource consumer groups.
DBMS_RLS	Offers an interface to the fine-grained access control administrative features of Oracle8*i*; only available with the Enterprise Edition.
DBMS_RULE DBMS_RULE_ADM DBMS_RULE_EXIMP	Administer export/import information in the Rules Engine Administrator.
DBMS_SPACE_ADMIN	Provides tablespace and segment space administration that is not available through the standard SQL statements.
DBMS_STATS	Provides a PL/SQL-based mechanism to allow users to view and modify optimizer statistics gathered on database objects.
DBMS_SUMMARY	Manages and refreshes table-based summaries.

Table 7-1. New Built-in Packages in Oracle8i (continued)

Package Name	Description
DBMS_TRACE	Allows PL/SQL developers to trace the execution of stored PL/SQL functions, procedures, and exceptions.
DBMS_TTS	Contains procedures and functions supporting the Pluggable Tablespace feature. These programs are mostly called by the import/export utilities.
OUTLN_PKG	Contains a functional interface for procedures and functions that are associated with the management of stored outlines.
UTL_COLL	Allows PL/SQL programs to use collection locators in order to perform queries and updates.

DBMS_PROFILER: Providing Code Profiling

In Oracle8*i*, Oracle adds a new package, DBMS_PROFILER, to facilitate performance and code coverage analysis of your PL/SQL application. Use this package to define one or more runs of your code and collect a wide range of information about the code that is executed in that run.

The API for this package is very simple. You start the profiler, run your code, and stop the profiler. The PL/SQL engine will have populated up to three different tables with the performance and code coverage information. You can then use SQL—either your own queries or one of the reports offered by Oracle—to examine the results of the run.

DBMS_PROFILER Programs

The DBMS_PROFILER package contains the two functions listed in Table 7-2.

Table 7-2. DBMS_PROFILER Programs

Program	Description
DBMS_PROFILER.START_PROFILER function	Starts profiling in the current connection. You can provide an optional string to give a name to the profiling session.
DBMS_PROFILER.STOP_PROFILER function	Ends profiling in the current connection.

Installing DBMS_PROFILER

The DBMS_PROFILER package may not have been installed automatically for you when the database was set up. In this case, you will need to install the package specification and body. After that, you will want to create profiler tables and packages to help you analyze the output (stored in the profiler tables) more effectively.

Table 7-3 shows all of the files related to DBMS_PROFILER that you will probably want to run. You will find most of these files on Windows NT in one of the following directories (the exceptions are the demo files *profrep.sql* and *profsum.sql*), depending on how you installed the database:

> *Oracle**Ora81**Rdbms**Admin*\
> *Ora81**Rdbms**Admin*\

Regardless of the higher-level directory structure, these files will always be found in the *Rdbms**Admin* subdirectory under the Oracle 8.1 home directory.

Table 7-3. DBMS_PROFILER Files

File	Description
dbmspbp.sql	DBMS_PROFILER package specification; this package should be created automatically when you install the Oracle8*i* database. You may want to examine this file to read the documentation.
prvtpbp.plb	DBMS_PROFILER package body/library definition. This is a wrapped file and should be executed automatically when you install the Oracle8*i* database.
profload.sql	Orchestrates the loading of *dbmspbp.sql* and *prvtpbp.plb*. This script must be run under a DBA account.

proftab.sql	Script to create the profiling tables. When you profile a program, data is written to one or more of these tables:
	    plsql_profiler_runs
	    plsql_profiler_units
	    plsql_profiler_data

profrep.sql	Creates a set of views and a reporting package named prof_report_utilities that offers an API to more easily extract reports from the profiling tables. Found under *plsql**demo*.
profsum.sql	A set of ad hoc queries and calls to programs in the prof_report_utilities package. Don't run the whole file unless you have a small volume of data in your profiling tables. Instead, go through the file and extract those queries that you want to run. Found under *plsql**demo*.

You can define the profiler tables in each individual schema developers want to profile. You can also define the profiler tables in a central schema, to be shared among multiple developers. In this case, you need to grant full access to all of the tables and to the sequence that defines the run number. You will also need to create public synonyms.

The profiler will not profile a PL/SQL block unless the current user has CREATE access on the block.

DBMS_PROFILER Example

It's certainly easy enough to use the PL/SQL profiler. Here's an example of the code you would execute:

```
/* Filename on companion disk: profiler.sql */
BEGIN
    DBMS_OUTPUT.PUT_LINE (
        DBMS_PROFILER.START_PROFILER (
            'showemps ' ||
            TO_CHAR (SYSDATE, 'YYYYMMDD HH24:MI:SS')
            )
        );
    showemps;
    DBMS_OUTPUT.PUT_LINE (
        DBMS_PROFILER.STOP_PROFILER);
END;
/
```

If you do not pass an argument to START_PROFILER, then the "name" of the profile run is SYSDATE. In the example just given, I want to record both the name of the program I am running and the date-time stamp so that I can distinguish this run from others for the same program.

Profiler Return Codes

Both START_PROFILER and END_PROFILER are functions that return a status code. A value of 0 means that the program was called successfully. A nonzero return code indicates a problem, and may be one of the values listed in Table 7-4.

Table 7-4. DBMS_PROFILER Return Codes

Database Constant	Value	Description
DBMS_PROFILER.SUCCESS	0	No problem!
DBMS_PROFILER.ERROR_PARM	1	A subprogram was called with an incorrect parameter.
DBMS_PROFILER.ERROR_IO	2	An attempt to flush profile data to the tables failed. Make sure the tables are present and accessible and have sufficient space for the inserts.
DBMS_PROFILER.ERROR_VERSION	-1	The engine has detected a mismatch between the profiler package and the database version. The only possible recovery is to install the correct version of the package.

Consider yourself warned: unless you are running a very simple application, the profiler will write thousands of rows of data to its tables. To make it easier for you to manage all this information, I have created the following scripts, located on the companion disk:

proftrunc.sql
> Truncates all three profiling tables

profdel.sql
> Deletes all rows from the three profiling tables for the specified run number

DBMS_TRACE: Providing a PL/SQL Trace Facility

Earlier versions of Oracle offered some PL/SQL trace capabilities, but Oracle8*i* provides an API that allows you to more easily specify and control the tracing of the execution of PL/SQL procedures, functions, and exceptions. DBMS_TRACE provides programs to start and stop PL/SQL tracing in a session. When tracing is turned on, the engine collects data as the program executes. The data is then written out to the Oracle Server trace file.

 The PL/SQL trace facility provides you with a trace file that shows you the specific steps executed by your code. The PL/SQL profiler (described earlier in this chapter) offers a much more comprehensive analysis of your application, including timing information and counts of the number of times a specific line was executed.

Installing DBMS_TRACE

This package may not have been installed automatically with the rest of the built-in packages. To determine whether DBMS_TRACE is present, connect to SYS and execute this command:

```
BEGIN DBMS_TRACE.CLEAR_PLSQL_TRACE; END;
/
```

If you see this error:

```
PLS-00201: identifier 'DBMS_TRACE.CLEAR_PLSQL_TRACE'
           must be declared
```

then you must install the package. To do this, remain connected as SYS and run the following files in the order specified:

> *\Oracle\Ora81\Rdbms\Admin\dbmspbt.sql*
> *\Oracle\Ora81\Rdbms\Admin\prvtpbt.plb*

The directory shown here is the default for a Windows NT installation. Your Oracle 8.1 home directory may be different, but these files will always be found in the *Rdbms\Admin* subdirectory under the Oracle 8.1 home directory.

DBMS_TRACE Programs

The programs in the DBMS_TRACE package are listed in Table 7-5.

Table 7-5. DBMS_TRACE Programs

Program	Description
SET_PLSQL_TRACE procedure	Starts PL/SQL tracing in the current session
CLEAR_PLSQL_TRACE procedure	Stops the dumping of trace data for that session
PLSQL_TRACE_VERSION procedure	Gets the major and minor version numbers of the DBMS_TRACE package

To trace execution of your PL/SQL code, you must first start the trace with a call to:

```
DBMS_TRACE.SET_PLSQL_TRACE (trace_level INTEGER);
```

in your current session, where *trace_level* is one of the following values:

```
DBMS_TRACE.trace_all_calls          CONSTANT INTEGER := 1;
DBMS_TRACE.trace_enabled_calls      CONSTANT INTEGER := 2;
DBMS_TRACE.trace_all_exceptions     CONSTANT INTEGER := 4;
DBMS_TRACE.trace_enabled_exceptions CONSTANT INTEGER := 8;
```

To turn on tracing from all programs executed in your session, issue this call:

```
DBMS_TRACE.SET_PLSQL_TRACE (DBMS_TRACE.trace_all_calls);
```

To turn on tracing for all exceptions raised during the session, issue this call:

```
DBMS_TRACE.SET_PLSQL_TRACE (DBMS_TRACE.trace_all_exceptions);
```

You then run your code; when you are done, you stop the trace session by calling:

```
DBMS_TRACE.CLEAR_PLSQL_TRACE;
```

You can then examine the contents of the trace file. The names of these files are generated by Oracle; you will mostly need to pay attention to the modification date of the files to figure out which file to examine. The location of the trace files is discussed in the later section "Format of Collected Data." You cannot use PL/SQL tracing with the multithreaded server (MTS).

Controlling Trace File Contents

The trace files produced by DBMS_TRACE can get *really* big. You can minimize the trace output and focus it by obtaining trace information only for specific programs that you have enabled for trace data collection.

 You cannot use this approach with remote procedure calls.

To enable a specific program for tracing, you can alter the session to enable any programs that are created or replaced in the session. To take this approach, issue this command:

```
ALTER SESSION SET PLSQL_DEBUG=TRUE;
```

If you don't want to alter your entire session, you can recompile a specific program unit in debug mode as follows (not applicable to anonymous blocks):

```
ALTER [PROCEDURE | FUNCTION | PACKAGE BODY] program_name COMPILE DEBUG;
```

After you have enabled the programs in which you're interested, the following call will initiate tracing just for those program units:

```
DBMS_TRACE.SET_PLSQL_TRACE (DBMS_TRACE.trace_enabled_calls);
```

You can also restrict the trace information to only those exceptions raised within enabled programs with this call:

```
DBMS_TRACE.SET_PLSQL_TRACE (DBMS_TRACE.trace_enabled_exceptions);
```

If you request tracing for all programs or exceptions and also request tracing only for enabled programs or exceptions, the request for "all" takes precedence.

Format of Collected Data

If you request tracing only for enabled program units and the current program unit is not enabled, then no trace data is written. If the current program unit is enabled for tracing, then call tracing writes out the program unit type, name, and stack depth. If the current program unit is not enabled, then call tracing writes out the program unit type, line number, and stack depth.

Exception tracing writes out the line number. Raising an exception records trace information on whether the exception is user defined or predefined, and records the exception number in the case of predefined exceptions. If you raise a user-defined exception, you will always see an error code of 1.

In Oracle8*i* under Windows NT, the trace files are written to the following directory (by default):

> *Oracle\Admin\Oracle81\udump*

Here is an example of the output from a trace of the procedure showemps:

```
*** 1999.06.14.09.59.25.394
*** SESSION ID:(9.7) 1999.06.14.09.59.25.344
------------ PL/SQL TRACE INFORMATION -----------
Levels set :  1
Trace:  ANONYMOUS BLOCK: Stack depth = 1
Trace:   PROCEDURE SCOTT.SHOWEMPS: Call to entry at line 5 Stack depth = 2
Trace:    PACKAGE BODY SYS.DBMS_SQL: Call to entry at line 1 Stack depth = 3
Trace:     PACKAGE BODY SYS.DBMS_SYS_SQL: Call to entry at line 1 Stack depth = 4
Trace:     PACKAGE BODY SYS.DBMS_SYS_SQL: ICD vector index = 21 Stack depth = 4
Trace:    PACKAGE PLVPRO.P: Call to entry at line 26 Stack depth = 3
Trace:    PACKAGE PLVPRO.P: ICD vector index = 6 Stack depth = 3
Trace:    PACKAGE BODY PLVPRO.P: Call to entry at line 1 Stack depth = 3
Trace:    PACKAGE BODY PLVPRO.P: Call to entry at line 1 Stack depth = 3
Trace:     PACKAGE BODY PLVPRO.P: Call to entry at line 1 Stack depth = 4
```

DBMS_RLS: Implementing Fine-Grained Access Control

Fine-grained access control (FGAC) is a new feature in Oracle8*i* that allows you to implement security policies with functions and then associate those security policies with tables or views. The database server enforces those policies automatically, no matter how the data is accessed. For lots more information on FGAC, see Chapter 8, *Deploying Fine-Grained Access Control*. I'll focus here on the new built-in package, DBMS_RLS.

Installing DBMS_RLS

The DBMS_RLS package should have been installed automatically with the rest of the built-in packages. If you are not able to execute the procedures in the package, you can install the package yourself. To do this, connect to the SYS schema and run the following files in the order specified:

> *\Oracle\Ora81\Rdbms\Admin\dbmsrlsa.sql*
> *\Oracle\Ora81\Rdbms\Admin\prvtrlsa.plb*

The directory shown here is the default for a Windows NT installation. Your Oracle 8.1 home directory may be different, but these files will always be found in the *Rdbms\Admin* subdirectory under the Oracle 8.1 home directory.

DBMS_RLS Programs

The DBMS_RLS package offers a set of procedures to administer your security policies. Fine-grained access control usually affects the rows a user can access—hence the name of the package, the Row-Level Security (RLS) administrative interface. Using this package, you can add, drop, enable, disable, and refresh the policies you create. Table 7-6 lists the programs in this package.

Table 7-6. DBMS_RLS Programs

Program	Description
ADD_POLICY procedure	Creates or registers a fine-grained access control policy for a table or view
DROP_POLICY procedure	Drops a fine-grained access control policy from a table or view
ENABLE_POLICY procedure	Enables or disables a fine-grained access control policy
REFRESH_POLICY procedure	Causes all the cached statements associated with the policy to be reparsed

Committing with DBMS_RLS

Each of the DBMS_RLS procedures causes the current transaction to commit before carrying out the specified operation. The procedures will also issue a commit at the end of their operations.

This commit processing does not occur if the DBMS_RLS action takes place within a DDL event trigger. In this case, the DBMS_RLS action becomes a part of the DDL transaction. You might, for example, place a trigger on the CREATE TABLE user event (another new Oracle8*i* capability, described in Chapter 6, *New Trigger Features in Oracle8i*). This trigger can then call DBMS_RLS.ADD_POLICY to add a policy on that table.

ADD_POLICY: Adding a Policy

Use the DBMS_RLS.ADD_POLICY procedure to add a policy for use in the FGAC architecture. Here is the header for this program:

```
DBMS_RLS.ADD_POLICY (
    object_schema    IN VARCHAR2 := NULL,
    object_name      IN VARCHAR2,
    policy_name      IN VARCHAR2,
    function_schema IN VARCHAR2 := NULL,
    policy_function IN VARCHAR2,
    statement_types IN VARCHAR2 := NULL,
    update_check     IN BOOLEAN  := FALSE,
    enable           IN BOOLEAN  := TRUE);
```

The parameters for this procedure are listed in Table 7-7.

Table 7-7. DBMS_RLS.ADD_POLICY Parameters

Parameter	Description
object_schema	Schema containing the table or view. The default is the currently connected schema (that returned by USER).
object_name	Name of the table or view to which the policy is added.
policy_name	Name of the policy to be added. It must be unique for the same table or view. If not, you will get this error: ORA-28101: policy already exists
function_schema	Schema of the function that is used to implement the policy. The default is the currently connected schema (that returned by USER).
policy_function	Name of the function that generates a predicate for the policy. If the function is defined within a package, then you must specify the function in the form *package.function*, as in the following example: 'personnel_rules.by_department'
statement_types	Statement types to which the policy will apply. Those types can be any combination of SELECT, INSERT, UPDATE, and DELETE. The default is to apply to all of these types. This is a comma-delimited list. If you provide a list with the wrong structure, you will receive one of these compile-time errors: ORA-00911: invalid character ORA-28106: input value for argument #6 is not valid
update_check	Optional argument for INSERT or UPDATE statement types. The default is FALSE. Setting update_check to TRUE causes the server to check the policy against the value after the insert or update has been performed.
enable	Indicates if the policy is enabled when it is added. The default is TRUE. If you specify FALSE, then you must also call DBMS_RLS.ENABLE_POLICY after you have added the policy.

The following rules apply when adding a policy:

- The policy function that generates a dynamic predicate is called by the Oracle server. Your function must conform to the following header:

```
FUNCTION policy_function (
   object_schema IN VARCHAR2,
   object_name VARCHAR2)
   RETURN VARCHAR2;
```

Where *object_schema* is the schema owning the table or view and *object_name* is the table or view to which the policy applies. Your function does not necessarily have to use those arguments, but they must be included in the parameter list.

- The maximum length of the predicate that the policy function can return is 2000 bytes.

- The policy function must have a purity level of WNDS (writes no database state), so that the function can be called within a SQL statement.

- If a SQL statement causes the generation of more than one dynamic predicate for the same object, these predicates are combined with an AND operator. In other words, all dynamic predicates must be satisfied.

- The definer rights model is used to resolve any references in the policy function. Any object lookups required are performed against the owner of the policy function, not the owner of the table or view on which the policy is based.

- If your function returns a NULL predicate, then the predicate is ignored. In other words, no filtering of rows takes place for the current user.

- In some cases, usually involving object types, Oracle requires an alias for the table name. In these cases, the name of the table or view itself must be used as the name of the alias.

- The policy function is not checked until runtime. The program you specify in the call to DBMS_RLS.ADD_POLICY does not need to exist or be compilable when the policy is added.

Here is an example of adding a policy:

```
BEGIN
    DBMS_RLS.ADD_POLICY (
        'SCOTT',
        'patient',
        'patient_privacy',
        'SCOTT',
        'nhc_pkg.person_predicate',
        'SELECT,UPDATE,DELETE');
END;
/
```

ENABLE_POLICY: Enabling or Disabling a Policy

You can enable or disable a policy with the DBMS_RLS.ENABLE_POLICY procedure:

```
DBMS_RLS.ENABLE_POLICY (
    object_schema IN VARCHAR2 := NULL,
    object_name   IN VARCHAR2,
    policy_name   IN VARCHAR2,
    enable        IN BOOLEAN);
```

The parameters for this procedure are listed in Table 7-8.

Table 7-8. DBMS_RLS.ENABLE_POLICY Parameters

Parameter	Description
object_schema	Schema containing the table or view. The default is the currently connected schema (that returned by USER).
object_name	Name of the table or view for which the policy is enabled or disabled.
policy_name	Name of the policy to be enabled or disabled. It must be unique for the same table or view. If not, you will get this error: `ORA-28101: policy already exists`
enable	TRUE to enable the policy, FALSE to disable the policy.

DROP_POLICY: Dropping a Policy

The DBMS_RLS package also provides the interface to drop security policies with the DBMS_RLS.DROP_POLICY procedure:

```
DBMS_RLS.DROP_POLICY (
    object_schema IN VARCHAR2 := NULL,
    object_name   IN VARCHAR2,
    policy_name   IN VARCHAR2);
```

Parameters have essentially the same meanings as those shown in Table 7-7.

The following procedure uses the DBMS_RLS package's DROP_POLICY procedure to drop all policies for a specific schema and database object:

```
/* Filename on companion disk: droppol.sp */
CREATE OR REPLACE PROCEDURE drop_policy (
    objname IN VARCHAR2,
    polname IN VARCHAR2 := '%',
    objschema IN VARCHAR2 := NULL)
    AUTHID CURRENT_USER
IS
BEGIN
    FOR rec IN (
        SELECT object_owner,
               object_name,
               policy_name
          FROM ALL_POLICIES
         WHERE object_owner LIKE NVL (objschema, USER)
           AND object_name LIKE objname
           AND policy_name LIKE polname)
    LOOP
        DBMS_RLS.DROP_POLICY (
            rec.object_owner, rec.object_name, rec.policy_name);
    END LOOP;
END;
/
```

In Oracle8*i* Release 8.1.5, the behavior of the DBMS_RLS.DROP_
POLICY procedure was erratic inside *droppol.sp* Sometimes it
worked, but often it raised an exception along these lines:

```
ORA-28106: input value for argument #2 is not valid
```

If you pass hardcoded string literals to DBMS_RLS_DROP_POLICY,
the procedure doesn't seem to have any difficulties.

REFRESH_POLICY: Refreshing a Policy

The DBMS_RLS.REFRESH_POLICY procedure causes all the cached SQL statements associated with the policy to be reparsed. This guarantees that the latest
change to this policy will have an immediate effect after the procedure is executed. This procedure is needed because parsed SQL statements are cached in the
System Global Area to improve performance. The header is as follows:

```
DBMS_RLS.REFRESH_POLICY (
    object_schema IN VARCHAR2 := NULL,
    object_name   IN VARCHAR2 := NULL,
    policy_name   IN VARCHAR2 := NULL);
```

Parameters have essentially the same meanings as those shown in Table 7-7.

Every time you change the set of policies associated with a table or view, you
should issue a refresh for that object. To ensure that this happens, you might consider building an encapsulation around DBMS_RLS so that a call to *your* ADD_
POLICY procedure would automatically add the policy and then refresh as well.
Your encapsulated add would then look like this:

```
/* Filename on companion disk: my_rls.pkg */
CREATE OR REPLACE PACKAGE BODY my_rls
IS
    ...
    PROCEDURE add_policy (
        object_schema   IN VARCHAR2 := NULL,
        object_name     IN VARCHAR2,
        policy_name     IN VARCHAR2,
        function_schema IN VARCHAR2 := NULL,
        policy_function IN VARCHAR2,
        statement_types IN VARCHAR2 := NULL,
        update_check    IN BOOLEAN  := FALSE,
        enable          IN BOOLEAN  := TRUE);
    IS
    BEGIN
        DBMS_RLS.ADD_POLICY (
            object_schema   ,
            object_name     ,
            policy_name     ,
```

```
            function_schema ,
            policy_function ,
            statement_types ,
            update_check    ,
            enable);

      IF enable
      THEN
         DBMS_RLS.REFRESH_POLICY (
             object_schema,
             object_name  ,
             policy_name);
      END IF;
   END;
END;
/
```

See Chapter 8 to explore in much more detail the features supported by DBMS_
RLS.

UTL_COLL: Using Collection Locators

The UTL_COLL package lets PL/SQL programs use collection locators to query and
update. This package currently has only a single program: the IS_LOCATOR function. It determines whether a collection item is actually a locator. The header for
this program is:

```
UTL_COLL.IS_LOCATOR (collection IN ANY)
   RETURNS BOOLEAN;
```

where *collection* is a nested table or variable array. This function returns TRUE if
the collection is a locator, FALSE if the collection is not a locator. It asserts the
WNDS (writes no database state), WNPS (writes no program state), and RNPS
(reads no package state) pragmas; thus, it can be used within SQL.

At the time of table creation, the user may specify that a collection locator is to be
returned when a nested table column or attribute is fetched. Use UTL_COLL.IS_
LOCATOR in your PL/SQL program to check whether a nested table attribute or
variable is locator based. You might want to do this before performing certain collection operations that could cause a large nested table value to be materialized in
memory.

The following script demonstrates the use of UTL_COLL.IS_LOCATOR. Its data is
based on a true story drawn from the pages of a major Midwestern newspaper. It
seems that in a recent election, a candidate pledged firm opposition to an expansion of gambling in the state. After receiving hundreds of thousands of dollars in
"contributions" from various gambling forces in that state, however, this candidate
(who won the election) changed that position and supported the expansion of
gambling venues.

```
/* Filename on companion disk: utlcoll.sql */
CREATE OR REPLACE TYPE legal_bribe_t as TABLE OF NUMBER;
/

CREATE OR REPLACE TYPE legal_briber_t AS OBJECT (
  source VARCHAR2(100), legal_bribes legal_bribe_t );
/

CREATE TABLE legal_briber OF legal_briber_t
  NESTED TABLE legal_bribes STORE AS nt_bribes;

INSERT INTO legal_briber VALUES (
  'RIVERBOAT CASINO INDUSTRY',
  legal_bribe_t (385584, 632000, 267000)
  );

CREATE TABLE legal_briber1 OF legal_briber_t
  NESTED TABLE legal_bribes STORE AS nt_bribes1
  RETURN LOCATOR;

INSERT INTO legal_briber1 VALUES (
  'RIVERBOAT CASINO INDUSTRY',
  legal_bribe_t (385584, 632000, 267000)
  );

DECLARE
  pocket_liners legal_bribe_t;
  pocket_liners1 legal_bribe_t;
BEGIN
  SELECT legal_bribes INTO pocket_liners
    FROM legal_briber
   WHERE source = 'RIVERBOAT CASINO INDUSTRY';

  SELECT legal_bribes INTO pocket_liners1
    FROM legal_briber1
   WHERE source = 'RIVERBOAT CASINO INDUSTRY';

  /* Boolean "put line" procedure */
  bpl (UTL_COLL.IS_LOCATOR (pocket_liners));

  bpl (UTL_COLL.IS_LOCATOR (pocket_liners1));
END;
/
```

How would you put this function to use in your code? Here is one example:

```
/* Filename on companion disk: utlcoll2.sql */
CREATE OR REPLACE FUNCTION getpets_like
    (petlist IN Pettab_t, like_str IN VARCHAR2)
    RETURN pettab_t
IS
    list_to_return Pettab_t := Pettab_t();
    onepet Pet_t;
    counter PLS_INTEGER := 1;
BEGIN
```

```
        IF UTL_COLL.IS_LOCATOR (petlist)
        THEN
           FOR theRec IN
              (SELECT VALUE(petList) apet
                 FROM TABLE(CAST(petlist AS Pettab_t)) petList
               WHERE petList.name LIKE like_str)
           LOOP
              list_to_return.EXTEND;
              list_to_return(counter) := theRec.apet;
              counter := counter + 1;
           END LOOP;
        ELSE
           FOR i IN 1..petlist.COUNT
           LOOP
              IF petlist(i).name LIKE like_str
              THEN
                 list_to_return.EXTEND;
                 list_to_return(i) := petlist(i);
              END IF;
           END LOOP;
        END IF;
        RETURN list_to_return;
     END;
     /
```

The getpets_like function accepts a list of pets and a filter or "like string." It returns a list of pets whose names match that filter. It uses the UTL_COLL.IS_LOCATOR function to optimize access to the nested table. If you have a locator, then the TABLE CAST operators are used to access the table contents via SQL. Otherwise, a numeric FOR loop is used to access each row individually. For large collections that return a locator, the TABLE CAST approach should be more efficient.

LOB Enhancements

Oracle8*i* offers several enhancements to the way you work with large objects (LOBs). It adds a new top-level function, TO_LOB, and also allows you to create and manipulate temporary LOBs.

The TO_LOB Function

Oracle offers a new built-in conversion function, TO_LOB, to convert a LONG or LONG RAW datatype to a LOB. You can apply this function only to a LONG or LONG RAW column, and only in the SELECT list of a subquery in an INSERT statement. This function was designed to allow you to migrate your LONG data to LOB columns, in anticipation of Oracle's discontinuing support for LONGs in a future release.

Before using this function, you must create a LOB column to receive the converted LONG values. To convert LONGs, the LOB column must be of type CLOB (character large object) or NCLOB (NLS character large object). To convert LONG RAWs, the LOB column must be of type BLOB (binary large object).

Given the following tables:

```
CREATE TABLE long_table (n NUMBER, long_col LONG);
CREATE TABLE lob_table (n NUMBER, lob_col CLOB);
```

use this function to convert LONG to LOB values as follows:

```
INSERT INTO lob_table
    SELECT n, TO_LOB(long_col) FROM long_table;
```

DBMS_LOB: Working with Temporary LOBs

Oracle8 provided support for permanently storing large unstructured data by means of LOB datatypes; these are known as *persistent LOBs*. But many applications have a need for *temporary LOBs* that act like local variables but do not exist permanently in the database. This section discusses temporary LOBs and the use of the DBMS_LOB built-in package to manipulate these data structures.

Oracle8*i* supports the creation, freeing, access, and update of temporary LOBs through the Oracle Call Interface (OCI) and DBMS_LOB calls. The default lifetime of a temporary LOB is a session, but such LOBs may be explicitly freed sooner by the application. Temporary LOBs are ideal as transient workspaces for data manipulation, and because no logging is done or redo records generated, they offer better performance than persistent LOBs. In addition, remember that whenever you rewrite or update a LOB, Oracle copies the entire LOB to a new segment. Applications that perform lots of piecewise operations on LOBs should see significant performance improvements with temporary LOBs.

A temporary LOB is empty when it is created—you don't need to (and, in fact, you will not be able to) use the EMPTY_CLOB and EMPTY_BLOB functions to initialize LOB locators for a temporary LOB. By default, all temporary LOBs are deleted at the end of the session in which they were created. If a process dies unexpectedly or if the database crashes, then temporary LOBs are deleted, and the space for temporary LOBs is freed.

Let's take a look at the DBMS_LOB programs provided to work with temporary LOBs, follow that with an example, and finish up by covering some of the administrative details.[*]

---

[*] For information about the DBMS_LOB package, see *Oracle Built-in Packages*; the next edition of that book will describe temporary LOBs.

CREATETEMPORARY: Creating a temporary LOB

Before you can work with a temporary LOB, you need to create it with a call to the CREATETEMPORARY procedure. This program creates a temporary BLOB or CLOB and its corresponding index in your default temporary tablespace. The header is:

```
DBMS_LOB.CREATETEMPORARY (
    lob_loc IN OUT NOCOPY [ BLOB | CLOB CHARACTER SET ANY_CS ],
    cache   IN BOOLEAN,
    dur     IN PLS_INTEGER := DBMS_LOB.SESSION);
```

The parameters are listed in Table 7-9.

Table 7-9. CREATETEMPORARY Parameters

Parameter	Description
lob_loc	Receives the locator to the LOB.
cache	Specifies whether the LOB should be read into the buffer cache.
dur	Controls the duration of the LOB. The dur argument can be one of the following two named constants: *DBMS_LOB.SESSION* Specifies that the temporary LOB created should be cleaned up (memory freed) at the end of the session. This is the default. *DBMS_LOB.CALL* Specifies that the temporary LOB created should be cleaned up (memory freed) at the end of the current program call in which the LOB was created.

FREETEMPORARY: Freeing the temporary LOB

The FREETEMPORARY procedure frees the temporary BLOB or CLOB in your default temporary tablespace. The header for this procedure is:

```
PROCEDURE DBMS_LOB.FREETEMPORARY (
    lob_loc IN OUT NOCOPY
        [ BLOB | CLOB CHARACTER SET ANY_CS ]);
```

After the call to FREETEMPORARY, the LOB locator that was freed (*lob_loc*) is marked as invalid. If an invalid LOB locator is assigned to another LOB locator through an assignment operation in PL/SQL, then the target of the assignment is also freed and marked as invalid.

ISTEMPORARY: Is it a temporary LOB?

The ISTEMPORARY function tells you if the LOB locator (*lob_loc*) points to a temporary or persistent LOB. The function returns an integer value: 1 means that it is a temporary LOB, 0 means that it is not (it's a persistent LOB instead):

```
DBMS_LOB.ISTEMPORARY (
    lob_loc IN [ BLOB | CLOB CHARACTER SET ANY_CS ])
    RETURN INTEGER;
```

This function is designed to be called from within SQL; that, presumably, is the reason that Oracle did not define ISTEMPORARY to be a Boolean function.

Example

Let's combine a number of these temporary LOB operations into a single example, found in the *cretemplob.sql* file on the disk. First, I create a directory; this is needed in order to reference a BFILE—a file locator pointing to an operating system file outside the database:

```
/* Filename on companion disk: cretemplob.sql */
CREATE DIRECTORY trainings AS 'E:\Oracle8i-Training';
```

Next, I declare my local data structures: a named constant to hide the integer value used to represent "TRUE" by the ISTEMPORARY function, a BLOB to hold the locator to my temporary LOB, a BFILE that points to one of my PowerPoint presentations, and the number of bytes of that presentation that I want to load to my temporary LOB:

```
DECLARE
   /* Hide the 1/0 values for ISTEMPORARY. */
   c_truetemp CONSTANT INTEGER := 1;

   tempBLOB BLOB;

   my_presentation BFILE :=
      /* Note: Must pass the directory in uppercase. */
      BFILENAME ('TRAININGS', 'collections.ppt');

   lobLength INTEGER := 150000;
BEGIN
```

Next, I create my temporary LOB and specify this call or block as the duration of the LOB. By taking this action, I avoid the need for an explicit call to DBMS_LOB. FREETEMPORARY to free the memory associated with the LOB:

```
DBMS_LOB.CREATETEMPORARY (
   tempBLOB, TRUE, DBMS_LOB.CALL);
```

Now let's see if this new LOB really *is* a temporary one:

```
IF DBMS_LOB.ISTEMPORARY (tempBLOB) = c_truetemp
THEN
   DBMS_OUTPUT.PUT_LINE (
      'It won''t be around for long...');
END IF;
```

On to the real work of the example: transfer a BFILE's contents to a temporary LOB. I will open the BFILE and then use the very convenient LOADFROMFILE procedure to do the transfer:

```
DBMS_LOB.OPEN (
   my_presentation, DBMS_LOB.LOB_READONLY);
```

```
DBMS_LOB.LOADFROMFILE (
    tempBLOB, my_presentation, lobLength);
```

Notice that I open the BFILE but not the temporary LOB. That's because the OPEN step is optional for the temporary LOB. Now that I have transferred the contents, I will find out the length of the temporary LOB to confirm the transfer, and then close the BFILE:

```
lobLength := DBMS_LOB.GETLENGTH (tempBLOB);
IF lobLength = 0
THEN
    DBMS_OUTPUT.PUT_LINE ('LOB is empty.');
ELSE
    DBMS_OUTPUT.PUT_LINE (
        'The length is ' || lobLength);
END IF;

DBMS_LOB.CLOSE(my_presentation);
END;
/
```

Managing temporary LOBs

Temporary LOBs are handled quite differently from normal, persistent, internal LOBs. With temporary LOBs, there is no support for transaction management, consistent read operations, rollbacks, and so forth. There are various consequences to this lack of support:

- If you encounter an error when processing with a temporary LOB, you must free that LOB and start your processing over again.

- You should not assign multiple LOB locators to the same temporary LOB. Lack of support for consistent read and undo operations can cause performance degradation with multiple locators.

- If a user modifies a temporary LOB while another locator is pointing to it, a copy (referred to by Oracle as a *deep copy*) of that LOB is made. The different locators will then no longer see the same data. To minimize these deep copies, use the NOCOPY compiler hint whenever passing LOB locators as arguments.

- To make a temporary LOB permanent, you must call the DBMS_LOB.COPY program and copy the temporary LOB into a permanent one.

- Temporary LOB locators are unique to a session. You cannot pass a locator from one session to another (through a database pipe, for example), and make the associated temporary LOB visible in that other session.

Oracle offers a new V$ view called V$TEMPORARY_LOBS that shows how many cached and uncached LOBs exist per session. Your DBA can combine information from V$TEMPORARY_LOBS and the DBA_SEGMENTS data dictionary view to see how much space a session is using for temporary LOBs.

New DBMS_AQ and DBMS_AQADM Features

DBMS_AQ provides an API to the enqueue and dequeue operations in the Oracle Advanced Queuing (AQ) facility. Oracle8*i* enhances AQ in a number of ways, many reflected in changes in the DBMS_AQ and DBMS_AQADM packages.

 A working knowledge of the Oracle Advanced Queuing facility and the DBMS_AQ and DBMS_AQADM packages is assumed for this section. If you need to learn more, you might want to check out Chapter 5 of *Oracle Built-in Packages.*

CREATE_QUEUE_TABLE and MIGRATE_QUEUE_TABLE: Setting Version Compatibility and Queue Migration

Oracle has changed the security model for Oracle AQ in Oracle8*i*. You can now set security at the system and queue level (discussed in the next section). These features are only available, however, for AQ 8.1-style queues.

To create queues in Oracle 8.1 that can make use of the new security features, you must set the *compatible* parameter in DBMS_AQADM.CREATE_QUEUE_TABLE to '8.1' or above. Here is the new, expanded header:

```
PROCEDURE DBMS_AQADM.CREATE_QUEUE_TABLE (
    queue_table        IN VARCHAR2,
    queue_payload_type IN VARCHAR2,
    storage_clause     IN VARCHAR2        DEFAULT NULL,
    sort_list          IN VARCHAR2        DEFAULT NULL,
    multiple_consumers IN BOOLEAN         DEFAULT FALSE,
    message_grouping   IN BINARY_INTEGER  DEFAULT NONE,
    comment            IN VARCHAR2        DEFAULT NULL,
    auto_commit        IN BOOLEAN         DEFAULT TRUE,
    primary_instance   IN BINARY_INTEGER  DEFAULT 0,
    secondary_instance IN BINARY_INTEGER  DEFAULT 0,
    compatible         IN VARCHAR2        DEFAULT NULL);
```

The first eight parameters are the same as in Oracle 8.0. The final three parameters have the meanings shown here:

primary_instance

The primary owner of the queue table. This instance performs the queue monitor scheduling and propagation for the queues in the queue table. The default is 0, which means scheduling and propagation will be performed in any available instance.

secondary_instance

> The queue table fails over to this instance if the primary instance is not available.

compatible

> The lowest database version with which the queue table is compatible: currently '8.0' or '8.1'. The default is '8.0'.

If you want to define a queue table with 8.1 compatibility, you will need to make a call like this:

```
BEGIN
    DBMS_AQADM.CREATE_QUEUE_TABLE (
        'workflow',
        'workflow_ot',
        compatible => '8.1');
END;
```

I have used named notation to skip over all the intervening parameters (thereby accepting their default values) and set the compatibility level.

If you want to use the AQ 8.1 security features on a queue that was defined originally in an 8.0 database, you must convert the queue table to 8.1 compatibility by executing DBMS_AQADM.MIGRATE_QUEUE_TABLE on the queue table. Here is the header for this procedure:

```
PROCEDURE DBMS_AQADM.MIGRATE_QUEUE_TABLE(
    queue_table IN VARCHAR2,
    compatible  IN VARCHAR2)
```

where *queue_table* is the name of the queue table to be migrated, and *compatible* indicates the direction of the migration, as shown in the following table.

Compatible Value	Meaning
'8.0'	Downgrade an 8.1 queue table to be 8.0 compatible.
'8.1'	Upgrade an 8.0 queue table to be 8.1 compatible.

System-Level Access Control

Back in Oracle 8.0, administrators granted access to AQ operations by assigning roles that provided execution privileges on the AQ procedures. There was no security at the database object level, which meant that in Oracle 8.0 a user with the AQ_USER_ROLE could enqueue and dequeue to *any* queue in the system. This is obviously inadequate, and in Oracle8i, AQ offers a much more granular approach to security. An owner of an 8.1-compatible queue can now grant or revoke queue-level privileges on the queue (described in the "Queue-Level Access Control" section). DBAs can grant or revoke new AQ system-level privileges to any database user. DBAs can also make any database user an AQ administrator.

The grant and revoke operations for AQ are not performed through the GRANT and REVOKE DDL statements. Instead, the DBMS_AQADM package provides a set of procedures. Some of these procedures were present in Oracle 8.0, but with limited capabilities.

GRANT_SYSTEM_PRIVILEGE: Granting system-level privileges

To set a system-level privilege, call the following procedure:

```
PROCEDURE DBMS_AQADM.GRANT_SYSTEM_PRIVILEGE (
    privilege    IN VARCHAR2,
    grantee      IN VARCHAR2,
    admin_option IN BOOLEAN := FALSE);
```

where *privilege* is the AQ system privilege to grant, *grantee* is the user or role (including PUBLIC) to which the privilege is granted, and *admin_option* controls whether the grantee is allowed to use this procedure to grant the system privilege to other users or roles. The options for *privilege* are shown here:

ENQUEUE_ANY

Users granted this privilege are allowed to enqueue messages to any queues in the database.

DEQUEUE_ANY

Users granted this privilege are allowed to dequeue messages from any queues in the database.

MANAGE_ANY

Users granted this privilege are allowed to run DBMS_AQADM calls on any schemas in the database.

Immediately after database installation, only SYS and SYSTEM have the privileges to run this program successfully. If you do not want to manage AQ from either of these schemas, you will want to grant MANAGE_ANY with the *admin_option* parameter set to TRUE to another schema (such as AQADMIN) and then work from there for future AQ administrative activities.

REVOKE_SYSTEM_PRIVILEGE: Revoking system-level privileges

You can revoke system privileges with the following procedure:

```
PROCEDURE DBMS_AQADM.REVOKE_SYSTEM_PRIVILEGE (
    privilege IN VARCHAR2,
    grantee   IN VARCHAR2);
```

where the parameters have the same meanings as for the GRANT_SYSTEM_PRIVI-LEGE procedure.

Example

Let's take a look at the steps a DBA will commonly take to set up a schema as an AQ administrator. First, create the user (I'll call it "WFADM" for "workflow administration") and grant the roles needed to function in the database and work as an AQ administrator:

```
CREATE USER WFADM IDENTIFIED BY WFADM;
GRANT CONNECT, RESOURCE, aq_administrator_role TO WFADM;
```

Next, make sure that this schema can execute both of the AQ packages:

```
GRANT EXECUTE ON dbms_aq TO WFADM;
GRANT EXECUTE ON dbms_aqadm TO WFADM;
```

Finally, give this schema the ability to work with any queues in the database:

```
BEGIN
    DBMS_AQADM.GRANT_SYSTEM_PRIVILEGE (
        'ENQUEUE_ANY', 'WFADM', FALSE);
    DBMS_AQADM.GRANT_SYSTEM_PRIVILEGE (
        'DEQUEUE_ANY', 'WFADM', FALSE);
END;
/
```

Queue-Level Access Control

This section describes how you can grant and revoke privileges at the queue level.

GRANT_QUEUE_PRIVILEGE: Granting queue-level privileges

To set a queue-level privilege, call the following procedure:

```
PROCEDURE DBMS_AQADM.GRANT_QUEUE_PRIVILEGE (
    privilege       IN VARCHAR2,
    queue_name      IN VARCHAR2,
    grantee         IN VARCHAR2,
    admin_option IN BOOLEAN := FALSE);
```

where *privilege* is the AQ system privilege to grant, *queue_name* is the name of the queue on which the grant is to be made, *grantee* is the user or role (including PUBLIC) to which the privilege is granted, and *admin_option* controls whether the grantee is allowed to use this procedure to grant the privilege to other users or roles.

The options for *privilege* are shown here:

ENQUEUE

Users granted this privilege are allowed to enqueue messages to this queue.

DEQUEUE

Users granted this privilege are allowed to dequeue messages from this queue.

ALL

Both ENQUEUE and DEQUEUE

REVOKE_QUEUE_PRIVILEGE: Revoking queue-level privileges

You can revoke queue privileges with the following procedure:

```
PROCEDURE DBMS_AQADM.REVOKE_QUEUE_PRIVILEGE (
    privilege  IN VARCHAR2,
    queue_name IN VARCHAR2,
    grantee    IN VARCHAR2);
```

where the parameters have the same meaning as for the GRANT_QUEUE_PRIVI-
LEGE procedure.

Example

Queue-level grants are crucial when you want to set up individual schemas to be
able to only enqueue or only dequeue for specific queues. Suppose, for example,
that I am constructing a system to support universal health care in the United
States. I want doctors to be able to enqueue a record of services performed, but I
don't want them to be able to dequeue that information. I want my administrators
to be able to dequeue that information, but not to enqueue it. I might execute a
block like this:

```
BEGIN
   DBMS_AQADM.GRANT_QUEUE_PRIVILEGE (
       'DEQUEUE', 'FEELGOOD_service_record_q', 'Doctor_Role', FALSE);

   DBMS_AQADM.GRANT_QUEUE_PRIVILEGE(
       'ENQUEUE', 'FEELGOOD_service_record_q', 'Admin_Role', FALSE);
END;
/
```

Improved Publish/Subscribe Support

Oracle AQ adds various features in Oracle 8.1 that allow you to develop an application based on a publish/subscribe model. This model allows different components of the application to communicate with each other in a very flexible way,
based on an important principle: publisher application components interact with
subscriber application components only through messages and message content.

This means that publisher applications don't have to know about, or ever have to
manage, recipient information. They "publish" their messages by putting information in queues. They don't worry about who is going to receive it, when, and how.
The subscriber applications receive messages through the dequeue operation,
based solely on the content of those messages. The identity of the publisher does
not play a role in determining the enqueue operation, and the identities and number of subscriber applications can be modified without affecting the messages.

This basic approach was available in Oracle 8.0, when the AQ facility was first introduced. Oracle8*i* significantly improves the ability to implement a publish/subscribe model with the following features:

- Rule-based subscribers

- The LISTEN procedure

- Notification capabilities, available currently only through OCI (the Oracle Call Interface) and not through PL/SQL

The following sections focus on the new PL/SQL features—rule-based subscribers and the new LISTEN procedure.

Rule-based subscribers

Oracle AQ has always let you define subscriber lists and add subscribers with the DBMS_AQADM.ADD_SUBSCRIBER procedure. The 8.1 implementation adds another parameter to this procedure, allowing you to associate a *rule* with a subscriber. Here is the new procedure header:

```
PROCEDURE DBMS_AQADM.ADD_SUBSCRIBER (
    queue_name   IN  VARCHAR2,
    subscriber   IN  sys.aq$_agent,
    rule         IN  VARCHAR2 DEFAULT NULL);
```

where *queue_name* is the name of the queue in which the subscriber is interested, *subscriber* is an object instance of type SYS.AQ$_AGENT that identifies the agent to be added to the subscription list, and *rule* is a string that contains a conditional expression.

The rule must be a string that is evaluated dynamically to a Boolean value: TRUE, FALSE, or NULL. The string may contain references to message properties (fields in the DBMS_AQ.MESSAGE_PROPERTIES_T record type), to attributes of the queue's payload (object payloads only, not RAW) and to PL/SQL functions (either built-in or your own).

Let's go over some rules and then look at some examples. The rule must conform to the following guidelines:

- The only message properties currently supported are PRIORITY and CORRID (correlation identifier).

- If you wish to reference attributes of the object payload in a queue, you must prefix each attribute with a qualifier of TAB.USER_DATA (a hardcoded string).

- The maximum length of the *rule* parameter is 4000 characters.

- Any PL/SQL functions you reference in the rule must be callable from within the WHERE clause of a SQL statement.

- If you need to surround a literal with single quotes inside the rule, then you must use two single quotes in sequence.

The following examples should clarify these rules and their application:

1. Add a subscriber to the War Criminals Prosecution queue who is interested only in dequeuing messages of top priority:

```
DECLARE
    most_urgent SYS.AQ$_AGENT :=
        SYS.AQ$_AGENT ('ChiefProsecutor', 'Cases_queue');
BEGIN
    DBMS_AQADM.ADD_SUBSCRIBER (
        'Cases_queue', most_urgent, 'PRIORITY = 1');
END;
```

2. The War Crimes Tribunal has just hired a junior prosecutor to handle cases involving atrocities in Latin America. The following block of code ensures that this agent will only handle low-priority cases from that region. Notice the use of multiple single quotes to ensure that the literal for region name is passed through properly:

```
DECLARE
    back_burner SYS.AQ$_AGENT :=
        SYS.AQ$_AGENT ('JuniorProsecutor', 'Cases_queue');
BEGIN
    DBMS_AQADM.ADD_SUBSCRIBER (
        'Cases_queue', back_burner,
        'PRIORITY > 3 AND CORRID = ''LATIN AMERICA''');
END;_
```

3. Big changes in the year 2015! Even as the fast food chains come to dominate the delivery of food to the world's population, the percentage of humans living in hunger increases. A worldwide protest movement rises up—and the three biggest chains are purchased by the United Nations. Now all that technology and food delivery capability will be used directly to make sure that no one in the world starves. But wait—we need to set up subscribers to receive orders for food in their specific regions. So I set up an object type to be used as the queue payload:

```
CREATE TYPE food_order_t AS OBJECT (
    country VARCHAR2(100),
    region VARCHAR2(100),
    child_population NUMBER,
    adult_population NUMBER
    );
```

I can now define a subscriber in the North American Midwest who is responsible for the distribution of food within an area that has a child population of more than 10,000:

```
DECLARE
    lotsa_kids SYS.AQ$_AGENT  :=
```

```
            SYS.AQ$_AGENT ('FoodManager', 'Food_distribution_queue');
BEGIN
   DBMS_AQADM.ADD_SUBSCRIBER (
      'Food_distribution_queue',
      lotsa_kids,
      'TAB.USER_DATA.country = ''USER'' AND
      TAB.USER_DATA.region = ''MIDWEST'' AND
      TAB.USER_DATA.child_population > 10000');
END;_
```

LISTEN: Listening for messages

Oracle8i adds a procedure to DBMS_AQ that you can use to listen for the enqueuing of a message to which one or more agents have subscribed. The header for this program is as follows:

```
PROCEDURE DBMS_AQ.LISTEN (
   agent_list IN  AQ$_AGENT_LIST_T,
   wait       IN  BINARY_INTEGER DEFAULT DBMS_AQ.FOREVER,
   agent      OUT SYS.AQ$_AGENT);
```

where *agent_list* is an index-by table defined in DBMS_AQ as follows:

```
TYPE DBMS_AQ.AQ$_AGENT_LIST_T IS TABLE of AQ$_AGENT
   INDEXED BY BINARY_INTEGER;
```

wait is the number of seconds the LISTEN procedure will wait or block as it waits for a message (the default is forever), and *agent* is the value returned by the procedure: an object.

The DBMS_AQ.LISTEN procedure is very similar to DBMS_ALERT.WAITANY. You can call the procedure to monitor one or more queues, which are identified by the address field of the agent object (only local queues are supported as addresses). When you call DBMS_AQ.LISTEN, your session will be blocked until a message is available in one of the queues, or until the wait time expires.

If a message is available for consumption on one of the queues indicated by the agents in *agent_list*, then that address will be returned in the *agent* OUT parameter. A successful completion of this call to DBMS_AQ.LISTEN does not, however, dequeue the message. Once you retrieve the agent, you must obtain the queue name and then issue an explicit DBMS_AQ.DEQUEUE call against that queue to get the payload.

If there are no messages found when the wait time expires in a call to DBMS_AQ. LISTEN, then the following error is raised:

```
ORA-25254: time-out in LISTEN while waiting for a message
```

Let's look at an example. All the members of my family love ice cream and we each have our own favorite flavor. We have installed Oracle8i on our local ice cream truck, along with a cellular modem. Whenever Sally, who drives the truck, is coming into our neighborhood, she will queue up messages indicating the flavors available that day. Every hot summer afternoon, we issue a call to DBMS_AQ.LIS-TEN and wait to hear who will have first (and hopefully not only) dibs on the ice cream. So let's walk through the code needed to accomplish this task (all to be found in the *aqlisten.sql* file on the companion disk).

Here is the payload for my queue:

```
/* Filename on companion disk: aqlisten.sql */
CREATE TYPE ice_cream_t IS OBJECT (
    flavor VARCHAR2(30),
    calories INTEGER);
/
```

Then I create a package to hold the queue-related data structures and also initialize my queue. The package specification contains a named constant for the queue name and the list of subscribers I will use in my call to DBMS_AQ.LISTEN:

```
CREATE OR REPLACE PACKAGE aqlisten
IS
    qname CONSTANT CHAR(15) := 'ice_cream_queue';
    tell_us DBMS_AQ.AQ$_AGENT_LIST_T;
END;
/
```

The package body defines a procedure that I use to define subscribers for my queue and also build the listen list:

```
PROCEDURE subscribe_me (
    name IN VARCHAR2, flavor IN VARCHAR2)
IS
    tell_me SYS.AQ$_AGENT
        := SYS.AQ$_AGENT (name, qname, NULL);
BEGIN
    DBMS_AQADM.ADD_SUBSCRIBER (
        qname,
        tell_me,
        'TAB.USER_DATA.flavor = ''' || flavor || '''');

    tell_us (NVL(tell_us.LAST,0)+1) := tell_me;
END;
```

Notice that each subscriber has a rule associated with it: his or her favorite flavor of ice cream. The assignment to the tell_us index-by table always adds to the end of the table.

There is nothing else in the package body but the initialization section. This section contains code that will be executed for each session the first time that session references any element in the package. In the case of aqlisten, there are only two ways to reference it: use aqlisten.qname or the aqlisten.tell_us table. The first step in the initialization is to clean out any old versions of my queue table and queue:

```
DBMS_AQADM.STOP_QUEUE (qname, TRUE, TRUE, FALSE);
DBMS_AQADM.DROP_QUEUE (qname);
DBMS_AQADM.DROP_QUEUE_TABLE ('ice_cream_qtable');
```

Then I can create the elements anew, making sure that they are defined as I need them for the example:

```
DBMS_AQADM.CREATE_QUEUE_TABLE (
    queue_table => 'ice_cream_qtable',
    queue_payload_type => 'ice_cream_t',
    multiple_consumers => TRUE,
    compatible => '8.1');

DBMS_AQADM.CREATE_QUEUE (qname, 'ice_cream_qtable');

DBMS_AQADM.START_QUEUE (qname);
```

Notice that I specify the ice cream queue table as an 8.1 queue table able to support multiple consumers. Great! Now I can define my subscribers and their favorite flavors and confirm the number of subscribers in my list:

```
subscribe_me ('Steven', 'ROCKY ROAD');
subscribe_me ('Veva', 'BUTTER PECAN');
subscribe_me ('Chris', 'VANILLA');
subscribe_me ('Eli', 'MINT CHOCOLATE CHIP');

DBMS_OUTPUT.PUT_LINE (tell_us.COUNT || ' subscribers in tell_us.');
```

Now I am ready to try it out. I create a procedure that allows me to enqueue a particular flavor and then listen for the corresponding agent. I then use DBMS_OUTPUT to confirm the agent by name and queue:

```
CREATE OR REPLACE PROCEDURE tasty_treat_time (
    flavor IN VARCHAR2)
IS
    tell_me SYS.AQ$_AGENT;
    queueOpts DBMS_AQ.ENQUEUE_OPTIONS_T;
    msgProps DBMS_AQ.MESSAGE_PROPERTIES_T;
    mmmmm ice_cream_t;
    msgid RAW(16);
BEGIN
    queueopts.visibility := DBMS_AQ.IMMEDIATE;

    /* Populate the object. */
    mmmmm := ice_cream_t (flavor, 10);

    DBMS_AQ.ENQUEUE (
       aqlisten.qname, queueOpts, msgProps, mmmmm, msgid);

    DBMS_AQ.LISTEN (aqlisten.tell_us, 0, tell_me);

    DBMS_OUTPUT.PUT_LINE (
       'Message for ' || tell_me.name ||
       ' in queue ' || tell_me.address);
END;
/
```

When I run this script I see the following output:

```
BEGIN
   tasty_treat_time ('MINT CHOCOLATE CHIP');
   tasty_treat_time ('VANILLA');
   tasty_treat_time ('STRAWBERRY');
EXCEPTION
   WHEN OTHERS
   THEN
      DBMS_OUTPUT.PUT_LINE (SQLERRM);
END;
/


Message for ELI in queue SCOTT.ICE_CREAM_QUEUE
Message for CHRIS in queue SCOTT.ICE_CREAM_QUEUE
ORA-24033: no recipients for message
```

If the address (queue) for an agent is a multiconsumer queue, then you must supply the agent name. If the queue is a single-consumer queue, then you must leave the agent name unspecified or NULL.

New DBMS_UTILITY Features

Oracle has added two functions to the DBMS_UTILITY package that allow you to obtain information about the currently connected instance as well as active instances.

CURRENT_INSTANCE: Returning the Instance Number

The CURRENT_INSTANCE function returns the currently connected instance number. Its header is:

```
FUNCTION DBMS_UTILITY.CURRENT_INSTANCE RETURN NUMBER;
```

This function returns NULL if the connected instance is unavailable (down).

ACTIVE_INSTANCES: Returning a List of Active Instances

The ACTIVE_INSTANCES procedure returns a list of all of the active instances. Its header is:

```
PROCEDURE DBMS_UTILITY.ACTIVE_INSTANCES (
   instance_table OUT DBMS_UTILITY.instance_table,
   instance_count OUT NUMBER);
```

instance_table will contain the returned list, and *instance_count* is the number of active instances. DBMS_UTILITY.INSTANCE_TABLE is defined as follows:

```
TYPE DBMS_UTILITY.INSTANCE_RECORD IS RECORD (
    inst_number NUMBER,
    inst_name   VARCHAR2(60));

TYPE DBMS_UTILITY.INSTANCE_TABLE IS
    TABLE OF instance_record INDEX BY BINARY_INTEGER;
```

This procedure behaves as follows:

- When no instance is available (or the parallel server is not in use), the list is empty.

- The *instance_count* argument contains the number of active instances, or 0 if none are found.

- The starting index of the *instance_table* is always 1 and the table is always densely filled. The only defined rows of the table, in other words, are 1 through *instance_count.*

8

Deploying Fine-Grained Access Control

Fine-grained access control (FGAC) is a new feature in Oracle8*i* that allows you to implement security policies with functions and then use those security policies to implement row-level security on tables and views. The database server automatically enforces these security policies, no matter how the data is accessed—through SQL*Plus or the Internet, as an ad hoc query, or as an update processed through an Oracle Forms application.

What, you might ask, is a *security policy*? Consider the following very simple scenario (I'll expand upon this scenario in the full example at the end of this chapter). Suppose that I have tables of hospital patients and their doctors defined as follows:

```
CREATE TABLE patient (
    patient_id NUMBER,
    name VARCHAR2(100),
    dob DATE,
    doctor_id INTEGER
    );

CREATE TABLE doctor (
    doctor_id NUMBER,
    name VARCHAR2(100)
    );
```

Now suppose that I want to let a doctor see only her own patients when she issues a query against the table. More than that, I don't want to let a doctor modify patient records unless those records belong to that doctor's patients.

You could achieve much of what is needed through the creation of a set of views, and many organizations have been doing just that for years. The view-based approach can become quite complex, especially if you want to make it foolproof.

Wouldn't it be so much more elegant if you could just let any doctor connect to her schema in Oracle, issue the following query:

```
SELECT * FROM patient;
```

and then make certain that the doctor sees information only about her patients? With this approach, you embed all the rules needed to enforce the appropriate privacy and security rules into the database itself as a security policy so that it is transparent to users of the data structures. Oracle uses that policy to modify the WHERE clause of any SQL statement executed against the table, thereby restricting access to data. This process is illustrated in Figure 8-1.

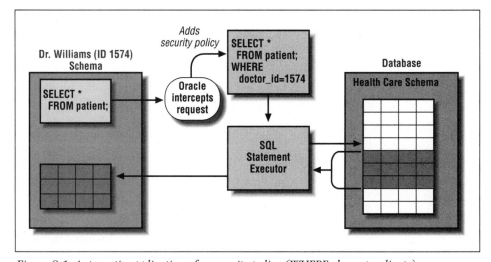

Figure 8-1. Automatic application of a security policy (WHERE clause predicate)

With Oracle8*i*'s fine-grained access control, you can apply different policies to SELECT, INSERT, UPDATE, and DELETE operations and use security policies only where you need them (for example, on salary information). You can also design and enforce more than one policy for a table, and can even construct layers of policies (one policy building on top of an existing policy) to handle complex situations.

FGAC Components

To take advantage of FGAC, you have to use programs and functionality from a wide variety of sources within Oracle, including the following:

CREATE CONTEXT DDL statement
> Allows you to define a system or application context by name, and associate that context with a PL/SQL package. A *context* is a named set of attribute/value pairs that are global to your session.

DBMS_SESSION.SET_CONTEXT procedure

Allows you to set the value for a specific attribute in a particular context.

SYS_CONTEXT function

Returns the value of a specific attribute of a context. These attributes can be system values, such as the schema name, or they can be application-specific elements that you define.

DBMS_SESSION.LIST_CONTEXT procedure

Returns the value of all attributes and values defined across all contexts in the current session.

DBMS_RLS package

A variety of programs you can use to define security policies and to associate those policies with specific PL/SQL functions that will generate WHERE clause predicates for use in fine-grained access queries. See Chapter 7, *New and Enhanced Built-in Packages in Oracle8i.*

The default database installation does *not* grant the EXECUTE privilege on the DBMS_RLS package to PUBLIC. Access is granted only to EXECUTE_CATALOG_ROLE, so schemas calling the package must have that role assigned to them.

Oracle discusses each of these topics in a different area of its documentation, making it difficult to pull them all together into a sensible, easy-to-deploy feature. This chapter takes a different approach. I will explain each area of functionality and the standalone steps needed to use them, but then immediately move to an extended example that will show you exactly how to implement FGAC in your own environment.

CREATE CONTEXT: *Creating Contexts*

Application contexts facilitate the implementation of fine-grained access control. They allow you to implement security policies with functions and then associate those security policies with applications. Each application can have its own application-specific context. Users are not allowed to arbitrarily change their context (for example, through SQL*Plus).

A context is a named set of attribute/value pairs associated with a PL/SQL package. A context is attached to, and is global within, a session. Your application can use a context to set values that are then accessed from within your code and, specifically, from within code that is used to generate WHERE clause predicates for fine-grained access control.

Suppose you are building a human resources application. You might create a context called HRINFO and define the following attributes for that context:

```
position
organizational_unit
country
```

You can then set values for each of these attributes from within your PL/SQL programs.

Oracle provides a Data Definition Language (DDL) statement to create the context used to validate and secure an application. The format of this statement is as follows:

```
CREATE [OR REPLACE] CONTEXT namespace USING [schema.]plsql_package;
```

You may deduce from this statement that a context has two attributes. Parameters are summarized in Table 8-1.

Table 8-1. CREATE_CONTEXT Parameters

Parameter	Description
namespace	The name of the context. Context namespaces are always stored in the schema SYS.
schema	Name of the schema owning the PL/SQL package. If this name is not included, Oracle uses the currently connected schema.
plsql_package	A package that can be used to set or modify the attributes of the associated context.

To create a context namespace, you must have the CREATE ANY CONTEXT system privilege. Here is the format for this grant:

```
GRANT CREATE ANY CONTEXT TO schema_name;
```

 To make it easier for you to construct contexts and the code to support them, Oracle does not verify the existence of the schema or the validity of the package at the time you create the context.

By the way, you do not have to use contexts only with the FGAC feature; they can be used simply to give you a more general and flexible way of setting and obtaining attributes for a session. I'll explore that capability in the later section, "SYS_CONTEXT and LIST_CONTEXT: Obtaining Context Information."

SET_CONTEXT: Setting Context Attribute Values

The DBMS_SESSION built-in package has been enhanced with the SET_CONTEXT procedure so that you can set the value for an attribute within a context. Here is the header for that procedure:

```
PROCEDURE DBMS_SESSION.SET_CONTEXT (
    namespace VARCHAR2,
    attribute VARCHAR2,
    value VARCHAR2);
```

The parameters are listed in Table 8-2.

Table 8-2. SET_CONTEXT Parameters

Parameter	Description
namespace	The name of the context
attribute	The attribute name
value	The value to be assigned to that attribute in the current session

This procedure can only be called inside the package specified for the namespace context in the CREATE CONTEXT statement. This relationship is shown in the following steps:

```
/* Filename on companion disk: earth.pkg */
    CREATE CONTEXT pollution_indicators USING earth_pkg;

CREATE OR REPLACE PACKAGE earth_pkg
IS
    PROCEDURE set_contexts;
END;
/
CREATE OR REPLACE PACKAGE BODY earth_pkg
IS
    c_context CONSTANT VARCHAR2(30) :=
        'pollution_indicators';

    PROCEDURE set_contexts IS
    BEGIN
        DBMS_SESSION.SET_CONTEXT (
            c_context, 'acidrain', 'corrosive');
        DBMS_SESSION.SET_CONTEXT (
            c_context, 'smog', 'dense');
    END;
END;
/
```

If you try to execute DBMS_SESSION.SET_CONTEXT "out of context," you will get an error, as shown here:

```
SQL> BEGIN
  2      DBMS_SESSION.SET_CONTEXT (
  3          'pollution_indicators', 'smog', 'dense');
  4  END;
  5  /
BEGIN
*
ERROR at line 1:
ORA-01031: insufficient privileges
```

SYS_CONTEXT and LIST_CONTEXT: Obtaining Context Information

You can obtain the value of a context's attribute in one of two ways:

SYS_CONTEXT
  A top-level PL/SQL function that returns the value of a specified attribute

DBMS_SESSION.LIST_CONTEXT
  A procedure that returns *all* of the attributes and values defined across all contexts in the current session

The SYS_CONTEXT Function

The header for the SYS_CONTEXT function is:

```
FUNCTION SYS_CONTEXT (
    namespace VARCHAR2,
    attribute VARCHAR2)
RETURN VARCHAR2;
```

It returns the value associated with *attribute* as defined in the specified context *namespace*.

In addition to your own application context information, you can retrieve information about your current connection by calling SYS_CONTEXT as follows:

```
SYS_CONTEXT ('USERENV', attribute)
```

where *attribute* can be any of the values listed in Table 8-3.

Table 8-3. SYS_CONTEXT Attributes

Attribute	Description
'CURRENT_SCHEMA'	Returns the current schema name, which may be changed with an ALTER SESSION SET SCHEMA statement

Table 8-3. SYS_CONTEXT Attributes (continued)

Attribute	Description
'CURRENT_SCHEMAID'	Returns the current schema ID
'CURRENT_USER'	Returns the current session username, which may be different from SESSION_USER from within a stored procedure (such as an invoker rights procedure)
'CURRENT_USERID'	Returns the current session user ID
'IP_ADDRESS'	Returns the IP address of the client only if the client is connected to Oracle using Net8 with the TCP protocol
'NLS_CALENDAR'	Returns the NLS calendar used for dates
'NLS_CURRENCY'	Returns the currency symbol
'NLS_DATE_FORMAT'	Returns the current date format
'NLS_DATE_LANGUAGE'	Returns the language used for days of the week, months, and so forth, in dates
'NLS_SORT'	Indicates whether the sort base is binary or linguistic
'NLS_TERRITORY'	Returns the territory
'SESSION_USER'	Returns the name of the user who logged on
'SESSION_USERID	Returns the logged-on user ID

Use the following script to examine each of these values:

```
/* Filename on companion disk: showucntxt.sql */
DECLARE
    PROCEDURE showenv (str IN VARCHAR2) IS
    BEGIN
        DBMS_OUTPUT.PUT_LINE (
            str || '=' || SYS_CONTEXT ('USERENV', str));
    END;
BEGIN
    showenv ('NLS_CURRENCY');
    showenv ('NLS_CALENDAR');
    showenv ('NLS_DATE_FORMAT');
    showenv ('NLS_DATE_LANGUAGE');
    showenv ('NLS_SORT');
    showenv ('SESSION_USER');
    showenv ('CURRENT_USER');
    showenv ('CURRENT_SCHEMA');
    showenv ('CURRENT_SCHEMAID');
    showenv ('SESSION_USERID');
    showenv ('CURRENT_USERID');
    showenv ('IP_ADDRESS');
END;
/
```

LIST_CONTEXT: Obtaining the List of Defined Context Attributes

The DBMS_SESSION built-in package provides a procedure that retrieves the list of defined attributes and values for all contexts in your session. Here is the header of that procedure:

```
PROCEDURE DBMS_SESSION.LIST_CONTEXT (
    list OUT DBMS_SESSION.AppCtxTabTyp,
    lsize OUT number);
```

where *lsize* is the number of elements in *list*, and *list* is an index-by table of records. Each record has this format:

```
TYPE DBMS_SESSSION.AppCtxRecTyp IS RECORD (
    namespace VARCHAR2(30),
    attribute VARCHAR2(30),
    value VARCHAR2(4000));
```

where *namespace* and *attribute* have the meanings described for SYS_CONTEXT.

Here is a program that utilizes this procedure to retrieve and display all defined context attributes:

```
/* Filename on companion disk: showcntxt.sp */
CREATE OR REPLACE PROCEDURE show_context_info
IS
    context_info DBMS_SESSION.AppCtxTabTyp;
    info_count PLS_INTEGER;
    indx PLS_INTEGER;
BEGIN
    DBMS_SESSION.LIST_CONTEXT (
        context_info,
        info_count);
    indx := context_info.FIRST;
    LOOP
        EXIT WHEN indx IS NULL;
        DBMS_OUTPUT.PUT_LINE (
            context_info(indx).namespace || '.' ||
            context_info(indx).attribute || ' = ' ||
            context_info(indx).value);
        indx := context_info.NEXT (indx);
    END LOOP;
END;
/
```

Here is a script and output that demonstrates the use of this procedure (building upon contexts and packages defined by first running the *earth.pkg* and *prison.pkg* scripts):

```
/* Filename on companion disk: showcntxt.tst */
BEGIN
    /* Set context information.*/
```

```
        earth_pkg.set_contexts;
        prison_pkg.set_contexts;
        show_context_info;
END;
/

INCARCERATION_FACTORS.CLASS = poor
POLLUTION_INDICATORS.SMOG = dense
INCARCERATION_FACTORS.EDUCATION = minimal
POLLUTION_INDICATORS.ACIDRAIN = corrosive
```

Context Data Dictionary Views

Oracle provides the data dictionary views listed in Table 8-4, which you can query to obtain information about policies defined in or accessible to your schema.

Table 8-4. Data Dictionary Views

View	Description
USER_POLICIES	All policies owned by the current schema.
ALL_POLICIES	All policies owned or accessible by the current schema.
DBA_POLICIES	All policies regardless of whether they are defined in or accessible in the current schema. Special privileges are required to access this view.
ALL_CONTEXT	All *active* context namespaces defined in the session. This view is based on the v$context virtual table.
DBA_CONTEXT	All context namespace information (active and inactive). Special privileges are required to access this view.

The columns for the *_POLICIES views are described in Table 8-5. These values are set through calls to the DBMS_RLS programs ADD_POLICY and ENABLE_POLICY, described in Chapter 7.

*Table 8-5. Columns of the *_POLICIES Data Dictionary Views*

Column Name	Datatype	Description
OBJECT_OWNER	VARCHAR2(30)	Owner of the object for which the policy is defined; only present in ALL_POLICIES and DBA_POLICIES.
OBJECT_NAME	VARCHAR2(30)	Name of the object for which the policy is defined.
POLICY_NAME	VARCHAR2(30)	Name of the policy.
PF_OWNER	VARCHAR2(30)	Owner of the packaged function.
PACKAGE	VARCHAR2(30)	Name of the package that contains the function.
FUNCTION	VARCHAR2(30)	Name of the function used to generate dynamic predicate.
SEL	VARCHAR2(3)	'YES' or 'NO'—Is this policy applied to SELECT statements?

Table 8-5. Columns of the *_POLICIES Data Dictionary Views (continued)

Column Name	Datatype	Description
INS	VARCHAR2(3)	'YES' or 'NO'—Is this policy applied to INSERT statements?
UPD	VARCHAR2(3)	'YES' or 'NO'—Is this policy applied to UPDATE statements?
DEL	VARCHAR2(3)	'YES' or 'NO'—Is this policy applied to DELETE statements?
CHK_OPTION	VARCHAR2(3)	'YES' or 'NO'—Is check option enforced for this policy?
ENABLE	VARCHAR2(3)	'YES' or 'NO'—Is the policy checked against the value after insert or update?

The columns for the *_CONTEXT views are described in Table 8-6.

Table 8-6. Columns of the *_CONTEXT Data Dictionary Views

Column Name	Datatype	Description
NAMESPACE	VARCHAR2(30)	Name of the namespace or context
SCHEMA	VARCHAR2(30)	The schema that owns the namepace
PACKAGE	VARCHAR2(30)	The package associated with the namespace

You can, of course, write queries and stored programs to access this information. Here is a procedure that you can use to drop one or all of your policies:

```
/* Filename on companion disk: droppol.sp */
CREATE OR REPLACE PROCEDURE drop_policies (
    objname IN VARCHAR2,
    polname IN VARCHAR2 := '%',
    objschema IN VARCHAR2 := NULL)
    AUTHID CURRENT_USER
IS
BEGIN
    FOR rec IN (
        SELECT object_owner,
               object_name,
               policy_name
          FROM ALL_POLICIES
         WHERE object_owner LIKE NVL (objschema, USER)
           AND object_name LIKE objname
           AND policy_name LIKE polname)
    LOOP
        DBMS_RLS.DROP_POLICY (
            rec.object_owner, rec.object_name, rec.policy_name);
    END LOOP;
END;
/
```

Notice that I use AUTHID CURRENT_USER to make sure that the procedure will only drop policies for the tables and views for which the CURRENT_USER has the right access privileges, regardless of who owns the procedure itself. The WHERE clause will further limit the policies to those created for the objects owned by the CURRENT_USER.

You can also use the DDL statement DROP CONTEXT to drop a context or policy directly within a SQL execution environment (or via dynamic SQL).

A Complete FGAC Example

To illustrate the steps you would follow to take advantage of fine-grained access control, I am going to share with you one of my dearest dreams. The year is 2010. A massive, popular uprising has forced the establishment of a national health care system. No more for-profit hospitals pulling billions of dollars out of the system; no more private insurance companies soaking up 30 cents on the dollar; all children are vaccinated; all pregnant women receive excellent prenatal care.

Of course, we need an excellent database to back up this system. Here are four of the many tables in that database (see *fgac.sql* on the companion disk for all the DDL statements and subsequent commands in this example section):

```
/* Filename on companion disk: fgac.sql */
CREATE TABLE patient  (
    patient_id NUMBER,
    schema_name VARCHAR2(30),
    last_name VARCHAR2(100),
    first_name VARCHAR2(100),
    dob DATE,
    home_clinic_id INTEGER,
    state CHAR(2)
    );

CREATE TABLE clinic (
    clinic_id INTEGER,
    name VARCHAR2(100),
    state CHAR(2)
    );

CREATE TABLE doctor (
    doctor_id NUMBER,
    schema_name VARCHAR2(30),
    last_name VARCHAR2(100),
    first_name VARCHAR2(100),
    home_clinic_id INTEGER
    );

CREATE TABLE regulator (
    regulator_id NUMBER,
    schema_name VARCHAR2(30),
    last_name VARCHAR2(100),
    first_name VARCHAR2(100),
    state CHAR(2)
    );
```

We also insist on privacy. So here are the following rules that I am going to enforce with FGAC:

- Doctors can see only those patients who are assigned to their clinic.

- Regulators can see only those patients who reside in the same state.

- Patients can see only information about themselves.

Sure, I can create views to build in some or all of these types of security rules. But I will instead use FGAC to accomplish the same objective at a more fundamental and comprehensive level. For example, with FGAC in place, any doctor can issue this query:

```
SELECT * FROM patient;
```

and only see her patients at the clinic. Regulators (whose job it is to make sure that patients receive top-notch care) can see all of (and only) *their* clients with the same query:

```
SELECT * FROM patient;
```

And if a patient issues an unqualified query against the patient table, she will see only her row. "Same" query, different results, processed transparently with FGAC.

Here are the steps I will take to get this job done:

1. Create all of the data structures and data in a central schema (SCOTT in the demonstration).

2. Create separate schemas for each of the doctors, regulators, and patients.

3. Create an application context for SCOTT that associates the named context with a package. This package will contain all the logic rules I need to enforce patient privacy.

4. Create the package, which will be called nhc_pkg (National Health Care package). Make it publicly available (owned by SCOTT). The package allows me to define a predicate for the patient table, but also to set and verify the context information for any schema.

5. Define an FGAC policy through DBMS_RLS that associates the patient table with the predicate-generating function.

6. Create a database trigger on the system LOGON event so that every time a user connects to the database, her context will be set, guaranteeing privacy.

Once all these pieces are in place, I can test my newly secured environment. All of these steps are contained in the *fgac.sql* script. In the following sections, I'll focus on the context-specific elements (as opposed to the CREATE TABLE statements and so on).

Creating the Security Package

I decided to create one package that would contain all of the programs I need to set and manage my context attributes and generate the security predicates. Here is the National Health Care package specification:

```
/* Filename on companion disk: fgac.sql */
CREATE OR REPLACE PACKAGE nhc_pkg
IS
    c_context CONSTANT VARCHAR2(30) := 'patient_restriction';
    c_person_type_attr CONSTANT VARCHAR2(30) := 'person_type';
    c_person_id_attr CONSTANT VARCHAR2(30) := 'person_id';
    c_patient CONSTANT CHAR(7) := 'PATIENT';
    c_doctor CONSTANT CHAR(6) := 'DOCTOR';
    c_regulator CONSTANT CHAR(9) := 'REGULATOR';

    PROCEDURE show_context;

    PROCEDURE set_context;

    FUNCTION person_predicate (
        schema_in VARCHAR2,
        name_in VARCHAR2)
    RETURN VARCHAR2;
END nhc_pkg;
/
```

The show_context procedure comes in handy when I want to verify the context information in a session. Here is the body of this program:

```
PROCEDURE show_context
IS
BEGIN
    DBMS_OUTPUT.PUT_LINE ('Type: ' ||
        SYS_CONTEXT (c_context, c_person_type_attr));
    DBMS_OUTPUT.PUT_LINE ('  ID: ' ||
        SYS_CONTEXT (c_context, c_person_id_attr));
    DBMS_OUTPUT.PUT_LINE ('Predicate: ' ||
        person_predicate (USER, 'PATIENT'));
END;
```

Here is the output from this procedure when run, for example, from the schema of Sandra Wallace, a doctor (see the *fgac.sql* INSERT statements to verify this data):

```
Type: DOCTOR
  ID: 1060
Predicate:
home_clinic_id IN
    (SELECT home_clinic_id FROM doctor
      WHERE doctor_id = SYS_CONTEXT (
          'patient_restriction', 'person_id'))
```

Setting the Context for the Schema

The nhc_pkg.set_context procedure sets the context based on the type of person
the current schema represents: patient, doctor, or regulator (you can only be one
in my simplified system). I set up two explicit cursors:

```
PROCEDURE set_context
IS
    CURSOR doc_cur IS
        SELECT doctor_id FROM doctor
         WHERE schema_name = USER;

    CURSOR reg_cur IS
        SELECT regulator_id FROM regulator
         WHERE schema_name = USER;

    l_person_type VARCHAR2(10) := c_patient;
    l_person_id INTEGER;
```

along with a local module to set the context of both of my attributes:

```
PROCEDURE set_both (
    persType IN VARCHAR2, persID IN VARCHAR2)
IS BEGIN
    DBMS_SESSION.SET_CONTEXT (
        c_context, c_person_type_attr, persType);
    DBMS_SESSION.SET_CONTEXT (
        c_context, c_person_id_attr, persID);
END;
```

The executable section then sets the attributes for a doctor, regulator, or patient,
depending on the schema name:

```
BEGIN
    OPEN doc_cur; FETCH doc_cur INTO l_person_id;
    IF doc_cur%FOUND
    THEN
        l_person_type := c_doctor;
    ELSE
        OPEN reg_cur; FETCH reg_cur INTO l_person_id;
        IF reg_cur%FOUND
        THEN
            l_person_type := c_regulator;
        END IF;
        CLOSE reg_cur;
    END IF;
    set_both (l_person_type, l_person_id);
    CLOSE doc_cur;
END;
```

Defining the Predicate

The main purpose of the National Health Care package is to generate the predicate that will be attached to any query against the patient table. This action is performed by the person_predicate function:

```
FUNCTION person_predicate (
    schema_in VARCHAR2,
    name_in VARCHAR2)
    RETURN VARCHAR2
```

As you will see later in this function's implementation, the schema_in and name_in parameters are not used at all. I still *must* include these parameters in the parameter list if it is to be callable by the FGAC mechanism. Now, in the declaration section, I obtain the value for the person type attribute (doctor, regulator, or patient):

```
IS
    l_context VARCHAR2(100) :=
        SYS_CONTEXT (c_context, c_person_type_attr);
    retval VARCHAR2(2000);
```

This value is set by a call to nhc_pkg.set_context that is made whenever a person connects to the database instance (explained in the next section). Once I have this value, I can create the appropriate predicate. For a doctor, I use the following:

```
BEGIN
    IF l_context = 'DOCTOR'
    THEN
        retval :=
            'home_clinic_id IN
                (SELECT home_clinic_id FROM doctor
                   WHERE doctor_id = SYS_CONTEXT (''' ||
                       c_context || ''', ''' || c_person_id_attr || '''))';
```

In other words, the doctor can only see patients whose clinic ID matches that of the doctor. Notice I call SYS_CONTEXT directly within the predicate (at runtime, not during the execution of this function) to obtain the doctor's ID number. I construct a very similar predicate for a regulator:

```
    ELSIF l_context = 'REGULATOR'
    THEN
        retval :=
            'state IN
                (SELECT state FROM regulator
                   WHERE regulator_id = SYS_CONTEXT (''' ||
                       c_context || ''', ''' || c_person_id_attr || '''))';
```

If the user is a patient, then the predicate is much simpler: she can only see information about herself, so I force a match on the schema_name column:

```
    ELSIF l_context = 'PATIENT'
    THEN
        retval := 'schema_name = ''' || USER || '''';
```

Finally, if the person type attribute is not set to one of the values just discussed, I've identified someone outside of the health care system entirely, so I refuse access to *any* patient information:

```
ELSE
    /* Refuse any access to information. */
    retval := 'person_id IS NULL';
END IF;
```

and then return the predicate:

```
    RETURN retval;
END person_predicate;
```

Defining the Policy

I still need to register the security policy (that is, the predicate to be attached to the patient table). To do this, I call DBMS_RLS.ADD_POLICY as follows:

```
BEGIN
    DBMS_RLS.ADD_POLICY (
        'SCOTT',
        'patient',
        'patient_privacy',
        'SCOTT',
        'nhc_pkg.person_predicate',
        'SELECT,UPDATE,DELETE');
END;
/
```

This program call specifies that whenever a SELECT, UPDATE, or DELETE on the SCOTT.patient table is executed, the SCOTT.nhc_pkg.person_predicate function is to be called to generate a predicate that will be added to the WHERE clause of the statement.

I could define a different security policy for the different SQL statements, but in this case, the same predicate would be applied to each.

Setting Up the LOGON Trigger

Now all the pieces are in place. To get things rolling, however, I need to create a trigger that will execute whenever anyone logs in to the database.

```
CONNECT sys/sys

/* Create a LOGON trigger that automatically sets
   the NHC privacy attributes. */
CREATE OR REPLACE TRIGGER set_id_on_logon
AFTER logon ON DATABASE
BEGIN
    nhc_pkg.set_context;
END;
/
```

With this trigger, I guarantee that no one can have unrestricted access to the patient data. Let's give it a try. I connect as Suni Maximo, a regulator:

```
CONNECT smaximo/smaximo
```

I'll show the context information before I try to get patient information:

```
SQL> exec nhc_pkg.show_context
Type: REGULATOR
  ID: 542
Predicate:
state IN
   (SELECT state FROM regulator
     WHERE regulator_id = SYS_CONTEXT (
        'patient_restriction', 'person_id'))
```

Let's confirm the state in which Suni Maximo is supposed to regulate health care activity:

```
SQL> SELECT last_name, state FROM regulator;
LAST_NAME            ST
-------------------- --
Halloway             IL
Maximo               NY
```

When I run a query against the patient table in this schema, we see that the predicate has been appended properly:

```
SQL> SELECT last_name, state FROM patient;
LAST_NAME            ST
-------------------- --
Walsh                NY
DeUrso               NY
```

Debugging FGAC Code

Getting this code to work can be tricky; there are lots of interdependencies and, of course, the very nature of the feature is that it automatically appends predicates to your SELECT statement. How do you watch *that* to see if it is working correctly?

Here are descriptions of some of the errors I encountered and what I did to fix the code:

- I created a trigger on the LOGON system event to automatically set various context attributes. In the early stages of testing, my package was failing—and as a result, I could not connect to any of my test schemas! I would simply get this error:

```
SQL> CONNECT csilva/csilva
ERROR:
ORA-04098: trigger 'SET_ID_ON_LOGON' is invalid
          and failed re-validation

Warning: You are no longer connected to ORACLE.
```

What's a fella to do? What I have to do is drop the trigger so that I can recreate the package and solve my problem. So I did it this way:

```
CONNECT INTERNAL/oracle
DROP TRIGGER set_id_on_logon;
```

and then I could get on with my test.

- If there is any kind of error in your function, you will see this error when you try to execute a query that includes the predicate:

```
SELECT * FROM patient
       *
ERROR at line 1:
ORA-28113: policy predicate has error
```

This is, obviously, a very generic error message. How do you figure out what went wrong and then fix it? The best thing to do at this point is execute the function *outside* the query to verify its contents. You will also want to display the various system context values. I created the nhc_pkg.show_context procedure for just this purpose.

- Your predicate function must take two string arguments for schema and object names, even if you do not use them. Otherwise, you get this error:

```
ORA-28112: failed to execute policy function
```

9

Calling Java from PL/SQL

In this chapter, I explore the exciting new feature of Oracle8*i* that allows a developer to call Java stored procedures (JSPs) from within PL/SQL. Java is a very powerful language, much more robust in many ways than PL/SQL. Java also offers hundreds of classes that provide clean, easy-to-use application programming interface (APIs) to a wide variety of functionality.

Oracle8i and Java

In Oracle8*i*, Oracle includes a new product called JServer, which consists of the following elements:

- Oracle's Java Virtual Machine (JVM), called Aurora, the supporting runtime environment, and Java class libraries

- Tight integration with PL/SQL and Oracle RDBMS functionality

- An Object Request Broker (the Aurora/ORB) and Enterprise JavaBeans (EJB)

- The JServer Accelerator (native compiler) (available in the 8.1.6 Enterprise Edition only)

The Aurora JVM executes Java methods (also known as Java stored procedures) and classes if they were stored in the database itself.

Java in the Oracle database is a big topic; Java programming all by itself is an even bigger topic. Complete treatment of either is outside the scope of this book. My objectives for this chapter are limited to the following:

- Providing the information you need to load Java classes into the Oracle database, manage those new database objects, and publish them for use inside PL/SQL

- Offering a basic tutorial in building Java classes that should give you enough guidance to let you construct simple classes to access underlying Java functionality

To access Java class methods from within Oracle, you must take the following steps:

1. Create the Java code elements. You can do this in Oracle's JDeveloper, or in any other Java Integrated Development Environment. (*notepad.exe* will also, of course, do the trick in a pinch!)

2. Load the Java class(es) into Oracle using the loadjava command-line utility or the CREATE JAVA statement.

3. Publish the Java class methods inside PL/SQL by writing wrapper programs in PL/SQL around the Java code.

4. Grant privileges as required on the PL/SQL wrapper programs and the Java class referenced by the PL/SQL wrapper.

5. Call the PL/SQL programs from any one of a number of environments, as illustrated in Figure 9-1.

Oracle8*i* offers a variety of components and commands to work with Java. Table 9-1 summarizes these different elements.

Table 9-1. Oracle8i Components and Commands for Java

Component	Description
Aurora JVM	The Java Virtual Machine (JVM) that Oracle implemented in its database server
loadjava	An operating system command-line utility that loads your Java code elements (classes, *.jar* files, etc.) into the Oracle database
dropjava	An operating system command-line utility that drops your Java code elements (classes, *.jar* files, etc.) from the Oracle database
CREATE JAVA DROP JAVA ALTER JAVA	New DDL statements that perform some of the same tasks as loadjava and dropjava
DBMS_JAVA	A built-in package that offers a number of utilities to set options and other aspects of the JVM
DBMS_JAVA_TEST	A built-in package you can use to more easily test your JSPs
JPublisher	A utility used to build Java classes around object types and REFs defined in the Oracle database

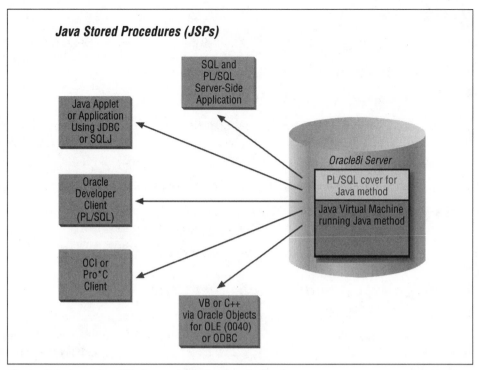

Figure 9-1. Accessing JSPs from within the Oracle database

The remainder of this chapter explains the steps outlined earlier and the components in Table 9-1. For more thorough coverage of Java in the Oracle database, please consult the Oracle documentation.

Getting Ready to Use Java in Oracle

Before you can call Java methods from within your PL/SQL programs you will need to do the following:

- Install a Java Development Kit (JDK™) 1.1.5 or above (check the Oracle documentation for the latest information about version support; some features of Java 1.2 are not, at the time of publication, supported inside Oracle).

- Build your Java classes and code elements, and then compile them into *.class* and *.jar* files.

- Set privileges on your Oracle schema.

Installing Java

You will need to install a Java Development Kit (JDK) 1.1.5 or above. You can do this by downloading a JDK from the Javasoft web site; Oracle also provides a JDK with Oracle8*i*. Here is the Javasoft URL:

> *http://www.javasoft.com/products/index.html*

You will need to make sure to set the CLASSPATH so that the Java compiler (javac) can locate any references to your classes—and to the Oracle classes. Visit the following URL to get more information about CLASSPATH:

> *http://www.javasoft.com/products/jdk/1.2/docs/tooldocs/win32/classpath.*
> *html#env var*

You can see an online version of the Java language specification at:

> *http://java.sun.com/docs/books/jls/html/index.html*

Building and Compiling Your Java Code

Many PL/SQL developers (including the author) have never worked with an object-oriented language of any kind, so coming up to speed on Java can be a bit of a challenge. In the short time in which I have studied and used Java, I have come to these conclusions:

- It doesn't take long to get a handle on the syntax needed to build simple classes in Java.

- It's not very difficult at all to start leveraging Java inside PL/SQL.

- Writing real object-oriented applications using Java requires significant rethinking for PL/SQL developers.

It would be impossible to offer a comprehensive primer on Java in this chapter. There are many (many, many, many) books available on various aspects of Java, and a number of them are excellent. I would recommend that you check out the following:

- *Exploring Java*, by Patrick Niemeyer and Joshua Peck (O'Reilly & Associates). One of more than a dozen O'Reilly books on Java, this text is a nice introduction, from the standpoint of both syntax and concepts.

- *The Java Programming Language, Second Edition*, by Ken Arnold and James Gosling (Addison Wesley). James Gosling is the creator of Java, so you'd expect the book to be helpful. It is. Written in clear, simple terms, it gives you a strong grounding in the language.

- *Thinking in Java*, by Bruce Eckel (Prentice Hall). A very readable and creative approach to explaining object-oriented concepts. If you liked the feel of my *Oracle PL/SQL Programming*, you will definitely enjoy *Thinking in Java*.

In the "Examples" section, later in this chapter, as I demonstrate how to call Java methods from within PL/SQL, I will also take you step by step through the creation of relatively simple classes. You will find that, in many cases, this discussion will be all you need to get the job done.

Setting Oracle Privileges

Oracle8*i* has created two new roles to support Java security. For many Java-based operations within the database, you will not have to work with these roles. If, on the other hand, you want to interact with the operating system (to access or modify operating system files, for example), you need to be granted one of the following roles:

```
JAVASYSPRIV
JAVAUSERPRIV
```

You grant these roles as you would any other database role. For example, if I want to allow SCOTT to perform any kind of Java-related operation, I would issue this command from a SYSDBA account:

```
GRANT JAVASYSPRIV TO SCOTT;
```

If I want to place some restrictions on what the user can do with Java, I might execute this grant instead:

```
GRANT JAVAUSERPRIV TO SCOTT;
```

Here's one example of the difference between the two roles. To create a file through Java, I need the JAVASYSPRIV role; to read or write a file, I only need the JAVAUSERPRIV role. See the Oracle documentation for more details, including a table listing the different check methods of Java and which role is required to run those methods.

When the Aurora JVM is initialized, it installs an instance of java.lang.SecurityManager, the Java Security Manager. Each Oracle user has a *dynamic ID*, which will correspond to the session owner when you access the Java methods from within PL/SQL.

If a user lacking the sufficient privileges granted by one of these roles tries to execute an illegal operation, then the JVM will throw the java.lang.SecurityException. Here is what you would see in SQL*Plus:

```
ORA-29532: Java call terminated by uncaught Java exception:
         java.lang.SecurityException
```

When you run Java methods inside the database, different security issues can arise, particularly when interacting with the server-side filesystem or other operating system resources. Oracle follows one of the following two rules when checking I/O operations:

- If the dynamic ID has been granted JAVASYSPRIV, then Security Manager allows the operation to proceed.

- If the dynamic ID has been granted JAVAUSERPRIV, then Security Manager follows the same rules that apply to the PL/SQL UTL_FILE package to determine if the operation is valid. In other words, the file must be in a directory (or subdirectory) specified by the UTL_FILE_DIR parameter in the database initialization file.

A Simple Demonstration

Before diving into the details, let's just walk through all the different steps needed to access Java from within PL/SQL. In the process, I'll introduce the various pieces of technology you need to get the job done.

So here is my challenge: I need to be able to delete a file from within PL/SQL. Prior to Oracle 8.1, I had the following options:

- Even in Oracle 7.3, I could send a message to a database pipe, and then have a C listener program grab the message ("Delete file X") and do all the work.

- In Oracle 8.0, I could set up a library that pointed to a C DLL or shared library, and then from within PL/SQL, call a program in that library to delete the file.

The pipe technique is handy, but it is a clumsy workaround. The external procedure implementation in Oracle 8.0 is a better solution, but it is far less than straightforward, especially if you don't know the C language.

Java, on the other hand, comes with prebuilt (*foundation*) classes that offer clean, easy-to-use APIs to a wide array of functionality, including file I/O.

Here are the steps I will perform in this demonstration:

1. Identify the Java functionality I need to access.

2. Build a class of my own to make the underlying Java feature callable through PL/SQL.

3. Compile the class and load it into the database.

4. Build a PL/SQL program to call the class method I created.

5. Delete files from within PL/SQL.

Finding the Java Functionality

My O'Reilly & Associates editor, Deborah Russell, was kind enough to send me a whole bunch of their Java books, so I grabbed the big, fat *Java Fundamental Class Reference*, by Mark Grand and Jonathan Knudsen, and looked up "File" in the index (sure, I could use HTML documentation, too, but I *like* books). The entry for "File class" caught my eye and I hurried to page 161.

There I found information about the class named java.io.File, namely, that it "provides a set of methods to obtain information about files and directories." Well, fortunately, it doesn't just let you obtain information. It also contains methods (procedures and functions) to delete and rename files, make directories, and so on. I had come to the right place!

Here is a portion of the API offered by the File class:

```
public class java.io.File {
    public boolean delete();
    public boolean mkdir ();
}
```

I will, in other words, call a Boolean function in Java to delete a file. It the file is deleted, the function returns TRUE; otherwise, it returns FALSE.

Building a Custom Java Class

Now, you might be asking yourself: why should Steven have to build his own Java class on top of the File class? Why can't I just call that function directly inside my PL/SQL wrapper? There are two reasons:

- A Java class method is, in almost every case (except for static methods), executed for a specific object instantiated from the class. From within PL/SQL, I cannot instantiate a Java object and then call the method against that object.

- Even though Java and PL/SQL both have Boolean datatypes (Java even offers a Boolean primitive and a Boolean class), they do not map to each other. I cannot pass a Boolean from Java back directly to a PL/SQL Boolean.

As a direct consequence, I need to build my own class that will:

- Instantiate an object from the File class

- Execute the delete method against that object

- Return a value that PL/SQL interprets properly

Here is the very simple class that I wrote to take advantage of the File.delete method:

```
/* Filename on companion disk: JDelete.java */
import java.io.File;
```

```
public class JDelete {

    public static int delete (String fileName) {
        File myFile = new File (fileName);
        boolean retval = myFile.delete();
        if (retval) return 1; else return 0;
        }
    }
```

Figure 9-2 explains each of the steps in this code, but the main effect is clear: the JDelete.delete method simply instantiates a dummy File object for the specified filename, so that I can call the delete method for that file. By declaring my method to be static, I make that method available without the need to instantiate an object. Static methods are associated with the *class* and not with objects declared from that class.

This class highlights a number of differences between Java and PL/SQL you should keep in mind:

- There are no BEGIN and END statements in Java for blocks, loops, or conditional statements. Instead, you use an open-brace ({) to start a block of related code, and a close-brace (}) to close the block.

- Java is case sensitive; "if" is definitely not the same thing as "IF".

- The assignment operator is a plain equals sign (=) rather than the complex symbol used in PL/SQL (:=).

- When you call a method that does not have any arguments (such as delete), you still must provide open and close parentheses. Otherwise, the Java compiler will try to interpret the method as a class member or data structure.

Hey, that was easy! Of course, you didn't watch me fumble around with Java for a day, getting over the nuisance of minor syntax errors, the agony of a case-sensitive language (I have a hard time with operating systems and programming languages that are case sensitive), and confusion concerning setting the CLASSPATH. I'll leave all that to the imagination of my readers—and your own day of fumbling!

Compiling and Loading into Oracle

Now that my class is written, I need to compile. To do this I open an MS-DOS session in Windows NT, change to the *d:\Java* directory, and compile the class:

```
D:\Java> javac JDelete.java
```

Now that it's compiled, I realize that it would make an awful lot of sense to test the function before I stick it inside Oracle and try it from PL/SQL. You are always better off building and testing *incrementally*. Java gives us an easy way to do this: the main method. If you provide a void method (procedure) called *main* in your

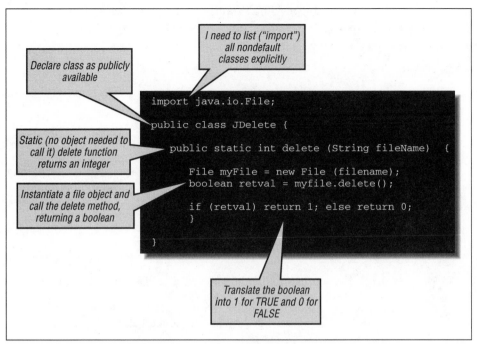

Figure 9-2. A simple Java class used to delete a file

class—and give it the right parameter list—you can then call the class, and this code will execute.

The main method is one example of how Java treats certain elements in a special way if they have the right signature. Another example is the toString method. If you add a method with this name to your class, then whenever you reference an object of that class where a string is needed, it will automatically call the toString method to display your custom description of the object.

So let's add a simple main method to JDelete (shown in bold in the following code):

```java
public class JDelete {
    public static int delete ...

    public static void main (String args[]) {
        System.out.println (
            delete (args[0])
        );
    }
}
```

In other words: call delete for the first value passed to the class and then display the value being returned. Now I will recompile the class and then run it, as shown (this example is taken from a DOS Window):

```
D:\Java>javac JDelete.java

D:\Java>java JDelete c:\temp\te_employee.pks
1

D:\Java>java JDelete c:\temp\te_employee.pks
0
```

Notice that the first time I run the main method it displays 1 (TRUE), indicating that the file was deleted. So it will come as no surprise that when I run the same command, main displays 0. It couldn't delete a file that had already been deleted.

That didn't take too much work or know-how, did it?

 In another demonstration of the superiority of Java over PL/SQL, please note that whereas you have to type 20 characters in PL/SQL to display output (DBMS_OUTPUT.PUT_LINE), you needn't type any more than 18 characters in Java (System.out.println). Give us a *break*, you language designers!

Now that my class compiles and I have verified that the delete method works, I will load it into the SCOTT schema of the Oracle database using the loadjava command:

```
D:\Java>loadjava -user scott/tiger -oci8 -resolve JDelete.class
```

I can even verify that the class is loaded by querying the contents of the USER_OBJECTS data dictionary via a utility I'll introduce later in this chapter:

```
SQL> exec myjava.showobjects
Object Name  Object Type   Status  Timestamp
------------------------------------------------
Hello        JAVA CLASS    VALID   1999-05-19:16:42
JDelete      JAVA CLASS    VALID   1999-06-07:13:20
JFile2       JAVA CLASS    VALID   1999-05-26:17:07
JFile3       JAVA CLASS    VALID   1999-05-27:12:53
```

That takes care of all the Java-specific steps, which means that it's time to return to the cozy world of PL/SQL.

Building a PL/SQL Wrapper

I will now make it easy for anyone connecting to my instance to delete files from within PL/SQL. To accomplish this goal, I will create a PL/SQL wrapper that looks like a PL/SQL function on the outside, but is really nothing more than a pass-through to the underlying Java code.

```
/* Filename on companion disk: fdelete.sf */
CREATE OR REPLACE FUNCTION fDelete (
     file IN VARCHAR2)
     RETURN NUMBER
AS LANGUAGE JAVA
     NAME 'JDelete.delete (
          java.lang.String)
          return int';
/
```

The implementation of the fdelete function consists of a string describing the Java method invocation. The parameter list must reflect the parameters of the method, but in place of each parameter I specify the fully qualified datatype name. In this case, that means that I cannot simply say "String", but instead must add the full name of the package containing the String class. The RETURN clause simply lists int for integer. The int is a primitive datatype and not a class, so that is the complete specification.

Deleting Files from PL/SQL

So I compile the function and then perform my magical, previously difficult if not impossible feat:

```
SQL> @fdelete.sf

Function created.

Input truncated to 12 characters
SQL> exec DBMS_OUTPUT.PUT_LINE (
     fdelete('c:\temp\te_employee.pkb'))
1

SQL> exec DBMS_OUTPUT.PUT_LINE (
     fdelete('c:\temp\te_employee.pkb'))
0
```

I can also build utilities on top of this function. How about a procedure that deletes all of the files found in the rows of a nested table? Even better, a procedure that accepts a directory name and filter ("all files like *.tmp", for example) and deletes all files found in that directory that pass the filter.

In reality, of course, what I should do is build a package and then put all this great new stuff in there. And that is just what I will do in the "Examples" section. Before we do that, however, let's take a closer look at each of the steps I just performed.

Using loadjava

The loadjava utility is an operating system command-line utility that uploads Java files into the database. The first time you run loadjava in a schema, it creates a number of elements for its own use:

CREATE$JAVA$LOB$TABLE
> A table created in each schema, containing Java code elements

JAVA$CLASS$MD5$TABLE
> A *hash table*, also referred to as the *digest table*, used to track the loading of Java elements into a given schema

LOADLOBS
> A package that is installed in each schema, used to load Java code elements as large objects (LOBs) into the database

Using LOADLOBS, loadjava moves Java files into a BLOB column in the database table CREATE$JAVA$LOB$TABLE. It also checks the JAVA$CLASS$MD5$TABLE. MD5 hash value to see if the loaded classes have been loaded previously and whether they have been changed (thereby minimizing the need to reload).* This is done to avoid unnecessary invalidation of dependent classes. It then calls the new DDL command CREATE JAVA to load the Java classes from the BLOB column of CREATE$JAVA$LOB$TABLE into the RDBMS as schema objects. This loading occurs only if:

- The class is being loaded for the first time
- The class has been changed
- The –force option is supplied

Figure 9-3 illustrates the loading of Java objects into the Oracle database.

Here is the syntax:

```
loadjava {-user | -u} username/password[@database]
   [-option_name [-option_name] ...] filename [filename ]...
```

where *option_name* stands for the following syntax:

```
{  {andresolve | a}
 | debug
 | {definer | d}
 | {encoding | e} encoding_scheme_name
 | {force | f}
 | {grant | g} {username | role_name}[,{username | role_name}]...
 | {oci8 | o}
```

---

* MD5 is RSA Data Security's MD5 Message-Digest Algorithm; more information can be found on *http://www.columbia.edu/~ariel/ssleay/rfc1321.html*.

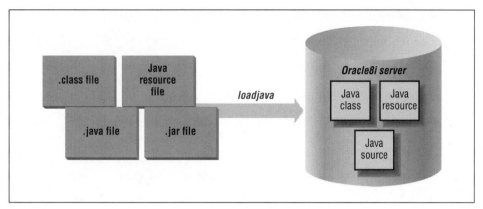

Figure 9-3. Loading Java elements into Oracle

```
| oracleresolver
| {resolve | r}
| {resolver | R} "resolver_spec"
| {schema | S} schema_name
| {synonym | s}
| {thin | t}
| {verbose | v} }
```

On the command line, you can enter the names of Java source, class, and resource files, SQLJ input files (*.sqlj* files), and uncompressed *.jar* files and *.zip* archives, in any order.

The following command, for example, loads the JFile class into the SCOTT schema:

```
loadjava -user scott/tiger -oci8 -resolve JFile.class
```

You can run this command from within a DOS window on Windows NT or from the command line in a Unix session. You can also execute it from within SQL*Plus as shown:

```
host loadjava -user scott/tiger -oci8 -resolve JFile.class
```

To make it easier for me to load classes into Oracle, I created a file named *lj.bat* for Windows NT as follows:

```
javac %1.java
loadjava -user %1 -oci8 -resolve %2.class
```

Now I can compile and load a Java class in one step:

```
D:\Java> lj scott/tiger JFile
```

Here are some things to keep in mind about loadjava. To display a help screen, use this syntax:

```
loadjava {-help | -h}
```

In a list of options or files, names must be separated only by spaces:

```
-force, -resolve, -thin  // No
-force -resolve -thin    // Yes
```

In a list of users or roles, however, names must be separated only by commas:

```
SCOTT, PAYROLL, BLAKE  // No
SCOTT,PAYROLL,BLAKE    // Yes
```

Table 9-2 describes the loadjava command-line options.

As you can probably imagine, there are a number of nuances to using loadjava, such as whether to load individual classes or compressed groups of elements in a *.zip* or *.jar* file. See the Oracle documentation for more information about the loadjava command.

Table 9-2. loadjava Options

Option	Description
-andresolve	Compiles source files and resolves each class file as it is loaded. This option and -resolve are mutually exclusive. If neither is specified, files are loaded but not compiled or resolved. In general, this mode is not recommended because it can leave classes that have unresolved references marked valid, causing an error at runtime.
-debug	Generates debug information. This option is equivalent to `javac -g`.
-definer	Specifies that the methods of uploaded classes will execute with the privileges of their definer, not their invoker. (By default, methods execute with the privileges of their invoker.) Different definers can have different privileges, and an application can have many classes, so make sure the methods of a given class execute only with the privileges they need. Note that Oracle8*i* Release 8.1.5 does not seem to conform to the Oracle documentation; the default seems to be to run with definer rights.
-encoding	Sets (or resets) the -encoding option in the database table JAVA$OPTIONS to the specified value, which must be the name of a standard JDK encoding scheme (the default is "latin1"). The compiler uses this value, so the encoding of uploaded source files must match the specified encoding.
-force	Forces the loading of Java class files, whether or not they have been loaded before. By default, previously loaded class files are rejected. You cannot force the loading of a class file if you previously loaded the source file. You must drop the source schema object first.
-grant	Grants the EXECUTE privilege on uploaded classes to the listed users or roles. (To call the methods of a class directly, users must have the EXECUTE privilege.) This option is cumulative. Users and roles are added to the list of those having the EXECUTE privilege. To revoke the privilege, either drop and reload the schema object without specifying -grant, or use the SQL REVOKE statement. To grant the privilege on an object in another user's schema, you must have the CREATE PROCEDURE WITH GRANT privilege.

Table 9-2. loadjava Options (continued)

Option	Description
-oci8	Directs loadjava to communicate with the database using the OCI JDBC driver. This option (the default) and -thin are mutually exclusive.
-oracleresolver	Binds newly created class schema objects to the following predefined resolver spec: `"((* definer's_schema) (* public))"` This option (the default) detects missing classes immediately. It and -resolver are mutually exclusive.
-resolve	After all class files on the command line are loaded and compiled (if necessary), resolves all external references in those classes. If this option is not specified, files are loaded but not compiled or resolved until runtime. Specify this option to compile (if necessary) and resolve a class that was loaded previously. You need not specify the -force option because resolution is done independently, after loading.
-resolver	Binds newly created class schema objects to a user-defined resolver spec. Because it contains spaces, the resolver spec must be enclosed by double quotes. This option and -oracleresolver (the default) are mutually exclusive.
-schema	Assigns newly created Java schema objects to the specified schema. If this option is not specified, then the logon schema is used. You must have the CREATE ANY PROCEDURE privilege to load into another user's schema.
-synonym	Creates a public synonym for uploaded classes, making them accessible outside the schema into which they are loaded. To specify this option, you must have the CREATE PUBLIC SYNONYM privilege. If you specify this option for source files, it also applies to classes compiled from those source files.
-thin	Directs loadjava to communicate with the database using the thin JDBC driver. This option and -oci8 (the default) are mutually exclusive.
-verbose	Enables the verbose mode, in which progress messages are displayed.

Using dropjava

The dropjava utility reverses the action of loadjava. It converts filenames into the names of schema objects, drops the schema objects, and finally deletes their digest table rows. Dropping a class invalidates classes that depend on it directly or indirectly. Dropping a source also drops classes derived from it.

Here is the syntax:

```
dropjava {-user | -u} username/password[@database]
    [-option_name [-option_name] ...] filename [filename] ...
```

where *option_name* stands for the following syntax:

```
{ {oci8 | o}
 | {schema | s} schema_name
```

```
| {thin | t}
| {verbose | v} }
```

On the command line, you can enter the names of Java source, class, and resource files, SQLJ input files, and uncompressed *.jar* files and *.zip* archives, in any order.

Table 9-3 describes the dropjava command-line options.

Table 9-3. dropjava Options

Option	Description
-oci8	Directs dropjava to communicate with the database using the OCI JDBC driver. This option (the default) and -thin are mutually exclusive.
-schema	Drops Java schema objects from the specified schema. If this option is not specified, then the logon schema is used. You must have the DROP ANY PROCEDURE privilege to drop objects from another user's schema.
-thin	Directs dropjava to communicate with the database using the thin JDBC driver. This option and -oci8 (the default) are mutually exclusive.
-verbose	Enables the verbose mode, in which progress messages are displayed.

Managing Java in the Database

This section explores in more detail issues related to the way Java elements are stored in the database, and how you can manage those elements.

The Java Namespace in Oracle

Oracle stores each Java class in the database as a schema object. The name of that object is *derived from* (but is not the same as) the fully qualified name of the class; this name includes the names of any containing packages. The full name of the class OracleSimpleChecker, for example, is as follows:

```
oracle.sqlj.checker.OracleSimpleChecker
```

In the database, however, the full name of the Java schema object would be:

```
oracle/sqlj/checker/OracleSimpleChecker
```

Once stored in the Oracle RDBMS, in other words, slashes replace dots.

An object name in Oracle, whether it is the name of a database table or a Java class, cannot be longer than 30 characters. Java does not have the same restriction; you can have much longer names. Oracle will allow you to load a Java class into Oracle with a name of up to 4000 characters. If the Java element name has more than 30 characters, Oracle will automatically generate a valid (less than 31 characters) alias for that element.

But don't worry! You never have to reference that alias. You can, instead, continue to use the real name for your Java element in your code. Oracle will map that long name automatically to its alias (the schema name) when necessary.

Examining Loaded Java Elements

Once you have loaded Java source, class, and resource elements into the database, information about those elements is available in several different data dictionary views, as shown in Table 9-4.

Table 9-4. Class Information in Data Dictionary Views

View	Description
USER_OBJECTS ALL_OBJECTS DBA_OBJECTS	Contains header information about your objects of JAVA SOURCE, JAVA CLASS, and JAVA RESOURCE types
USER_ERRORS ALL_ERRORS DBA_ERRORS	Contains any compilation errors encountered for your objects
USER_SOURCE	Contains the source code for your Java source if and only if you used the CREATE JAVA SOURCE command to create the Java schema object

You can write queries against these views or you can build programs to access the information in a variety of useful ways. For example, here is a query that shows me all of the Java-related objects in my schema:

```
/ *Filename on companion disk: myjava.pkg */
COLUMN object_name FORMAT A30
SELECT object_name, object_type, status, timestamp
  FROM user_objects
 WHERE (object_name NOT LIKE 'SYS_%'
        AND object_name NOT LIKE 'CREATE$%'
        AND object_name NOT LIKE 'JAVA$%'
        AND object_name NOT LIKE 'LOADLOB%')
   AND object_type LIKE 'JAVA %'
 ORDER BY object_type, object_name;
```

The WHERE clause filters out those objects created by Oracle for managing Java objects. Here is some sample output:

```
SQL> @showjava
OBJECT_NAME              OBJECT_TYPE   STATUS   TIMESTAMP
---------------------    -----------   -------  -------------------
Hello                    JAVA CLASS    VALID    1999-05-19:16:42:27
JFile2                   JAVA CLASS    VALID    1999-05-26:17:07:11
JFile3                   JAVA CLASS    VALID    1999-05-27:12:53:46
plsolutions/java/putLn   JAVA SOURCE   VALID    1999-05-19:16:30:29
```

The *myjava.pkg* file on the companion disk contains a packaged version of this query, allowing you to view your Java objects with this procedure call:

```
SQL> exec myjava.showobjects
```

The following lets you see a list of all the Java elements whose names start with OE:

```
SQL> exec myjava.showobjects ('OE%')
```

The USER_OBJECTS view's object_name column contains the full names of Java schema objects, unless the name is longer than 30 characters or contains an untranslatable character from the Unicode character set. In this case, the short name is displayed in the object_name column. To convert short names to full names, you can use the LONGNAME function in the utility package DBMS_JAVA, which is explored in the next section.

Here are some things to keep in mind about Java schema elements stored in the database:

- When you use the loadjava command to load your Java element into the database, the source of your Java element is not transferred to Oracle. Only the *.class*, *.jar*, *.zip*, *.java*, etc., files are moved into the database.

- If you use the CREATE JAVA DDL command, then the source for your Java element is stored in the database. You will then find an entry in your USER_ OBJECTS (as well as DBA_OBJECTS and ALL_OBJECTS) view for that element with type "JAVA SOURCE". You can then use the DBMS_JAVA.EXPORT_ SOURCE procedure to extract that source into PL/SQL data structures and display or manipulate the text. See the *showjava.sp* file, discussed later in this chapter, for an example of such a procedure.

Using DBMS_JAVA and DBMS_JAVA_TEST

The new Oracle built-in package DBMS_JAVA gives you access to, and the ability to modify, various characteristics of the Aurora Java Virtual Machine. The DBMS_ JAVA_TEST package lets you test your Java stored procedures.

The DBMS_JAVA package contains a large number of programs, many of which are intended for Oracle internal use only. Nevertheless, there are a number of very useful programs that we can take advantage of. Most of these programs can also be called within SQL statements. Table 9-5 summarizes the programs.

Table 9-5. DBMS_JAVA Programs

Program	Description
LONGNAME function	Obtains the full (long) Java name for a given Oracle short name

Table 9-5. DBMS_JAVA Programs (continued)

Program	Description
GET_COMPILER_ OPTION function	Looks up an option in the Java options table
SET_COMPILER_ OPTION procedure	Sets a value in the Java options table and creates the table, if one does not exist
RESET_COMPILER_ OPTION procedure	Resets a compiler option in the Java options table
SET_OUTPUT procedure	Redirects Java output to the DBMS_OUTPUT text buffer
EXPORT_SOURCE procedure	Exports a Java source schema object into an Oracle large object (LOB)
EXPORT_RESOURCE procedure	Exports a Java resource schema object into an Oracle large object (LOB)
EXPORT_CLASS procedure	Exports a Java class schema object into an Oracle large object (LOB)

LONGNAME: Converting Java Long Names

Java class and method names can easily exceed the maximum SQL identifier length of 30 characters. In such cases, Oracle creates a unique "short name" for the Java code element and uses that name for SQL- and PL/SQL-related access.

Use the following function to obtain the full (long) name for a given short name:

```
FUNCTION DBMS_JAVA.LONGNAME (shortname VARCHAR2) RETURN VARCHAR2
```

The following query displays the long name for all Java classes defined in the currently connected schema for which the long name and short names do not match:

```
/* Filename on companion disk: longname.sql */
SELECT object_name shortname,
       DBMS_JAVA.LONGNAME (object_name) longname
  FROM USER_OBJECTS
 WHERE object_type = 'JAVA CLASS'
   AND object_name != DBMS_JAVA.LONGNAME (object_name);
```

This query is also available inside the myJava package found in the *myJava.pkg* file; its use is shown here. Suppose that I define a class with this name:

```
public class DropAnyObjectIdentifiedByTypeAndName {
```

That is too long for Oracle, and we can verify that Oracle creates its own short name as follows:

```
SQL> exec myjava.showlongnames
Short Name | Long Name
---------------------------------------------------
Short: /247421b0_DropAnyObjectIdentif
Long:  DropAnyObjectIdentifiedByTypeAndName
```

GET_, SET_, and RESET_COMPILER OPTIONS: Getting and Setting Compiler Options

You can also set compiler option values in the database table JAVA$OPTIONS (called the *options table* from here on). Then, you can selectively override those settings using loadjava command-line options. A row in the options table contains the names of source schema objects to which an option setting applies. You can use multiple rows to set the options differently for different source schema objects.

The compiler looks up options in the options table unless they are specified on the loadjava command line. If there is no options-table entry or command-line value for an option, the compiler uses the following default values (you can find more information about nondefault values in the *Oracle8i SQLJ Developer's Guide and Reference* documentation):

```
encoding = latin1
online = true      // applies only to SQLJ source files
```

You can get and set options-table entries using the following DBMS_JAVA functions and procedures:

```
FUNCTION DBMS_JAVA.GET_COMPILER_OPTION (
    what VARCHAR2, optionName VARCHAR2)

PROCEDURE DBMS_JAVA.SET_COMPILER_OPTION (
    what VARCHAR2, optionName VARCHAR2, value VARCHAR2)

PROCEDURE DBMS_JAVA.RESET_COMPILER_OPTION (
    what VARCHAR2, optionName VARCHAR2)
```

The parameter *what* is the name of a Java package, the full name of a class, or the empty string. After searching the options table, the compiler selects the row in which *what* most closely matches the full name of the schema object. If *what* is the empty string, it matches the name of any schema object.

optionName is the name of the option being set. Initially, a schema does not have an options table. To create one, use the procedure DBMS_JAVA.SET_COMPILER_OPTION to set a *value*. The procedure creates the table if it does not exist. Enclose parameters in single quotes, as shown in the following example:

```
SQL> DBMS_JAVA.SET_COMPILER_OPTION ('X.sqlj', 'online', 'false');
```

SET_OUTPUT: Enabling Output from Java

The System.out and System.err classes send their output to the current trace files (when executed within the Oracle database). This is certainly not a very convenient repository if you simply want to test your code to see if it is working properly. DBMS_JAVA supplies a procedure you can call to redirect output to the

DBMS_OUTPUT text buffer so that it can be flushed to your SQL*Plus screen automatically. The syntax of this procedure is:

```
PROCEDURE DBMS_JAVA.SET_OUTPUT (buffersize NUMBER);
```

Here is an example of how you would use this program:

```
//* Filename on companion disk:  ssoo.sql */
SET SERVEROUTPUT ON SIZE 1000000
CALL DBMS_JAVA.SET_OUTPUT (1000000);
```

Documentation on the interaction between these two commands is skimpy; my testing has uncovered the following rules:

- The minimum (and default) buffer size is a measly 2000 bytes; the maximum size is 1,000,000 bytes. You can pass a number outside of that range without causing an error (unless the number is *really* big); it will simply be ignored.

- The buffer size specified by SET SERVEROUTPUT supersedes that of DBMS_JAVA.SET_OUTPUT. If, in other words, you provide a smaller value for the DBMS_JAVA call, it will be ignored, and the larger size used.

- If your output in Java exceeds the buffer size, you will *not* receive the error you get with DBMS_OUTPUT, namely:

  ```
  ORU-10027: buffer overflow, limit of nnn bytes
  ```

  The output will instead be truncated to the buffer size specified, and execution of your code will continue.

As is the case with DBMS_OUTPUT, you will not see any output from your Java calls until the stored procedure through which they are called finishes executing.

EXPORT_SOURCE, _RESOURCE, and _CLASS: Exporting Schema Objects

Oracle's DBMS_JAVA package offers the following set of procedures to export source, resources, and classes:

```
PROCEDURE DBMS_JAVA.EXPORT_SOURCE (
   name VARCHAR2,
   [ blob BLOB | clob CLOB ]
   );

PROCEDURE DBMS_JAVA.EXPORT_SOURCE (
   name VARCHAR2,
   schema VARCHAR2,
   [ blob BLOB | clob CLOB ]
   );

PROCEDURE DBMS_JAVA.EXPORT_RESOURCE (
   name VARCHAR2,
   [ blob BLOB | clob CLOB ]
   );
```

```
PROCEDURE DBMS_JAVA.EXPORT_RESOURCE (
   name VARCHAR2,
   schema VARCHAR2,
   [ blob BLOB | clob CLOB ]
   );

PROCEDURE DBMS_JAVA.EXPORT_CLASS (
   name VARCHAR2,
   blob BLOB
   );

PROCEDURE DBMS_JAVA.EXPORT_CLASS (
   name VARCHAR2,
   schema VARCHAR2,
   blob BLOB
   );
```

In all cases, *name* is the name of the Java schema object to be exported, *schema* is the name of the schema owning the object (if not supplied, then the current schema is used), and *blob|clob* is the large object that receives the specified Java schema object.

You cannot export a class into a CLOB, only into a BLOB. In addition, the internal representation of the source uses the UTF8 format, so that format is used to store the source in the BLOB as well.

The following prototype procedure offers an idea of how you might use the export programs to obtain source code of your Java schema objects, when appropriate:

```
/* Filename on companion disk: showjava.sp */
CREATE OR REPLACE PROCEDURE show_java_source (
    name IN VARCHAR2,
    schema IN VARCHAR2 := NULL
    )
IS
   b CLOB;
   v VARCHAR2(2000) ;
   i INTEGER ;
BEGIN
   /* Move the Java source code to a CLOB. */
   DBMS_LOB.CREATETEMPORARY (b, FALSE);
   DBMS_JAVA.EXPORT_SOURCE (name, NVL (schema, USER), b);

   /* Read the CLOB to a VARCHAR2 variable and display it. */
   i := 1000;
   DBMS_LOB.READ (b, i, 1, v);
   pl (v); /* run pl.sp to create this procedure */
END;
/
```

If I then create a Java source object using the CREATE JAVA statement as follows:

```
CREATE OR REPLACE JAVA SOURCE NAMED "Hello"
AS
```

```
public class Hello {
   public static String hello() {
      return "Hello Oracle World";
      }
   };
/
```

I can view the source code as shown here (assuming that DBMS_OUTPUT has been enabled):

```
SQL> exec show_java_source ('Hello')
public class Hello {
     public static String hello() {
         return "Hello
 Oracle World";
          }
     };
```

Using DBMS_JAVA_TEST

DBMS_JAVA_TEST provides a facility for testing your Java stored procedures. It contains a single, overloaded function named FUNCALL, as in "function call." It has this header:

```
FUNCTION DBMS_JAVA_TEST.FUNCALL (
class   IN VARCHAR2,
method IN VARCHAR2,
s1  IN VARCHAR2 := NULL, s2   IN VARCHAR2 := NULL,
s3  IN VARCHAR2 := NULL, s4   IN VARCHAR2 := NULL,
s5  IN VARCHAR2 := NULL, s6   IN VARCHAR2 := NULL,
s7  IN VARCHAR2 := NULL, s8   IN VARCHAR2 := NULL,
s9  IN VARCHAR2 := NULL, s10 IN VARCHAR2 := NULL,
s11 IN VARCHAR2 := NULL, s12 IN VARCHAR2 := NULL,
s13 IN VARCHAR2 := NULL, s14 IN VARCHAR2 := NULL,
s15 IN VARCHAR2 := NULL, s16 IN VARCHAR2 := NULL,
s17 IN VARCHAR2 := NULL, s18 IN VARCHAR2 := NULL,
s19 IN VARCHAR2 := NULL, s20 IN VARCHAR2 := NULL)
RETURN VARCHAR2
```

In actuality, DBMS_JAVA_TEST contains 20 overloadings of FUNCALL, each with a different number of s1 through s20 parameters, without any NULL default values. That interface is required for the call through to Java.

Here is an example of calling this function:

```
BEGIN
   p.l (DBMS_JAVA_TEST.FUNCALL (
         'JFile2', 'length', 'd:\java\jfile2.java'));
END;
/
```

At the time of publication, calls to DBMS_JAVA_TEST.FUNCALL did not return any values; it is unclear whether this functionality is to be used by PL/SQL developers.

Publishing and Using Java in PL/SQL

Once you have written your Java classes and loaded them into the Oracle RDBMS, you can call their methods from within PL/SQL (and SQL)—but only after you "publish" those methods via a PL/SQL wrapper.

Call Specs

You only need to build wrappers in PL/SQL for those Java methods you want to make available through a PL/SQL interface. Java methods can access other Java methods in the Java Virtual Machine directly, without any need for a wrapper. To publish a Java method, you write a *call spec*—a PL/SQL program header (function or procedure) whose body is actually a call to a Java method via the LANGUAGE JAVA clause. This clause contains the following information about the Java method: its full name, its parameter types, and its return type. You can define these call specs as standalone functions or procedures, as programs within a package, and as methods in an object type:

```
CREATE [OR REPLACE] --Only if a standalone program
<Standard PL/SQL procedure/function header>
{IS | AS} LANGUAGE JAVA
NAME 'method_fullname (java_type_fullname[, java_type_fullname]...)
   [return java_type_fullname]';
```

Where *java_type_fullname* is the full name of the Java type, such as java.lang. String.

The NAME clause string identifies uniquely the Java method being wrapped. The fully qualified Java names and the call spec parameters, which are mapped by position only, must correspond, one to one, with the parameters in the program. If the Java method takes no arguments, code an empty parameter list for it but not for the function or procedure.

Here are a few examples:

*   A standalone function calling a method:

```
CREATE OR REPLACE FUNCTION fDelete (
    file IN VARCHAR2)
    RETURN NUMBER
AS LANGUAGE JAVA
```

```
NAME 'JDelete.delete (
        java.lang.String)
        return int';
```

- A packaged procedure with the LANGUAGE clause in the specification that passes an object type as a parameter:

```
CREATE OR REPLACE PACKAGE nat_health_care
IS
    PROCEDURE consolidate_insurer (ins Insurer)
        AS LANGUAGE JAVA
        NAME 'NHC_consolidation.process(oracle.sql.STRUCT)';
END nat_health_care;
```

- An object type method with the LANGUAGE clause in the specification:

```
CREATE TYPE WarCriminal AS OBJECT (
    name VARCHAR2(100),
    victim_count NUMBER,
    MEMBER FUNCTION sentencing_date (
        name_in IN VARCHAR2) RETURN DATE
        AS LANGUAGE JAVA
        NAME 'warCriminal.dos (java.lang.String)
                return java.sql.Timestamp'
```

Some Rules for Java Wrappers

Note the following rules for Java wrappers:

- A PL/SQL call spec and the Java method it publishes must reside in the same schema.

- A call spec exposes a Java method's top-level entry point to Oracle. As a result, you can publish only public static methods, unless you are defining a member method of a SQL object type. In this case, you can publish instance methods as member methods of that type.

- A method in object-oriented languages cannot assign values to objects passed as arguments; the point of the method is to apply to the object to which it is attached. When you want to call a method from SQL or PL/SQL and change the value of an argument, you must declare it as an OUT or IN OUT parameter in the call spec. The corresponding Java parameter must then be a one-element array.

- You can replace the element value with another Java object of the appropriate type, or (for IN OUT parameters only) modify the value if the Java type permits. Either way, the new value propagates back to the caller. For example, you might map a call spec OUT parameter of type NUMBER to a Java parameter declared as `float[] p`, then assign a new value to `p[0]`.

A function that declares OUT or IN OUT parameters cannot be called from SQL DML statements.

Mapping Datatypes

Earlier, I showed you one very simple example of a PL/SQL wrapper. That delete function passed a VARCHAR2 value to a java.lang.String parameter. The Java method returned an int, which was then passed back through the RETURN NUMBER clause of the PL/SQL function. Those are two straightforward examples of datatype *mapping*, that is, setting up a correspondence between a PL/SQL datatype and a Java datatype.

When you build a PL/SQL call spec, the PL/SQL and Java parameters, as well as the function result, are related by position and must have compatible datatypes. Table 9-6 lists all the datatype mappings currently allowed between PL/SQL and Java. If you rely on a supported datatype mapping, Oracle will convert from one to the other automatically.

As you can see with a quick glance at the mapping table, Oracle supports only automatic conversion for SQL datatypes. PL/SQL-specific datatypes, including BINARY_INTEGER, PLS_INTEGER, BOOLEAN, and index-by table types, are not supported. In those cases, you will have to perform manual conversion steps to transfer data between these two execution environments. See the "Examples" section for examples of nondefault mappings; see Oracle documentation for even more detailed examples involving the use of JDBC.

Table 9-6. Legal Datatype Mappings

SQL Type	Java Class
CHAR, NCHAR, LONG, VARCHAR2, NVARCHAR2	oracle.sql.CHAR java.lang.String java.sql.Date java.sql.Time java.sql.Timestamp java.lang.Byte java.lang.Short java.lang.Integer java.lang.Long java.lang.Float java.lang.Double java.math.BigDecimal byte, short, int, long, float, double

Table 9-6. Legal Datatype Mappings (continued)

SQL Type	Java Class
DATE	oracle.sql.DATE java.sql.Date java.sql.Time java.sql.Timestamp java.lang.String
NUMBER	oracle.sql.NUMBER java.lang.Byte java.lang.Short java.lang.Integer java.lang.Long java.lang.Float java.lang.Double java.math.BigDecimal byte, short, int, long, float, double
RAW, LONG RAW	oracle.sql.RAW byte[]
ROWID	oracle.sql.CHAR oracle.sql.ROWID java.lang.String
BFILE	oracle.sql.BFILE
BLOB	oracle.sql.BLOB oracle.jdbc2.Blob
CLOB, NCLOB	oracle.sql.CLOB oracle.jdbc2.Clob
OBJECT	oracle.sql.STRUCT oracle.SqljData oracle.jdbc2.Struct
REF	oracle.sql.REF oracle.jdbc2.Ref
TABLE, VARRAY	oracle.sql.ARRAY oracle.jdbc2.Array
Any of the above SQL types	oracle.sql.CustomDatum oracle.sql.Datum

Calling a Java Method in SQL

You can call PL/SQL functions of your own creation from within SQL DML statements. You can also call Java methods wrapped in PL/SQL from within SQL. However, these methods must conform to the following purity rules:

- If you call a method from a SELECT statement or a parallelized INSERT, UPDATE, or DELETE statement, the method is not allowed to modify any database tables.

- If you call a method from an INSERT, UPDATE, or DELETE statement, the method cannot query or modify any database tables modified by that statement.

- If you call a method from a SELECT, INSERT, UPDATE, or DELETE statement, it cannot execute SQL transaction control statements (such as COMMIT), session control statements (such as SET ROLE), or system control statements (such as ALTER SYSTEM). You also cannot execute DDL statements, since they automatically perform a commit in your session.

The objective of these restrictions is to control side effects that might disrupt your SQL statements. If you try to execute a SQL statement that calls a method violating any of these rules, you will receive a runtime error when the SQL statement is parsed.

It is also possible to call Java from PL/SQL via the SQL layer using the CALL command syntax and native dynamic SQL, as shown in the following code (the implementation of dropany is shown in the next section):

```
DECLARE
    Tp varchar2(30):='TABLE';
    Nm varchar2(30):='mytable';
BEGIN
    EXECUTE IMMEDIATE 'CALL dropany(:tp,:nm)' USING tp, nm;
END;
```

Exception Handling with Java

On the one hand, the Java exception handling architecture is very similar to that of PL/SQL. In Java-speak, you throw an exception and then catch it. In PL/SQL-speak, you raise an exception and then handle it.

On the other hand, exception handling in Java is much more robust. Java offers a foundation class called Exception. All exceptions are objects based on that class, or on classes derived from (extending) Exception. You can pass exceptions as parameters and manipulate them pretty much as you would objects of any other class.

When a Java stored method executes a SQL statement and an exception is thrown, then that exception is an object from a subclass of java.sql.SQLException. That class contains two methods that return the Oracle error code and error message: getErrorCode( ) and getMessage( ).

If a Java stored procedure called from SQL or PL/SQL throws an exception that is *not* caught by the JVM, the caller gets an exception thrown from a Java error message. This is how all uncaught exceptions (including non-SQL exceptions) are reported. Let's take a look at different ways of handling errors and the resulting output.

Suppose that I create a class that relies on JDBC to drop objects in the database (this is drawn from an example in Oracle documentation):

```
/* Filename on companion disk: dropany.java */
import java.sql.*;
import java.io.*;
import oracle.jdbc.driver.*;

public class DropAny {
  public static void object (String object_type, String object_name)
  throws SQLException {
    // Connect to Oracle using JDBC driver
    Connection conn = new OracleDriver().defaultConnection();
    // Build SQL statement
    String sql = "DROP " + object_type + " " + object_name;
    try {
      Statement stmt = conn.createStatement();
      stmt.executeUpdate(sql);
      stmt.close();
    } catch (SQLException e) {System.err.println(e.getMessage());}
  }
}
```

> Of course, it doesn't really make any sense to rely on JDBC to per-
> form a drop object action, since this can be done much more easily
> in native PL/SQL. On the other hand, building it in Java does make
> the functionality available to other Java programs.

This version traps and displays any SQLException with this line:

```
} catch (SQLException e) {System.err.println(e.getMessage());}
```

I wrap this class inside a PL/SQL procedure as follows:

```
CREATE OR REPLACE PROCEDURE dropany (
    tp IN VARCHAR2,
    nm IN VARCHAR2
    )
AS LANGUAGE JAVA
    NAME 'DropAny.object (
            java.lang.String,
            java.lang.String)';
/
```

When I attempt to drop a nonexistent object, I will see one of the following two
outcomes:

```
SQL> CONNECT scott/tiger
Connected.
SQL> SET SERVEROUTPUT ON
SQL> BEGIN dropany ('TABLE', 'blip'); END;
/
PL/SQL procedure successfully completed.

SQL> CALL DBMS_JAVA.SET_OUTPUT (1000000);
```

```
Call completed.

SQL> BEGIN dropany ('TABLE', 'blip'); END;
/
ORA-00942: table or view does not exist
```

What you are seeing in these examples is a reminder that output from System.err. println will *not* appear on your screen until you explicitly enable it with a call to DBMS_JAVA.SET_OUTPUT. In either case, however, no exception was raised back to the calling block, since it was caught inside Java. After the second call to dropany, you can see that the error message supplied through the getMessage() method is one taken directly from Oracle.

If I comment out the try and catch lines in the DropAny.obj method, I will get very different behavior, as shown:

```
SQL> BEGIN
  2      dropany ('TABLE', 'blip');
  3   EXCEPTION
  4      WHEN OTHERS
  5      THEN
  6         DBMS_OUTPUT.PUT_LINE (SQLCODE);
  7         DBMS_OUTPUT.PUT_LINE (SQLERRM);
  8   END;
  9   /
java.sql.SQLException: ORA-00942: table or view does not exist
   at oracle.jdbc.kprb.KprbDBAccess.check_error(KprbDBAccess.java)
   at oracle.jdbc.kprb.KprbDBAccess.parseExecuteFetch(KprbDBAccess.java)
   at oracle.jdbc.driver.OracleStatement.doExecuteOther(OracleStatement.java)
   at oracle.jdbc.driver.OracleStatement.doExecuteWithBatch(OracleStatement.java)
   at oracle.jdbc.driver.OracleStatement.doExecute(OracleStatement.java)
   at oracle.jdbc.driver.OracleStatement.doExecuteWithTimeout(OracleStatement.java)
   at oracle.jdbc.driver.OracleStatement.executeUpdate(OracleStatement.java)
   at DropAny.object(DropAny.java:14)

-29532
ORA-29532: Java call terminated by uncaught Java exception: java.sql.SQLException:
ORA-00942: table or view does not exist
```

This takes a little explaining. Everything between:

```
.java.sql.SQLException: ORA-00942: table or view does not exist
```

and

```
-29532
```

represents an error stack dump generated by Java and sent to standard output, *regardless* of how you handle the error in PL/SQL. In other words, even if my exception section looked like this:

```
EXCEPTION WHEN OTHERS THEN NULL;
```

I would still get all that output to the screen, and then processing in the outer block (if any) would continue. The last three lines of output displayed are generated by the calls to DBMS_OUTPUT.PUT_LINE. Notice that the Oracle error is *not* ORA-00942, but instead is ORA-29532, a generic Java error. This is a problem. If you trap the error, how can you discover what the real error is? Looks like it's time for Write-A-Utility Man!

It appears to me that the error returned by SQLERRM is of this form:

```
ORA-29532: Java call ...: java.sql.SQLException: ORA-NNNNN ...
```

So I can scan for the presence of "java.sql.SQLException" and then SUBSTR from there. Here is a procedure that returns the error code and message for the current error, building in the smarts to compensate for the Java error message format:

```
/* Filename on companion disk: getErrorInfo.sp */
CREATE OR REPLACE PROCEDURE getErrorInfo (
    errcode OUT INTEGER,
    errtext OUT VARCHAR2)
IS
    c_keyword CONSTANT CHAR(23) := 'java.sql.SQLException: ';
    c_keyword_len CONSTANT PLS_INTEGER := 23;
    v_keyword_loc PLS_INTEGER;
    v_msg VARCHAR2(1000) := SQLERRM;
BEGIN
    v_keyword_loc := INSTR (v_msg, c_keyword);
    IF v_keyword_loc = 0
    THEN
        errcode := SQLCODE;
        errtext := SQLERRM;
    ELSE
        errtext := SUBSTR (
            v_msg, v_keyword_loc + c_keyword_len);
        errcode :=
            SUBSTR (errtext, 4, 6 /* ORA-NNNNN */);
    END IF;
END;
/
```

The following block demonstrates how I might use this procedure (it relies on the log81 package, created by the *log81.pkg* file, to write the error information to the log):

```
/* Filename on companion disk: dropany2.tst */
BEGIN
    dropany ('TABLE', 'blip');
EXCEPTION
    WHEN OTHERS
    THEN
        DECLARE
            v_errcode PLS_INTEGER;
            v_errtext VARCHAR2(1000);
        BEGIN
```

```
            getErrorInfo (v_errcode, v_errtext);
            log81.saveline (v_errcode, v_errtext);
        END;
   END;
   /
```

 Even though I am saving error information to the database log table, the Java exception stack will still be returned to the host session. If, for example, I were running the script in SQL*Plus, the Java exception stack would be displayed on the screen.

Examples

The main focus in this section is an expansion of the JDelete class into the JFile class, providing significant new file-related features in PL/SQL. Following that, I'll explore how to write Java classes and PL/SQL programs around them to manipulate Oracle objects.

Extending File I/O Capabilities

The UTL_FILE package of Oracle is notable more for what is missing than for what it contains. With UTL_FILE, you can read and write the contents of files sequentially. That's it. You can't delete files, change privileges, copy a file, obtain the contents of a directory, set a path, etc., etc. Java to the rescue! Java offers lots of different classes to manipulate files. You've already met the File class, and seen how easy it is to add the "delete a file" capability to PL/SQL.

I am now going to take my lessons learned from JDelete and the rest of this chapter and create a new class called JFile that will allow PL/SQL developers to answer the questions and take the actions listed here:

- Can I read from a file? Write to a file? Does a file exist? Is the named item a file or a directory?

- What is the number of bytes in a file? What is the parent directory of a file?

- What are the names of all the files in a directory that match a specified filter?

- How can I make a directory? Rename a file? Change the extension on a file?

I'm not going to explain all the methods in the JFile class and its corresponding package. There is a *lot* of repetition; most of the Java methods look just like the delete( ) function I built at the beginning of the chapter. I will, instead, focus on the unique issues addressed in different areas of the class and package. You can find the full definition of the code in the following files on the companion disk:

JFile.java

A Java class that draws together various pieces of information about operating system files and offers it through an API accessible from PL/SQL.

xfile.pkg

The PL/SQL package that wraps the JFile class. Stands for "eXtra stuff for FILEs."

Polishing up the delete method

Before we move on to new and exciting stuff, we should make sure that what we've done so far is optimal—and the way I defined the JDelete.delete() method and the delete_file function is far from ideal. Here's the code I showed you earlier:

```
public static int delete (String fileName) {
    File myFile = new File (fileName);
    boolean retval = myFile.delete();
    if (retval) return 1; else return 0;
    }


CREATE OR REPLACE FUNCTION fDelete (
    file IN VARCHAR2) RETURN NUMBER
AS LANGUAGE JAVA
    NAME 'JDelete.delete (java.lang.String)
            return int';
/
```

You might be asking yourself, so what's the problem? The problem is that I have been forced to use clumsy, numeric representations for TRUE/FALSE values. I must as a result write code like this:

```
IF fdelete ('c:\temp\temp.sql') = 1 THEN ...
```

and that is very ugly, hardcoded software. Not only is it ugly, but the person writing the PL/SQL code must know about the values for TRUE and FALSE embedded within a Java class.

I would much rather define a delete_file function with this header:

```
FUNCTION fDelete (
    file IN VARCHAR2) RETURN BOOLEAN;
```

So let's see what it would take to be able to present that clean, easy-to-use API for users of the xfile package.

First, I will rename the JDelete class to JFile to reflect its growing scope. Then, I will add methods that encapsulate the TRUE/FALSE values its other methods will return—and call those inside the delete() method. Here is the result:

```
/* Filename on companion disk: JFile.java */
import java.io.File;

public class JFile {
```

```
public static int tVal () { return 1; };
public static int fVal () { return 0; };

public static int delete (String fileName) {
    File myFile = new File (fileName);
    boolean retval = myFile.delete();
    if (retval) return tVal();
        else return fVal();
    }
}
```

That takes care of the Java side of things; it's time to shift attention to my PL/SQL package. Here's the first pass at the specification of xfile:

```
/* Filename on companion disk: xfile.pkg */
CREATE OR REPLACE PACKAGE xfile
IS
    FUNCTION delete (file IN VARCHAR2)
        RETURN BOOLEAN;
END xfile;
```

So now we have the Boolean function specified. But how do we implement it? I have two design objectives:

1. Hide the fact that I am relying on numeric values to pass back TRUE or FALSE.

2. Avoid hardcoding the 1 and 0 values in the package.

To achieve these objectives, I will define two global variables in my package to hold the numeric values:

```
/* Filename on companion disk: xfile.pkg */
CREATE OR REPLACE PACKAGE BODY xfile
IS
    g_true INTEGER;
    g_false INTEGER;
```

And way down at the end of the package body, I will create an initialization section that calls these programs to initialize my globals. By taking this step in the initialization section, I avoid unnecessary calls (and overhead) to Java methods:

```
BEGIN
    g_true := tval;
    g_false := fval;
END xfile;
```

Back up in the declaration section of the package body, I will define two private functions, whose only purpose is to give me access in my PL/SQL code to the JFile methods that have encapsulated the 1 and 0:

```
FUNCTION tval RETURN NUMBER
AS LANGUAGE JAVA
    NAME 'JFile.tVal () return int';

FUNCTION fval RETURN NUMBER
```

```
AS LANGUAGE JAVA
    NAME 'JFile.fVal () return int';
```

I have now succeeded in soft-coding the TRUE/FALSE values in the JFile package. To enable the use of a true Boolean function in the package specification, I create a private "internal delete" function that is a wrapper for the JFile.delete( ) method. It returns a number:

```
FUNCTION Idelete (file IN VARCHAR2) RETURN NUMBER
AS LANGUAGE JAVA
    NAME 'JFile.delete (java.lang.String) return int';
```

Finally, my public delete function can now call Idelete and convert the integer value to a Boolean by checking against the global variable:

```
FUNCTION delete (file IN VARCHAR2) RETURN BOOLEAN
AS
BEGIN
    RETURN Idelete (file) = g_true;
EXCEPTION
    WHEN OTHERS
    THEN
        RETURN FALSE;
END;
```

And that is how you convert a Java Boolean to a PL/SQL Boolean. You will see this same method employed again and again in the xfile package body.

Obtaining directory contents

One of my favorite features of JFile is its ability to return a list of files found in a directory. It accomplishes this feat by calling the File.list( ) method; if the string you used to construct a new File object is the name of a directory, it returns a String array of filenames found in that directory. Let's see how I can make this information available in PL/SQL.

I create a String method called dirContents, as follows:

```
/* Filename on companion disk: JFile.java */
public static String dirContents (String dir) {
    File myDir = new File (dir);
    String[] filesList = myDir.list();
    String contents = new String();
    for (int i = 0; i < filesList.length; i++)
        contents = contents + listDelimiter + filesList[i];
    return contents;
    }
```

This method instantiates a File object called myDir and then assigns the myDir.list( ) to a String array called filesList. I then use a Java "for" loop to concatenate each of the files into a single String, separated by the listDelimiter, and return that String.

Over on the PL/SQL side of the world, I will create a wrapper that calls this method:

```
FUNCTION dirContents (dir IN VARCHAR2)
    RETURN VARCHAR2
    AS LANGUAGE JAVA
        NAME 'JFile.dirContents (java.lang.String)
                 return java.lang.String';
```

But what am I do with this string? Let's build some additional code elements on top of my wrapper functions to make the information more developer friendly. First, I'd like to let users of xfile manipulate files either as string lists or as nested tables (much more structured data; easier to scan and manipulate). So I will define a nested table type as follows:

```
CREATE TYPE file_list_t IS TABLE OF VARCHAR2(2000);
/
```

Then I define a procedure to return the files in a directory in a nested table of this type. Note the call to the dirContents wrapper function and also the reference to g_listdelim, which contains the delimiter passed back from JFile (just like the numeric values for TRUE and FALSE):

```
PROCEDURE getDirContents (
    dir IN VARCHAR2,
    files IN OUT file_list_t)
IS
    file_list VARCHAR2(32767);
    next_delim PLS_INTEGER;
    start_pos PLS_INTEGER := 1;
BEGIN
    files.DELETE;
    file_list := dirContents (dir);
    LOOP
        next_delim :=
            INSTR (file_list, g_listdelim, start_pos);
        EXIT WHEN next_delim = 0;
        files.EXTEND;
        files(files.LAST) :=
            SUBSTR (file_list,
                start_pos,
                next_delim - start_pos);
        start_pos := next_delim + 1;
    END LOOP;
END;
```

From there, it's all just fun and games with PL/SQL. You will find in the xfile package the following programs built on top of getDirContents:

getDirContents, the filter version

> Allows the user to pass a filter, such as "*.tmp" or "%.tmp", and retrieve only files that match the filter. The character "_" will be treated as a single-character wildcard, following the SQL standard.

showDirContents

Displays all the files found in the specified directory that match your filter.

chgext

Changes the extension of the specified files.

In the xfile package, you will also find all of the entry points of the UTL_FILE package, such as FOPEN and PUT_LINE. I add those so that you can avoid the use of UTL_FILE for anything but declarations of file handles as UTL_FILE.FILE_TYPE.

Passing Objects to Java

Suppose that a union-busting firm is meeting with some of the largest corporations in the United States to develop a strategy to diminish the power of unions in this country. They need to keep track of different sources of labor and how much they plan to pay them, so the computer geek present, name of Steven, creates the following object type in Oracle:

```
/* Filename on companion disk: collsql2.sql */
CREATE TYPE labor_source_t AS OBJECT
    (labor_type VARCHAR2(30), hourly_rate NUMBER);
/
```

Steven is an object-oriented devotee and is committed to taking 100% advantage of both the limited object features of Oracle and the full object-oriented capabilities of Java. He needs, as a result, to be able to pass an object defined inside Oracle straight through to Oracle. How would he go about this?

One approach he can take is to utilize a special class provided by Oracle called oracle.sql.STRUCT. This class relies on default JDBC mappings for the attribute types. (See Oracle's and Java's documentation for more information about JDBC.) The STRUCT class offers a getAttributes() method that returns an array of Java objects, one object for each attribute in the Oracle object type, each object containing the value of the attribute. Given the labor source type just shown, for example, a call to getAttributes() would return an array with objects defined at indexes 0 and 1 (Java arrays always start at 0).

The following class demonstrates how you can build a Java class to pass an Oracle object and use the getAttributes() method to retrieve object attribute values. Notice the long list of import commands; whenever you use Oracle classes and JDBC, you will need to include these lines (or variations thereof). The java.math.* classes are imported because Oracle attributes of type NUMBER map to Java's BigDecimal class, which is not available by default.

```
/* Filename on companion disk: UnionBuster.java */
import java.sql.*;
import java.io.*;
import oracle.sql.*;
```

```
import oracle.jdbc.driver.*;
import oracle.oracore.*;
import oracle.jdbc2.*;
import java.math.*;

public class UnionBuster {

  public static void wageStrategy (STRUCT e)
    throws java.sql.SQLException {

    // Get the attributes of the labor_source object.
    Object[] attribs = e.getAttributes();

    // Access individual attributes by array index,
    // starting with 0.
    String laborType = (String)(attribs[0]);
    BigDecimal hourly_rate = (BigDecimal)(attribs[1]);

    // We'll simply display the two attribute values.
    System.out.println (
       "Pay " + laborType + " $" +
       hourly_rate + " per hour");
  }
}
```

This line probably looks quite odd to you:

```
BigDecimal hourly_rate = (BigDecimal)(attribs[1]);
```

What you are seeing here is a *cast* from one class to another. The attribs array is composed of "generic" objects. The object contains nothing more, however, than the attribute value. So if I want to extract the number from this object, I prefix the reference to the array element with the name of the class to which I want the object converted. Oracle, by the way, also supports the cast operation to a more limited degree with the SQL CAST operator, described in Chapter 10, *More Goodies for Oracle8i PL/SQL Developers*.

Once Steven has compiled and loaded this class into the Oracle database, he creates his PL/SQL cover, a procedure in this case, since the wageStrategy() method does not return any data:

```
/* Filename on companion disk: passobj.tst */
CREATE OR REPLACE PROCEDURE bust_em_with (
    labor_source_in IN labor_source)
AS LANGUAGE JAVA
    NAME 'UnionBuster.wageStrategy (oracle.sql.STRUCT)';
/
```

Notice that Steven must include the fully qualified datatype in his PL/SQL cover program, even though the Java class parameter is specified only as STRUCT.

And now companies all over the world can use this procedure to depress the hourly wages of workers generally, and destroy unions in particular, as shown here:

```
/* Filename on companion disk: passobj.tst */
BEGIN
    bust_em_with (
        labor_source ('Workfare', 0));
    bust_em_with (
        labor_source ('Prisoners', '5'));
END;
/
```

We see this output in SQL*Plus when this script is run:

```
makeOne: [B@2862355c 109 SCOTT.LABOR_SOURCE class oracle.sql.STRUCT
makeOne returns: class oracle.sql.STRUCT
Pay Workfare 0 per hour

makeOne: [B@eb7eefb2 109 SCOTT.LABOR_SOURCE class oracle.sql.STRUCT
makeOne returns: class oracle.sql.STRUCT
Pay Prisoners 5 per hour
```

10

In this chapter:
- *The NOCOPY Parameter Mode Hint*
- *Calling Packaged Functions in SQL*
- *SQL99 Compliance*
- *SQL Operations on Collections*
- *Miscellaneous and Minor Improvements*

More Goodies for Oracle8i PL/SQL Developers

I've already covered a veritable cornucopia of new features available for PL/SQL developers in Oracle8*i*. Even if that were all that Oracle8*i* offered to developers, we would all be very happy—and very busy learning how to use all the new stuff. Yet there is still more! This chapter covers other features that improve either the performance or the usability of PL/SQL in Oracle8*i*:

The NOCOPY compiler hint

> You can avoid the overhead of copying IN OUT parameter values with this enhancement. When you are working with large collections and records, NOCOPY can have a noticeable impact on program performance.

Calling PL/SQL functions from SQL

> Oracle8*i* offers some big relief for PL/SQL developers when it comes to calling their own functions: you no longer have to use the RESTRICT_REFERENCES pragma! Oracle8*i* also offers two new keywords, DETERMINISTIC and PARALLEL ENABLE, to help you integrate your PL/SQL, C, and Java code into all aspects of your database.

SQL99 compliance

> Oracle8*i* adds or expands the TRIM and CAST operators to better support the SQL99 standard.

SQL operations on collections

> Oracle8*i* makes it even easier to integrate PL/SQL (transient) collections into SQL statements.

I also review transparent improvements, that is, changes to the language that improve the performance or behavior of your PL/SQL-based applications without necessitating any modifications to your code.

The NOCOPY Parameter Mode Hint

PL/SQL 8.1 offers a new option for definitions of parameters: the NOCOPY clause. NOCOPY is a *hint* to the compiler about how you would like the PL/SQL engine to work with the data structure being passed in as an OUT or IN OUT parameter. To understand NOCOPY and its potential impact, it will help to review how PL/SQL handles parameters. Let's start with some definitions:

Formal parameter

> The parameter defined in the parameter list and used in the program.

Actual parameter

> The actual expression or variable passed to the program when it is called.

By reference

> When an actual parameter is passed *by reference*, it means that a pointer to the actual parameter is passed to the corresponding formal parameter. Both the actual and formal parameters then reference, or point to, the same location in memory that holds the value of the parameter.

By value

> When an actual parameter is passed *by value*, the value of the actual parameter is copied into the corresponding formal parameter. If the program then terminates without an exception, the formal parameter value is copied back to the actual parameter. If an error occurs, the changed values are *not* copied back to the actual parameter.

Parameter passing in PL/SQL (without the use of NOCOPY) follows the rules shown in the following table.

Parameter Mode	Passed by Value or Reference? (Default Behavior)
IN	By reference
OUT	By value
IN OUT	By value

We can infer from all of these definitions and rules that when you pass a large data structure (such as a collection, record, or instance of an object type) as an OUT or IN OUT parameter, your application could experience performance and memory degradation due to all of this copying.

PL/SQL 8.1 offers the NOCOPY hint as a way for you to attempt to avoid this copying. The syntax of this feature is as follows:

```
parameter_name [ IN | IN OUT | OUT | IN OUT NOCOPY | OUT NOCOPY ] parameter_datatype
```

You can specify NOCOPY only in conjunction with the OUT or IN OUT mode. Here, for example, is a parameter list that uses the NOCOPY hint for both of its IN OUT arguments:

```
PROCEDURE analyze_results (
   date_in IN DATE,
   values IN OUT NOCOPY numbers_varray,
   validity_flags IN OUT NOCOPY validity_rectype
   );
```

Remember that NOCOPY is a hint, not a command. This means that the compiler might silently decide that it cannot fulfill your request for a NOCOPY parameter treatment. The next section lists the restrictions on NOCOPY that might cause this to happen.

Restrictions on NOCOPY

A number of situations will cause the PL/SQL compiler to ignore the NOCOPY hint and instead use the default by-value method to pass the OUT or IN OUT parameter. These situations are the following:

- The actual parameter is an element of an index-by table (which could be an entire record structure). You can request NOCOPY for an entire index-by table, but not for an individual element in the table. A suggested workaround is to copy the structure to a standalone variable, either scalar or record, and then pass *that* as the NOCOPY parameter. That way, at least you aren't copying the entire structure.

- Certain constraints applied to actual parameters will result in the NOCOPY hint being ignored. These constraints include a scale specification for a numeric variable and the NOT NULL constraint. You can, however, pass a string variable that has been constrained by size.

- Both the actual and formal parameters are record structures. One or both records were declared using %ROWTYPE or %TYPE, and the constraints on corresponding fields in these two records are different.

- The actual and formal parameters are record structures. The actual parameter was declared by the PL/SQL engine as the index of a cursor FOR loop, and the constraints on corresponding fields in the records are different.

- In passing the actual parameter, the PL/SQL engine must perform an implicit datatype conversion. A suggested workaround is this: you are always better off performing explicit conversions, so do that and then pass the converted value as the NOCOPY parameter.

- The subprogram requesting the NOCOPY hint is used in an external or remote procedure call. In these cases, PL/SQL will always pass the actual parameter by value.

Impact of NOCOPY Use

Depending on your application, NOCOPY can improve the performance of programs with IN OUT or OUT parameters. As you might expect, these potential gains are only available with a trade-off: if a program terminates with an unhandled exception, you cannot trust the values in a NOCOPY actual parameter.

What do I mean by trust? Let's review how PL/SQL behaves concerning its parameters when an unhandled exception terminates a program. Suppose that I pass an IN OUT record to my calculate_totals procedure. The PL/SQL runtime engine first makes a copy of that record and then, during program execution, makes any changes to that *copy*. The actual parameter itself is not modified until calculate_totals ends successfully (without propagating back an exception). At that point, the local copy is copied back to the actual parameter, and the program that called calculate_totals can access that changed data. If calculate_totals terminates with an unhandled exception, however, the calling program can be certain that the actual parameter's value has not been changed.

That certainty disappears with the NOCOPY hint. When a parameter is passed by reference (the effect of NOCOPY), any changes made to the formal parameter are also made immediately to the actual parameter. Suppose that my calculate_totals program reads through a 10,000-row collection and makes changes to each row. If an error is raised at row 5000, and that error is propagated out of calculate_totals unhandled, my actual parameter collection will be only half-changed. How will I know what is good data and what is bad?

The following test script (available in *nocopy.tst* on the companion disk) demonstrates this problem. I create two versions of the same program, each of which moves through a five-row collection, doubling the value of each row. When they hit row 3, however, I raise a VALUE_ERROR exception. I then examine the contents of the collection before and after each program call.

Here are the programs:

```
/* Filename on companion disk: nocopy.tst */
CREATE OR REPLACE PACKAGE BODY nocopy_test
IS
   PROCEDURE pass_by_value (nums IN OUT number_varray)
   IS
   BEGIN
      FOR indx IN nums.FIRST .. nums.LAST
      LOOP
         nums(indx) := nums(indx) * 2;
         IF indx > 2 THEN RAISE VALUE_ERROR; END IF;
      END LOOP;
   END;

   PROCEDURE pass_by_ref (nums IN OUT NOCOPY number_varray)
   IS
```

```
       BEGIN
          FOR indx IN nums.FIRST .. nums.LAST
          LOOP
             nums(indx) := nums(indx) * 2;
             IF indx > 2 THEN RAISE VALUE_ERROR; END IF;
          END LOOP;
       END;

   END;
   /
```

Here is the block that exercises these two programs:

```
   DECLARE
       nums1 number_varray := number_varray (1, 2, 3, 4, 5);
       nums2 number_varray := number_varray (1, 2, 3, 4, 5);

       PROCEDURE shownums (
          str IN VARCHAR2, nums IN number_varray) IS
       BEGIN
          DBMS_OUTPUT.PUT_LINE (str);
          FOR indx IN nums.FIRST .. nums.LAST
          LOOP
             DBMS_OUTPUT.PUT (nums(indx) || '-');
          END LOOP;
          DBMS_OUTPUT.NEW_LINE;
       END;
   BEGIN

       shownums ('Before By Value', nums1);
       BEGIN
          nocopy_test.pass_by_value (nums1);
       EXCEPTION
          WHEN OTHERS THEN shownums ('After By Value', nums1);
       END;

       shownums ('Before NOCOPY', nums2);
       BEGIN
          nocopy_test.pass_by_ref (nums2);
       EXCEPTION
          WHEN OTHERS THEN shownums ('After NOCOPY', nums2);
       END;

   END;
   /
```

And here are the results:

```
   Before By Value
   1-2-3-4-5-
   After By Value
   1-2-3-4-5-
   Before NOCOPY
   1-2-3-4-5-
   After NOCOPY
   2-4-6-4-5-
```

As you can see from the last set of output numbers, the first three rows of the nums2 variable array have been modified, even though the pass_by_ref procedure did not finish its job.

One concern about this trade-off is that the behavior of your application can change even when you don't actually change any of your code. Suppose that you are running in a distributed database environment, and you rely on remote procedure calls (RPCs). In the current implementation of PL/SQL, the NOCOPY hint is always ignored for RPCs. For the last six months, your application has been calling a program that happened to reside on the same database instance as your application. Then a DBA reconfigured databases and the distribution of code, and now your application is calling a remote procedure—which may cause your application to behave differently, at least when an exception occurs.

On the other hand, you are not likely to encounter this scenario or others that might cause a change in behavior: for example, parameter aliasing (discussed in the next section) or reliance on the values of parameters after a program call fails with an unhandled exception. Standard, reasonable coding practices should keep you away from such problems.

Parameter Aliasing

Potential corruption of your data structures is not the only complication with NOCOPY. This hint also increases the possibility that you will encounter programs with a situation known as *parameter aliasing*, where two different identifiers in your program refer to the same memory location (two *aliases* for the same data), and the behavior of your code does not match your expectations.

Parameter aliasing as a potential issue predates the introduction of the NOCOPY feature. Programs should not rely on aliasing behavior, and you should examine your code carefully to ferret out such dependencies.

Here is an example of parameter aliasing and the trouble it can cause (see *parmalias.sql* for the contiguous code). First, I declare a record type containing information about a prisoner (name and number of years incarcerated). Then I declare a variable type array of those records:

```
/* Filename on companion disk: parmalias.sql */
DECLARE
    TYPE prisoner IS RECORD (
        name VARCHAR2(100),
        years_incarcerated NUMBER);
```

```
TYPE prisoner_list IS VARRAY(2000) OF prisoner;
innocents_on_deathrow prisoner_list := prisoner_list();
```

Since the death penalty was reinstated in the state of Illinois in 1977, 10 men have been executed (as of May 1999). Eleven men have been found to be innocent of the crimes for which they were to be killed and have been released, but often after spending many years on Death Row (Anthony Porter was there for 18 years!). Now that is what I call a travesty of justice. So here's a procedure—defined within the same PL/SQL block or scope—to add a travesty to the list:

```
PROCEDURE add_travesty (
    illinois_inhumanity IN OUT NOCOPY prisoner_list)
IS
BEGIN
    illinois_inhumanity(1).name := 'Rolando Cruz';
    illinois_inhumanity(1).years_incarcerated := 10;

    innocents_on_deathrow(1).name := 'Anthony Porter';
    innocents_on_deathrow(1).years_incarcerated := 17.75;
END;
```

This program populates the first rows of what seem to be two different variable arrays: illinois_inhumanity and innocents_on_deathrow. Nothing wrong with that, right? Well, let's see how we are going to use this program:

```
BEGIN
    innocents_on_deathrow.EXTEND;
    add_travesty (innocents_on_deathrow);
    DBMS_OUTPUT.PUT_LINE (innocents_on_deathrow(1).name);
END;
/
```

I extend the global innocents_on_deathrow array and then call add_travesty, passing in that variable array. Then I display the name of the person in the first row.

You will see in *parmalias.sql* that I have two different versions of this block: one that uses NOCOPY for the parameter in add_travesty, and another that relies on the default parameter passing mechanism (by value). When I run these two blocks, I see this result on my screen:

```
With NOCOPY: Anthony Porter
Without NOCOPY: Rolando Cruz
```

Why do I get these different results? We'll first analyze the action with the NOCOPY option (see Figure 10-1):

1. When I call add_travesty, I pass innocents_on_deathrow as the IN OUT prisoner list. Since it is passed using NOCOPY, any changes made to the array take place immediately.

2. I set the first row of illinois_inhumanity with information about Rolando Cruz.

3. Then I set the first row of innocents_on_deathrow with the information about Anthony Porter. Since I have used NOCOPY, the two arrays are the same, and so illinois_inhumanity is modified as well.

4. When the program ends, no copying takes place and so I see "Anthony Porter" when I display the contents of the innocents_on_deathrow array.

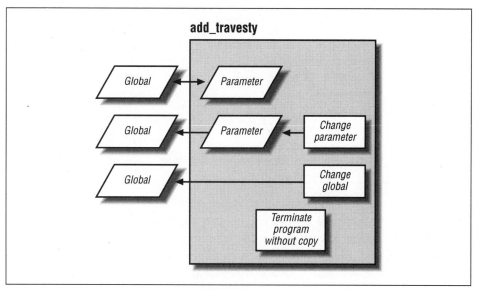

Figure 10-1. Parameter aliasing with NOCOPY

Now let's step through the default processing (no use of NOCOPY):

1. When I call add_travesty, I pass innocents_on_deathrow by value.

2. I set the first row of my formal parameter (a local copy of innocents_on_ deathrow) with information about Rolando Cruz.

3. Then I set the first row of my global collection (innocents_on_deathrow itself) with the information about Anthony Porter.

4. When the program ends, any changes made to the formal parameter are copied to the actual parameter, innocents_on_deathrow. This action *overwrites* the Anthony Porter information. Consequently, after the program is run, I see "Rolando Cruz" when I display the contents of the innocents_on_deathrow array.

Figure 10-2 illustrates the sequence of events without the use of NOCOPY.

You can see that the results of my program depend on the method of parameter passing chosen by the compiler. The compiler might change its mind, when and if circumstances change and a recompile is required. This introduces a level of uncertainty in your application. How can you avoid this problem?

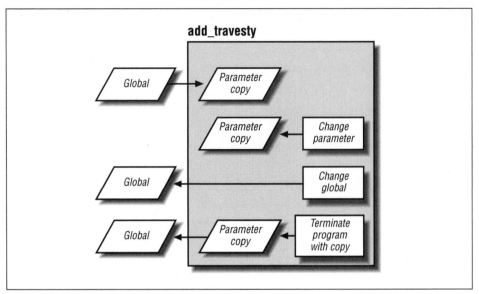

Figure 10-2. Parameter aliasing without NOCOPY

You should be very careful in your use of both the NOCOPY hint and global variables. You are almost always better off passing global data structures through a parameter list rather than referencing them directly within a program unit. When this is not practical, set clear rules about how and when your globals can be used.

Performance Gains with NOCOPY

How much faster might your application run if you use the NOCOPY hint? It will certainly depend very much on your data structures: the number of rows in your collections, the size of your records, and so on.

I put together a test comparing the management of an index-by table of records with NOCOPY and the default by-value passing method. Here is the procedure, combining both versions within the [ ] brackets to save some space (see *nocopy3. tst* for the full script):

```
/* Filename on companion disk: nocopy3.tst */
PROCEDURE pass_by_[value | ref ] (
    emps IN OUT [NOCOPY] emp_tabtype,
    raise_err IN BOOLEAN := FALSE)
IS
BEGIN
    FOR indx IN emps.FIRST .. emps.LAST
    LOOP
        emps(indx).last_name := RTRIM (emps(indx).last_name || ' ');
        emps(indx).salary := emps(indx).salary + 1;
    END LOOP;
```

```
    IF raise_err THEN RAISE VALUE_ERROR; END IF;
END;
```

Notice that I have set the procedure up to run so that I can allow it to end successfully or terminate with an unhandled exception. I ran these programs in a variety of ways, one of which is shown below:

```
PLVtmr.capture;
BEGIN
    FOR indx IN 1 .. num
    LOOP
        pass_by_[value | ref ] (emptab, TRUE);
    END LOOP;
EXCEPTION
    WHEN OTHERS THEN
        PLVtmr.show_elapsed ('By value raising error ' || num);
END;
```

Here are the results of executing the script 10 and then 100 times (with correspondingly larger volumes of data in the index-by table:

```
By value no error 10 Elapsed: .65 seconds.
NOCOPY no error 10 Elapsed: .06 seconds.

By value raising error 10 Elapsed: .03 seconds.
NOCOPY raising error 10 Elapsed: .01 seconds.

By value no error 100 Elapsed: 317.78 seconds.
NOCOPY no error 100 Elapsed: 6.67 seconds.

By value raising error 100 Elapsed: 1.57 seconds.
NOCOPY raising error 100 Elapsed: .07 seconds.
```

As you can see, there is a significant improvement in performance with NOCOPY, especially for the largest-scale test. I have run other tests, with less dramatic gains (see *nocopy2.tst*); you can easily modify my test scripts to test your own code to verify the impact of NOCOPY in your application.

Calling Packaged Functions in SQL

In Oracle8*i*, Oracle has made changes in the way you define programs and assert their *purity levels*, or lack of side effects.

RESTRICT_REFERENCES Pragma

Back in Oracle 7.3, PL/SQL offered a new pragma (compiler directive) called RESTRICT_REFERENCES. This pragma was used to assert to the PL/SQL compiler the purity level of a packaged procedure or function. The RESTRICT_REFERENCES pragma had to be included in the package specification if you were to use that program inside a SQL statement (directly or indirectly).

This pragma has always been a major headache for PL/SQL developers, and as of Oracle 8.1 it is no longer required. The SQL engine will determine at the time you run your SQL statement whether or not the function call is valid. Many of the restrictions on how and when you can use functions in SQL have been relaxed, but the following rules still apply:

- Named notation is not supported; you can only use positional notation. However, you cannot provide actual parameters for formal parameters with default values.

- A function called from a query or DML statement may not end the current transaction, commit or roll back to a savepoint, or ALTER the system or session.

- A function called from a SELECT statement or from a parallelized DML statement may not execute a DML statement or otherwise modify the database.

- A function called from a DML statement may not read or modify the particular table being modified by that DML statement.

The last three restrictions can be avoided if you take advantage of PL/SQL 8.1's autonomous transaction feature (described in Chapter 2, *Choose Your Transaction!*) in your function. With this approach, the function executes in its own transaction space, so a commit or DML statement has no impact on the "calling" SQL statement.

Oracle 8.1 also offers much better error messages. Instead of the double-negative, mind-bending:

```
ORA-06571: Function TOTCOMP does not guarantee not to update database
```

you will see this much more sensible message:

```
ORA-14551: cannot perform a DML operation inside a query
```

You can still include the PRAGMA RESTRICT_REFERENCES if you wish. You might, for example, want to use the PL/SQL compiler as a verification mechanism. It will tell you if your function has the side effects that you would expect, informing you of potential complications in underlying layers of code.

Related New Developments

Oracle has added several new options to the way you define programs and assert their purity levels to make it easier to deploy stored code in the new world of integration with Java and C, as well as with parallel databases.

The TRUST option

You no longer need to use PRAGMA RESTRICT_REFERENCES to enable PL/SQL programs for use in SQL; the runtime engine will figure it out all by itself. However, what if you want to call Java or C routines from within SQL? You can now build wrappers around code written in those languages to make them accessible in PL/SQL. But the SQL engine cannot analyze those programs to determine freedom from side effects.

Oracle has, therefore, added a new option in the PRAGMA RESTRICT_REFERENCES statement: TRUST. The complete syntax for this pragma is now as follows:

```
PRAGMA RESTRICT_REFERENCES (
    function_name, WNDS [, WNPS] [, RNDS] [, RNPS] [, TRUST] );
```

The TRUST option makes it easier to call Java and C routines from functions that have a RESTRICT_REFERENCES pragma. When TRUST is used in the pragma, the restrictions listed in that pragma are not actually enforced. They are, instead, simply trusted to be true. Now that's flexibility!

You can deploy the TRUST option on the top-level program that then calls other programs, or you can use TRUST with each of the lower-level programs, allowing you to then assert whatever purity levels are necessary on routines that call them. Let's look at some examples.

When calling from a section of code that is using pragmas to a section that is not, there are two likely usage styles. One is to place a pragma on the routine to be called, for example, on a call specification for a Java method. Calls from PL/SQL to this method will then complain if the method is less restricted than the calling function.

The following package declares two programs. The maxsal function is based on a Java method; it uses the TRUST option to assert WNDS (writes no database state) and RNDS (reads no database state). The analyze_compensation procedure, which needs to assert WNDS so that it can be called from within a SQL query (indirectly), can then call maxsal. Note that if I wanted to assert WNPS or use this procedure in a function that is called in a WHERE clause, it would be rejected because the underlying pragma does not assert this purity level:

```
CREATE OR REPLACE PACKAGE personnel
IS
    FUNCTION maxsal (ssn_in IN VARCHAR2) RETURN NUMBER
    IS
        LANGUAGE JAVA NAME
            'Person.max_salary (Java.lang.String) return long';
        PRAGMA RESTRICT_REFERENCES (maxsal, WNDS, RNDS, TRUST);

    PROCEDURE analyze_compensation (ssn_in IN VARCHAR2);

    PRAGMA RESTRICT_REFERENCES (analyze_compensation, WNDS);
END;
```

In the next example, I have rewritten the personnel package specification to demonstrate the second usage style. Here, the top-level program, analyze_compensation, is the only program with a RESTRICT_REFERENCES pragma. I still won't have

any problem calling maxsal and deploying it inside SQL, because I have added the
TRUST option:

```
CREATE OR REPLACE PACKAGE personnel
IS
    FUNCTION maxsal (ssn_in IN VARCHAR2) RETURN NUMBER
    IS
       LANGUAGE JAVA NAME
          'Person.max_salary (Java.lang.String) return long';

    PROCEDURE analyze_compensation (ssn_in IN VARCHAR2);

    PRAGMA RESTRICT_REFERENCES (
       analyze_compensation, WNDS, WNPS, TRUST);
END;
```

The SQL runtime engine will not even check the purity level of maxsal; it has been
instructed to "trust" the program.

Deterministic functions

What, you might ask, is a *deterministic function?* It's a program that doesn't have
any free will. If you pass it *X* and *Y* values for its arguments, it always returns the
same value(s). According to Oracle documentation:

> A function that is dependent solely on the values passed into it as arguments, and
> does not meaningfully reference or modify the contents of package variables or
> the database, or have any other side-effects, is termed deterministic.

Here is an example of a deterministic function:

```
CREATE FUNCTION ceo_compensation (
    stock_increase IN NUMBER,
    layoffs IN NUMBER)
    RETURN NUMBER
IS
BEGIN
    RETURN 1000000 * (layoffs + stock_increase);
END;
```

Even if the company's assembly line killed three workers due to faulty wiring, as
long as the stock price goes up and the CEO lays off a bunch of people, he
receives a huge paycheck.

What's the big deal about this sort of function? If Oracle can be sure that the function will return the same value for a given set of arguments, then it can avoid re-
executing the function if it remembers the value from the last execution with those
arguments.

If you tell Oracle that a function is deterministic, this declaration becomes an optimization hint. The Oracle8*i* engine then knows that this function does not need to

be called repetitively for the same arguments. It can instead cache the results and then simply use those results again and again.

This feature is especially useful within a parallelized query or parallelized DML statement. In addition, two new features in Oracle8*i* require that any function used with them be declared deterministic:

- Any function used in a function-based index is required to be deterministic.

- Any function used in a materialized view must be deterministic if that view is to be marked ENABLE QUERY REWRITE.

How do you declare a function to have this property? Simply place the DETER-MINISTIC keyword after the return value type in the header of your function. In the following block, I have redefined the ceo_compensation function to be deterministic:

```
CREATE FUNCTION ceo_compensation (
    stock_increase IN NUMBER,
    layoffs IN NUMBER)
    RETURN NUMBER DETERMINISTIC
IS
BEGIN
  RETURN 1000000 * (layoffs + stock_increase);
END;
```

You can add this DETERMINISTIC clause in a header of any of the following:

- A standalone function

- A packaged function

- An object type function

Do not place the DETERMINISTIC keyword in the header of the function in the package body or object type body. You can also declare a procedure to be deterministic. There are several situations in which deterministic functions are not required but are strongly recommended by Oracle:

- Any materialized view or snapshot that is declared REFRESH FAST should only call deterministic functions.

- If your function is called in a WHERE, ORDER BY, or GROUP BY clause, or is a MAP or ORDER method of a SQL type, or in any other way helps determine whether or where a row should appear in a result set, that function should be deterministic. (This characteristic was specified through the RESTRICT_REFER-ENCES pragma in earlier versions of Oracle with the WNDS and WNPS purity levels.)

All you have to do is include the DETERMINISTIC keyword in your program declaration, and the SQL engine will automatically take one of a number of optimization steps. Yet the PL/SQL compiler really doesn't have any way to tell whether a function truly is deterministic. So if you label a program as deterministic erroneously, the results of any queries that call that function may also be erroneous.

PARALLEL_ENABLE functions

The execution of a SQL statement can involve many distinct actions (for example, updating multiple indexes on an INSERT). Oracle's parallel execution feature allows these multiple operations to be executed simultaneously on different processes. If a function is called in a SQL statement that is run in parallel, then Oracle may make and run a separate copy of the function in each process.

Oracle's parallel execution feature divides the work of executing a SQL statement across multiple processes. Functions called from a SQL statement that is run in parallel may have a separate copy run in each of these processes, with each copy called for only the subset of rows handled by that process. Each process has its own copy of package data structures, as well as Java STATIC class attributes. Oracle cannot assume that it is safe to parallelize the execution of user-defined functions if they might possibly modify any of those variables.

Prior to Oracle8*i*, a packaged function could be run in a parallel DML statement if its RESTRICT_REFERENCES pragma asserted all purity levels: WNDS, RNDS, WNPS, and RNPS. Those same purity levels also needed to be applicable to a standalone function if it were to be called in parallelized SQL. A parallel query required RNPS and WNPS, in addition to WNDS.

In Oracle8*i*, since RESTRICT_REFERENCES is no longer required and parallel function execution is still desired, a new and optional keyword, PARALLEL_ENABLE, has been added for the program header. This keyword is placed before the IS or AS keyword as shown in this example:

```
CREATE FUNCTION ceo_compensation (
    stock_increase IN NUMBER,
    layoffs IN NUMBER)
    RETURN NUMBER PARALLEL_ENABLE
IS
BEGIN
  RETURN 1000000 * (layoffs + stock_increase);
END;
/
```

You can use this keyword in a function defined in a CREATE FUNCTION statement, in a function's declaration in a CREATE PACKAGE statement, or on a method's declaration in a CREATE TYPE statement. You do *not* repeat this keyword in the function's or method's body in a CREATE PACKAGE BODY or CREATE TYPE BODY statement.

You don't *have* to use the PARALLEL_ENABLE keyword to identify functions that are eligible for parallel execution; Oracle suggests, however, that you use it, rather than a RESTRICT_REFERENCES pragma, when you need to achieve this effect. Here are some things to keep in mind:

- If you define a standalone function with the CREATE FUNCTION statement, it may still be eligible for parallel execution if the SQL runtime engine can determine that the function neither reads nor writes package variables, nor calls any function that might do so.

- A Java method or C function can never be seen by Oracle as safe to run in parallel *unless* the programmer explicitly indicates PARALLEL_ENABLE on the call specification or provides a PRAGMA RESTRICT_REFERENCES indicating that the function is pure enough for the operation.

- If your function executes in parallel as part of a parallelized DML statement, it is not permitted to execute another DML statement. This function is, in fact, subject to the same restrictions enforced on functions that are run inside a query.

- You can combine PARALLEL_ENABLE and DETERMINISTIC in the same program header.

SQL99 Compliance

PL/SQL 8.1 adds support for several functions to come into compliance with the SQL99 standard.

The TRIM Function

The TRIM function allows you to trim leading or trailing characters (or both) from a character string. Here is the header of the function:

```
FUNCTION TRIM ( [LEADING | TRAILING | BOTH] trim_chars FROM trim_source )
    RETURN VARCHAR2;
```

where *trim_chars* is the number of characters to trim from *trim_source*.

This function conforms to these rules:

- If *trim_chars* or *trim_source* is a character literal, you must enclose it in single quotes.

- If you specify LEADING, Oracle removes any leading characters that are found in the *trim_chars* string (equivalent to the LTRIM built-in function).

- If you specify TRAILING, PL/SQL removes any trailing characters found in *trim_chars* (equivalent to the RTRIM built-in function).

- If you specify BOTH or none of the three, Oracle removes leading and trailing characters found in *trim_chars*.

- If you do not specify *trim_chars*, the default value is a blank space.

- The maximum length of the value is the length of *trim_source*.

The following block exercises the various forms of the TRIM command:

```
/* Filename on companion disk: trim.sql */
DECLARE
    mystr VARCHAR2(10);
    yourstr VARCHAR2(10) := 'Toronto';
BEGIN
    DBMS_OUTPUT.PUT_LINE (
        TRIM (LEADING 'x' FROM 'xyzabc'));
    DBMS_OUTPUT.PUT_LINE (
        TRIM (TRAILING 'cb' FROM 'xyzabc'));
    DBMS_OUTPUT.PUT_LINE (
        TRIM (BOTH 'x1' FROM '1x1yzabc111x'));
    DBMS_OUTPUT.PUT_LINE (
        TRIM ('x1' FROM '1x1yzabc111x'));
    DBMS_OUTPUT.PUT_LINE (
        TRIM (mystr FROM yourstr));
END;
/
```

and results in this output:

```
yzabc
xyza
yzabc
yzabc
Toronto
```

Oracle documentation states that "if either trim_source or trim_chars is a NULL value, then the TRIM function returns a null value." My tests indicate, however, that if trim_chars is NULL, then trim_source is returned unchanged.

The CAST Function

The CAST function converts one built-in datatype or collection-typed value into another built-in datatype or collection-typed value. CAST was first made available in Oracle 8.0 and has been extended in a variety of ways in Oracle8*i*. CAST, in essence, offers a single program name (and different syntax) to replace a variety of conversion programs, such as ROWIDTOHEX, TO_DATE, TO_CHAR, and so on. Here is the general syntax of the CAST statement:

```
CAST (expression AS type)
```

where *expression* is the expression to be converted and *type* is the name of the datatype to which the expression is converted.

You can cast an unnamed expression (such as a date or the result set of a subquery) or a named collection (such as a VARRAY or a nested table) into a type-compatible datatype or named collection. The type must be the name of a built-in datatype or collection type and the expression must be a built-in datatype or must evaluate to a collection value.

The expression can be either a built-in datatype or a collection type, and a subquery must return a single value of the collection type or the built-in type. If you are casting the result set of a subquery, you must then specify the MULTISET keyword to tell Oracle to return a collection value. MULTISET is illustrated in the last example in the section "Collection examples."

Table 10-1 shows which built-in datatypes can be cast into which other built-in datatypes.

Table 10-1. Conversions Supported by CAST

From/To	CHAR, VARCHAR2	NUMBER	DATE	RAW	ROWID, UROWID	NCHAR, NVARCHAR2
CHAR, VARCHAR2	✓	✓	✓	✓	✓	
NUMBER	✓	✓				
DATE	✓		✓			
RAW	✓			✓		
ROWID, UROWID	✓				✓[a]	
NCHAR, NVARCHAR2		✓	✓	✓	✓	✓

[a] You can't cast a UROWID to a ROWID if the UROWID contains the value of a ROWID of an index-organized table.

Note the following about using CAST:

- CAST does not support LONG, LONG RAW, or any of the LOB datatypes.

- If the UROWID contains the value of a ROWID of an index-organized table, you cannot cast that UROWID to a ROWID.

- To cast a named collection type into another named collection type, the elements of both collections must be of the same TYPE.

- If the result set of a subquery can evaluate to multiple rows, you must specify the MULTISET keyword. The rows resulting from the subquery form the elements of the collection value into which they are cast. Without the MULTISET keyword, the subquery is treated as a scalar subquery, which is not supported in the CAST expression. In other words, scalar subqueries as arguments of the CAST operator are not valid in Oracle8*i*.

- In many cases, you will not be able to use CAST directly within PL/SQL. It is primarily a SQL operator.

Let's take a look at some examples (you will find all of these grouped together in the *cast.sql* file on the disk).

Built-in datatype examples

You can use CAST instead of other datatype conversion functions:

```
/* Filename on companion disk: cast.sql */
BEGIN
    /* CAST for TO_DATE...no way to pass format mask.
       Instead, the database default or session setting of
       NLS_DATE_FORMAT is used. */
    DBMS_OUTPUT.PUT_LINE (CAST ('10-JAN-99' AS DATE));

    /* CAST as TO_NUMBER...no way to pass format mask.  */
    DBMS_OUTPUT.PUT_LINE (CAST ('107898888' AS NUMBER));
END;
/
```

As noted, there isn't any way to include a format mask with which to drive the conversion. If I use a different format for my date string, I get an error:

```
SQL>
  1  BEGIN
  2     DBMS_OUTPUT.PUT_LINE (
  3        CAST ('1/1/99' AS DATE));
  4* END;
  5  /

ERROR at line 1:
ORA-01843: not a valid month
```

I can use CAST to convert a ROWID to a string as follows:

```
SQL> SELECT CAST (ROWID AS VARCHAR2(20)) Vrowid
       FROM department;

VROWID
--------------------
AAADIKAACAAAAMeAAA
AAADIKAACAAAAMeAAB
AAADIKAACAAAAMeAAC
AAADIKAACAAAAMeAAD
```

Yet I cannot run this same query inside PL/SQL:

```
SQL> DECLARE
  2      my_rowid VARCHAR2(20);
  3  BEGIN
  4      FOR rec IN (
  5          SELECT CAST (ROWID AS VARCHAR2(20)) Vrowid
  6              FROM department)
  7      LOOP
  8          DBMS_OUTPUT.PUT_LINE (rec.Vrowid);
  9      END LOOP;
 10  END;
 11  /
ERROR at line 1:
PLS-00220: simple name required in this context
```

So I am not sure how useful CAST will ever be for PL/SQL developers for conversion of scalar datatypes.

Collection examples

CAST will almost certainly come in very handy when you want to convert between types of collections, or if you want to convert a subquery directly into a collection.

To demonstrate these capabilities, I will use the following structures (see *cast.sql* for all of these statements and the actual exercises):

```
/* Filename on companion disk: cast.sql */
CREATE TYPE address_t AS OBJECT
    (street VARCHAR2(100), city VARCHAR2(100));
/
CREATE TYPE address_book_t AS TABLE OF address_t;
/
CREATE TYPE address_array_t AS VARRAY(3) OF address_t;
/
CREATE TABLE addresses OF address_t;

INSERT INTO addresses VALUES (
    address_t('19th St', 'St. Louis'));
INSERT INTO addresses VALUES (
    address_t('Biglanes Blvd', 'Dallas'));
INSERT INTO addresses VALUES (
    address_t('Upanddown Lane', 'San Francisco'));
```

I now have a nested table, variable array, and database table all with the same structure. I can then use CAST—along with the MULTISET operator in SQL—to move between the different structures.

Suppose, for example, that I have a nested table declared in PL/SQL, and I want to move that to a VARRAY. Here are the steps I would take:

```
/* Filename on companion disk: cast.sql */
DECLARE
```

```
      addr_varray address_array_t;

      addr_ntable address_book_t :=
         address_book_t (
            address_t('Madison Ave', 'Chicago'),
            address_t('Devon Ave', 'Chicago'));
  BEGIN
     SELECT CAST (addr_ntable AS address_array_t)
       INTO addr_varray
       FROM dual;
```

I would love to be able to do this:

```
   addr_varray := CAST (addr_ntable AS address_array_t); /* INVALID! */
```

Unfortunately, the CAST operator cannot be used directly (natively) in PL/SQL to operate on collections.

I can also transform the result set of a query into a nested table or VARRAY using CAST and MULTISET, as shown in the following:

```
/* Filename on companion disk: cast.sql */
DECLARE
    addr_varray address_array_t;
BEGIN
    SELECT CAST (MULTISET (
              SELECT street, city
                FROM addresses p
               ORDER BY city)
        AS address_array_t)
      INTO addr_varray
      FROM dual;
```

Notice that I have included an ORDER BY in my query; it will generally be much more efficient to rely on SQL to do your sorting *before* moving your data to a PL/SQL structure.

SQL Operations on Collections

In Oracle 8.1, you can now more easily use SQL to operate on PL/SQL collections (nested tables and variable arrays). This feature, built upon the CAST operator, allows you to employ SQL capabilities against data stored in such structures, and also to integrate data in these collections with data in tables.

Here is the syntax needed to reference a collection inside a query:

```
SELECT column_list
  FROM TABLE (CAST (
       collection AS collection_type))
       [collection_alias]
```

Where *collection* is a collection declared in a PL/SQL block, *collection_type* is the TYPE from which the collection is declared, and *collection_alias* is an optional alias for the collection-cast-into-table.

column_list is a list of expressions returned by the query. If the collection TYPE is a nested table or variable array based on a scalar, then *column_list* must be the keyword COLUMN_VALUE, as shown:

```
SELECT COLUMN_VALUE FROM TABLE (CAST ...);
```

If the collection is based on an object, then the column list can directly reference individual elements of the object by name.

Let's look at a few examples. I will create a type of nested table and a database table to use in the scripts (see *collsql.sql* for the full set of steps):

```
/* Filename on companion disk: collsql.sql */
CREATE TYPE cutbacks_for_taxcuts AS TABLE OF VARCHAR2(100);
/
CREATE TABLE lobbying_results (
    activity VARCHAR2(200));

INSERT INTO lobbying_results
    VALUES ('No tax on stock transactions');
INSERT INTO lobbying_results
    VALUES ('Cut city income taxes');
```

Then I can merge the data for these two structures together, as follows:

```
/* Filename on companion disk: collsql.sql */
DECLARE
    nyc_devolution cutbacks_for_taxcuts :=
        cutbacks_for_taxcuts (
            'Stop rat extermination programs',
            'Fire building inspectors',
            'Close public hospitals');
BEGIN
    DBMS_OUTPUT.PUT_LINE (
        'How to Make the NYC Rich Much, Much Richer:');
    FOR rec IN (
        SELECT COLUMN_VALUE ohmy
          FROM TABLE (CAST (
                    nyc_devolution AS cutbacks_for_taxcuts))
        UNION
        SELECT activity FROM lobbying_results)
    LOOP
        DBMS_OUTPUT.PUT_LINE (rec.ohmy);
    END LOOP;
END;
/
```

And out comes the following data:

```
How to Make the NYC Rich Much, Much Richer:
Close public hospitals
```

```
Cut city income taxes
Fire building inspectors
No tax on stock transactions
Stop rat extermination programs
```

As you can see, the data is sorted, as will happen automatically with a UNION.

Now let's try this capability with a nested table of objects (see *collsql2.sql*):

```
CREATE TYPE labor_source AS OBJECT
  (labor_type VARCHAR2(30), hourly_rate NUMBER);
/
CREATE TYPE union_busters AS TABLE OF labor_source;
/
```

In the following block, I query both members of the object individually, employing an ORDER BY clause to rearrange the data:

```
/* Filename on companion disk: collsql2.sql */
DECLARE
    low_wage_pressure union_busters :=
        union_busters (
            labor_source ('Workfare', 0),
            labor_source ('Prisoner', '5'));
BEGIN
  FOR rec IN (
     SELECT labor_type, hourly_rate
       FROM TABLE (
          CAST (low_wage_pressure AS union_busters))
       ORDER BY labor_type)
  LOOP
     DBMS_OUTPUT.PUT_LINE (
        rec.labor_type || '-$' || rec.hourly_rate);
  END LOOP;
END;
/
```

And we see this output:

```
Prisoner-$5
Workfare-$0
```

Miscellaneous and Minor Improvements

The Oracle PL/SQL development team has been busy! In addition to all of the other features covered in this and other chapters, they have also improved PL/SQL in the following ways:

- Optimization of the STANDARD package's built-in programs. A lot of our code calls these low-level programs (TO_CHAR, SUBSTR, INSTR, etc.), so Oracle has focused on improving the performance of this package.

- Faster anonymous block execution.

- Faster RPC parameter passing.

- Caching of dynamic link libraries (DLLs) for improved external procedure performance. External procedures can now cache up to 10 DLLs in a session; subsequent calls to a C function in a cached DLL will not cause the DLL to be reloaded.

And there's more!

Dramatically Higher Limits on Body Size

You will also be very glad to know that the maximum size of package and object type bodies is now greatly increased. Prior to Oracle8*i*, the limitation on program size was determined by the maximum number of nodes supported in internal parsing tree structures: 2^{15}. This translated to a maximum byte size of approximately 128K (sometimes much less).

With Oracle8*i*, the compiler will now support up to 2^{26} nodes in its internal tree structure, giving us room to grow our code to something like 16MB! Of course, we will probably hit other limits before our code gets to be that large anyway.

Improved ORA-06502 Error Messages

Oh, that annoying ORA-06502 error! How many times have we seen this message:

```
ORA-06502: numeric or value error
```

only to wonder whether the error was caused by an attempt to put too large a string into a character variable or an attempt to stuff a non-numeric value into a numeric variable?

Now, the PL/SQL runtime engine will let you know for sure:

```
/* Filename on companion disk: ora6502.sql */
DECLARE
    this_world VARCHAR2(5);
BEGIN
    /* No room for justice... */
    this_world := 'Justice';
END;
/

ORA-06502: PL/SQL: numeric or value error:
    character string buffer too small

DECLARE
    bills_fortune NUMBER;
BEGIN
    bills_fortune := 'UNIMAGINABLE';
END;
/

ORA-06502: PL/SQL: numeric or value error: character to number conversion error
```

Appendix: What's on the Companion Disk?

The disk that accompanies this book contains the Companion Reference, an online tool designed by RevealNet, Inc. to help you find additional resources. The guide offers point-and-click access to approximately 100 files of source code I've prepared to accompany this book, as well as a copy of the PLVtmr package (described in the Preface). The goal of providing this material in electronic form is to give you a leg up on the development of your own PL/SQL programs for Oracle8*i*.

Installing the Reference

Before you begin installation, be sure to read the *readme* file on the disk. This file will tell you how to obtain a DLL that you need for installation.

In a Microsoft Windows environment (95, 98, or NT 4.0), you begin installation by double-clicking on the *Revealnet_08i_Guide_Setup.exe* file to run the installation program. If you are working in a non-Windows environment, please visit the RevealNet PL/SQL Pipeline Archives (*http://www.revealnet.com/plsql-pipeline*) to obtain a compressed file containing the examples on this disk.

The installation script will lead you through the necessary steps. The first screen you will see is the install screen, shown in Figure A-1.

You can change the default directory in which the files will be placed. Once this step is complete and the software has been copied to your drive, an icon will appear in the folder you specified. Double-click on the icon to start using the Companion Reference. You will then see the main menu, shown in Figure A-2.

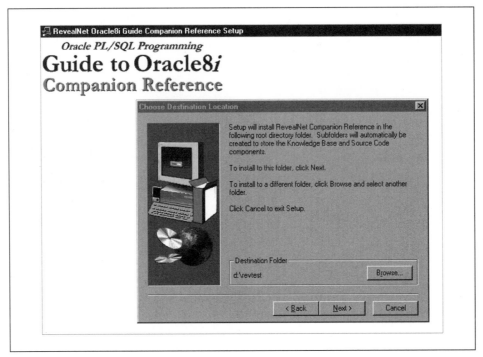

Figure A-1. Installing the Companion Guide

Using the Reference

The four buttons on the main menu take you to the companion information for this book:

About the Companion Reference

A brief description of the contents of this disk.

About the Indexes

An explanation of the information provided for each file: name, chapter reference, and description.

Source Code Index by File Name

The guide gives you point-and-click access to each of the files on the companion disk. Here the files are listed alphabetically. Source code listings in the book, indicated by the disk icon, begin with comment lines keyed to these filenames on the disk. Figure A-3 shows a portion of the Source Code Index by Filename.

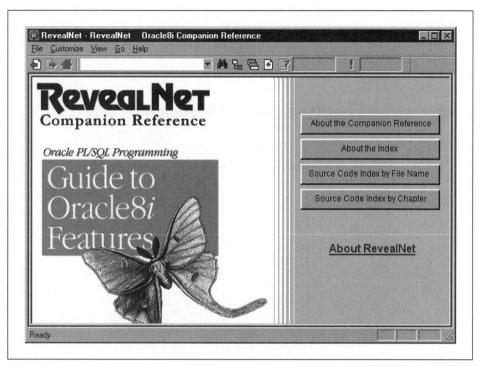

Figure A-2. The main menu

Chapter	File Name	Description
2	autondlock.sql	Demonstrates how you can cause a deadlock in your program when working with autonomous transactions.
2	trcfunc.sf	Demonstrates use of function to trace SQL activity; as an autonomous transaction, it can even do a commit.
2	autonserial.sql	Demonstrates the SERIALIZABLE isolation option for autonomous transactions.
2	autontrigger.sql	Demonstrates the use of autonomous transactions in database triggers.
2	autontrigger2.sql	Second iteration demonstrating the use of autonomous transactions in database triggers.
2	autontrigger3.sql	Third iteration demonstrating the use of autonomous transactions in database triggers This version shows that a RAISE in the AUTONOMOUS_TRANSACTION procedure will cause an automatic rollback of the DML. Makes sense; it's the top-level block in the transaction.
6	aq.sql	Runs through several steps required to set up an Advanced Queuing queue table and queue and then demonstrates how to use AQ to set up a database trigger to track logins to the database.
7	aqlisten.sql	Demonstrates the new LISTEN capability of Advanced Queuing.
3	authid.*	A set of files used to demonstrate the AUTHID feature of Oracle8i. The authid.sql file runs all commands in one sequence. You can run the other authid.* files to execute specific actions.
3	authid2.sql	Contains a basic demonstration of AUTHID CURRENT_USER feature.
3	authid3.sql	Contains a basic demonstration of AUTHID CURRENT_USER feature.
3	authid4.sql	Demonstration of AUTHID/Invoker functionality in which I blend shared access to perpetrator table with individualized schema tables for stolen_lives. This script assumes that you have already built the chicago, new york and HQ schemas, along with their tables and procedures.
3	authid5.sql	Demonstration of combination of DEFINER and CURRENT_USER access to blend shared and individual data.
U	bpl.sp	Utility that allows you to pass a Boolean expression to DBMS_OUTPUT.PUT_LINE to be displayed.
5	bulktiming.sql	Compares performance of normal per-statement INSERTs and bulk INSERTs. Shows...

Figure A-3. The Source Code Index by File Name

Source Code Index by Chapter

Here the files are listed in chapter order to make it easy for you to move between the book and the guide. Figure A-4 shows a portion of the Source Code Index by Chapter.

```
┌──────────────────────────────────────────────────────────────────────────────────────┐
│                                                                                        │
│  ┌──────────────────────────────────────────────────────────────────────────────┐──┐  │
│  │ ⓘ Source Code Index by Chapter                                      _ □ ×   │▲ │  │
│  │                    Click on file names in BLUE to display its contents ...    │  │  │
│  │                                                                              │  │  │
│  │   Chapter   File Name      Description                                        │  │  │
│  │   2         autondlock.sql Demonstrates how you can cause a deadlock in your program when working with autonomous │  │  │
│  │                            transactions.                                      │  │  │
│  │   2         trcfunc.sf     Demonstrates use of function to trace SQL activity; as an autonomous transaction, it can │  │  │
│  │                            even do a commit.                                  │  │  │
│  │   2         autonserial.sql Demonstrates the SERIALIZABLE isolation option for autonomous transactions. │  │  │
│  │   2         autontrigger.sql Demonstrates the use of autonomous transactions in database triggers. │  │  │
│  │   2         autontrigger2.sql Second iteration demonstrating the use of autonomous transactions in database triggers. │  │  │
│  │   2         autontrigger3.sql Third iteration demonstrating the use of autonomous transactions in database triggers This │  │  │
│  │                            version shows that a RAISE in the AUTONOMOUS_TRANSACTION procedure will cause an │  │  │
│  │                            automatic rollback of the DML. Makes sense; it's the top-level block in the transaction. │  │  │
│  │   2         log81.pkg      Package that demonstrates logging as an autonomous transaction. │  │  │
│  │   2         log81a.tst     Demonstrates use of the log81 package.            │  │  │
│  │   2         log81b.tst     Analyzes the overhead of using autonomous transactions. │  │  │
│  │   2         log81c.tst     Demonstrates nesting of autonomous transactions   │  │  │
│  │   2         retry.pkg      A package that demonstrates a "retry" utility using autonomous transactions │  │  │
│  │   2         retry.tst      Test script to demonstrate the retry package      │  │  │
│  │             run9am.sp      Demonstration of dynamic PL/SQL block execution with native dynamic SQL │  │  │
│  │   3         authid.*       A set of files used to demonstrate the AUTHID feature of Oracle8i. The authid.sql file runs all │  │  │
│  │                            commands in one sequence. You can run the other authid.* files to execute specific actions. │  │  │
│  │   3         authid2.sql    Contains a basic demonstration of AUTHID CURRENT_USER feature. │  │  │
│  │   3         authid3.sql    Contains a basic demonstration of AUTHID CURRENT_USER feature. │  │  │
│  │   3         authid4.sql    Demonstration of AUTHID/Invoker functionality in which I blend shared access to perpetrator │  │  │
│  │                            table with individualized schema tables for stolen_lives. This script assumes that you have │  │  │
│  │                            already built the chicago, new york and HQ schemas, along with their tables and procedures. │  │  │
│  │   3         authid5.sql    Demonstration of combination of DEFINER and CURRENT_USER access to blend shared │▼ │  │
│  │                            and individual data.                               │  │  │
│  └──────────────────────────────────────────────────────────────────────────────┘──┘  │
│                                                                                        │
└──────────────────────────────────────────────────────────────────────────────────────┘
```

Figure A-4. The Source Code Index by Chapter

Index

About the Author

Steven Feuerstein is considered one of the world's leading experts on the Oracle PL/SQL language. He is the author or coauthor of *Oracle PL/SQL Programming, Oracle Built-in Packages, Advanced Oracle PL/SQL Programming with Packages,* and several pocket reference books (all from O'Reilly & Associates). Steven has been developing software since 1980 and worked for Oracle Corporation from 1987 to 1992. As Chief Technology Officer of RevealNet, Inc., he has designed several products for PL/SQL developers, including the PL/SQL Knowledge Base, PL/Vision, and PL/Generator. Steven hosts RevealNet's PL/SQL Pipeline, an online community for PL/SQL developers (*http://www.revealnet.com/plsql-pipeline*). You can reach Steven via email at *feuerstein@revealnet.com* or visit him at *http://www.StevenFeuerstein.com*.

Steven is president of the PL/Solutions training and consulting company (*http://www.plsolutions.com*). He shares a Rogers Park, Chicago, Georgian with his wife, Veva, his youngest son, Eli, two cats (Sister Itsacat and Moshe Jacobawitz), and Mercury (a Congo Red African Gray parrot). His older son, Chris, is busy making music and creating art nearby. Steven is a member of the Board of Directors of the Crossroads Fund, which provides grants to organizations in Chicago working for social change.

Colophon

Our look is the result of reader comments, our own experimentation, and feedback from distribution channels. Distinctive covers complement our distinctive approach to technical topics, breathing personality and life into potentially dry subjects.

The insect on the cover of *Oracle PL/SQL Programming: Guide to Oracle8i Features* is a luna moth. One of the 100,000 species of moth, the luna moth (*Actius luna*) is found only in North America. The pale green color and delicate swirled tails of its wings make the luna moth one of the loveliest species of moth.

Like the wings of all moths, the luna moth's wings are covered with tiny, flattened, overlapping scales. The two pairs of wings move in tandem and operate as a single pair. When resting, these wings are spread open, unlike the butterfly's wings, which fold closed in rest. The eye spots on the luna moth's wings are intended to frighten away potential predators.

The adult luna moth has a very short lifespan—approximately one week. During that short life, adult luna moths do not eat at all; they get all of their nourishment during the caterpillar stage. Luna moth caterpillars feed on tree leaves, and tend not to be very picky about what kind of tree.

Although rarely sighted, the beautiful luna moth is not currently listed on the U.S. Fish and Wildlife Services Endangered Species List.

Madeleine Newell was the production editor for this book, and Cindy Kogut of Editorial Ink was the copyeditor. Ellie Cutler and Nancy Kotary provided quality assurance, and Jeff Holcomb and Abby Myers provided production assistance. Pamela Murray wrote the index.

Edie Freedman designed the cover of this book, using a nineteenth-century engraving from the Dover Pictorial Archive. Kathleen Wilson produced the cover layout and designed and produced the diskette label with QuarkXPress 3.3, using the ITC Garamond font. Whenever possible, our books use a durable and flexible lay-flat binding. If the page count exceeds the limit, perfect binding is used.

The inside layout was designed by Alicia Cech, based on a series design by Nancy Priest, and implemented in FrameMaker 5.5 by Mike Sierra. The text and heading fonts are ITC Garamond Light and Garamond Book. The illustrations that appear in this book were produced by Robert Romano and Rhon Porter using Macromedia Freehand 8 and Adobe Photoshop 5. This colophon was written by Clairemarie Fisher O'Leary.

Oracle

Oracle Performance Tuning, 2nd Edition

By Mark Gurry & Peter Corrigan
2nd Edition November 1996
964 pages, Includes diskette
ISBN 1-56592-237-9

The first edition of this book became a classic
for developers and DBAs. This edition offers
400 pages of updated material on Oracle
features, including parallel server, parallel
query, Oracle Performance Pack, disk striping and mirroring,
RAID, MPPs, SMPs, distributed databases, backup and recovery,
and much more. Includes a diskette containing the SQL and shell
scripts described in the book.

Oracle Scripts

By Brian Lomasky & David C. Kreines
1st Edition May 1998
204 pages, Includes CD-ROM
ISBN 1-56592-438-X

A powerful toolset for Oracle DBAs and
developers, these scripts will simplify
everyday tasks – monitoring databases,
protecting against data loss, improving
security and performance, and helping to diagnose problems and
repair databases in emergencies. The accompanying CD-ROM
contains complete source code and additional monitoring and
tuning software.

Oracle Security

By Marlene Theriault & William Heney
1st Edition October 1998
446 pages, ISBN 1-56592-450-9

This book covers the field of Oracle security
from simple to complex. It describes basic
RDBMS security features (e.g., passwords,
profiles, roles, privileges, synonyms) and
includes many practical strategies for securing
an Oracle system, developing auditing and backup plans, and using
the Oracle Enterprise Manager and Oracle Security Server. Also
touches on advanced security features, such as encryption, Trusted
Oracle, and Internet and Web protection.

Oracle Database Administration: The Essential Reference

By David Kreines & Brian Laskey
1st Edition April 1999
580 pages, ISBN 1-56592-516-5

This book provides a concise reference to
the enormous store of information Oracle8
or Oracle7 DBAs need every day. It covers
DBA tasks (e.g., installation, tuning, backups,
networking, auditing, query optimization)
and provides quick references to initialization parameters, SQL
statements, data dictionary tables, system privileges, roles, and
syntax for SQL*Plus, Export, Import, and SQL*Loader.

Oracle Distributed Systems

By Charles Dye
1st Edition April 1999
548 pages, Includes diskette
ISBN 1-56592-432-0

This book describes how you can use
multiple databases and both Oracle8 and
Oracle7 distributed system features to best
advantage. It covers design, configuration of
SQL*Net/Net8, security, and Oracle's distributed options (advanced
replication, snapshots, multi-master replication, updateable snapshots, procedural replication, and conflict resolution). Includes a
complete API reference for built-in packages and a diskette many
helpful scripts and utilities.

Oracle SAP Administration

By Donald K. Burleson
1st Edition November 1999 (est.)
200 pages (est.), ISBN 1-56592-696-X

This book provides tried-and-true advice
for administrators and developers who use
the SAP business system and the Oracle
database system (Oracle8 or Oracle7) in
combination. It covers SAP's SAPDBA and
SAPGUI utilities and describes effective data file placement,
initialization parameters, and monitoring techniques, as well
as high-performance table reorganization, backup, recovery,
tuning, and parallel processing.

Hand-held Computing

Palm Programming: The Developer's Guide

By Neil Rhodes & Julie McKeehan
1st Edition December 1998
482 pages, Includes CD-ROM
ISBN 1-56592-525-4

Emerging as the bestselling hand-held computers of all time, PalmPilots have spawned intense developer activity and a fanatical following. Used by Palm in their developer training, this tutorial-style book shows intermediate to experienced C programmers how to build a Palm application from the ground up. Includes a CD-ROM with source code and third-party developer tools.

PalmPilot: The Ultimate Guide, 2nd Edition

By David Pogue
2nd Edition June 1999
624 pages, Includes CD-ROM
ISBN 1-56592-600-5

This new edition of O'Reilly's runaway bestseller is densely packed with previously undocumented information. The bible for users of Palm VII and all other Palm models, it contains hundreds of timesaving tips and surprising tricks, plus an all-new CD-ROM (for Windows 9x, NT, or Macintosh) containing over 3,100 PalmPilot programs from the collection of palmcentral.com, the Internet's largest Palm software site.

How to stay in touch with O'Reilly

1. Visit Our Award-Winning Web Site

http://www.oreilly.com/

★ "Top 100 Sites on the Web" —*PC Magazine*
★ "Top 5% Web sites" —*Point Communications*
★ "3-Star site" —*The McKinley Group*

Our web site contains a library of comprehensive product information (including book excerpts and tables of contents), downloadable software, background articles, interviews with technology leaders, links to relevant sites, book cover art, and more. File us in your Bookmarks or Hotlist!

2. Join Our Email Mailing Lists

New Product Releases
To receive automatic email with brief descriptions of all new O'Reilly products as they are released, send email to:
listproc@online.oreilly.com
Put the following information in the first line of your message (*not* in the Subject field):
subscribe oreilly-news

O'Reilly Events
If you'd also like us to send information about trade show events, special promotions, and other O'Reilly events, send email to:
listproc@online.oreilly.com
Put the following information in the first line of your message (*not* in the Subject field):
subscribe oreilly-events

3. Get Examples from Our Books via FTP

There are two ways to access an archive of example files from our books:

Regular FTP
- ftp to:
  ftp.oreilly.com
  (login: anonymous
  password: your email address)
- Point your web browser to:
  ftp://ftp.oreilly.com/

FTPMAIL
- Send an email message to:
  ftpmail@online.oreilly.com
  (Write "help" in the message body)

4. Contact Us via Email

order@oreilly.com
To place a book or software order online. Good for North American and international customers.

subscriptions@oreilly.com
To place an order for any of our newsletters or periodicals.

books@oreilly.com
General questions about any of our books.

software@oreilly.com
For general questions and product information about our software. Check out O'Reilly Software Online at **http://software.oreilly.com/** for software and technical support information. Registered O'Reilly software users send your questions to: **website-support@oreilly.com**

cs@oreilly.com
For answers to problems regarding your order or our products.

booktech@oreilly.com
For book content technical questions or corrections.

proposals@oreilly.com
To submit new book or software proposals to our editors and product managers.

international@oreilly.com
For information about our international distributors or translation queries. For a list of our distributors outside of North America check out:
http://www.oreilly.com/www/order/country.html

O'Reilly & Associates, Inc.
101 Morris Street, Sebastopol, CA 95472 USA
TEL   707-829-0515 or 800-998-9938
            (6am to 5pm PST)
FAX   707-829-0104

Titles from O'Reilly

International Distributors

UK, Europe, Middle East and Africa (except France, Germany, Austria, Switzerland, Luxembourg, Liechtenstein, and Eastern Europe)

INQUIRIES
O'Reilly UK Limited
4 Castle Street
Farnham
Surrey, GU9 7HS
United Kingdom
Telephone: 44-1252-711776
Fax: 44-1252-734211
Email: josette@oreilly.com

ORDERS
Wiley Distribution Services Ltd.
1 Oldlands Way
Bognor Regis
West Sussex PO22 9SA
United Kingdom
Telephone: 44-1243-779777
Fax: 44-1243-820250
Email: cs-books@wiley.co.uk

FRANCE

ORDERS
GEODIF
61, Bd Saint-Germain
75240 Paris Cedex 05, France
Tel: 33-1-44-41-46-16 (French books)
Tel: 33-1-44-41-11-87 (English books)
Fax: 33-1-44-41-11-44
Email: distribution@eyrolles.com

INQUIRIES
Éditions O'Reilly
18 rue Séguier
75006 Paris, France
Tel: 33-1-40-51-52-30
Fax: 33-1-40-51-52-31
Email: france@editions-oreilly.fr

GERMANY, SWITZERLAND, AUSTRIA, EASTERN EUROPE, LUXEMBOURG, AND LIECHTENSTEIN

INQUIRIES & ORDERS
O'Reilly Verlag
Balthasarstr. 81
D-50670 Köln
Germany
Telephone: 49-221-973160-91
Fax: 49-221-973160-8
Email: anfragen@oreilly.de (inquiries)
Email: order@oreilly.de (orders)

CANADA (French language books)
Les Éditions Flammarion ltée
375, Avenue Laurier Ouest
Montréal (Québec) H2V 2K3
Tel: 00-1-514-277-8807
Fax: 00-1-514-278-2085
Email: info@flammarion.qc.ca

HONG KONG
City Discount Subscription Service, Ltd.
Unit D, 3rd Floor, Yan's Tower
27 Wong Chuk Hang Road
Aberdeen, Hong Kong
Tel: 852-2580-3539
Fax: 852-2580-6463
Email: citydis@ppn.com.hk

KOREA
Hanbit Media, Inc.
Sonyoung Bldg. 202
Yeksam-dong 736-36
Kangnam-ku
Seoul, Korea
Tel: 822-554-9610
Fax: 822-556-0363
Email: hant93@chollian.dacom.co.kr

PHILIPPINES
Mutual Books, Inc.
429-D Shaw Boulevard
Mandaluyong City, Metro
Manila, Philippines
Tel: 632-725-7538
Fax: 632-721-3056
Email: mbikikog@mnl.sequel.net

TAIWAN
O'Reilly Taiwan
No. 3, Lane 131
Hang-Chow South Road
Section 1, Taipei, Taiwan
Tel: 886-2-23968990
Fax: 886-2-23968916
Email: taiwan@oreilly.com

CHINA
O'Reilly Beijing
Room 2410
160, FuXingMenNeiDaJie
XiCheng District
Beijing, China PR 100031
Tel: 86-10-86631006
Fax: 86-10-86631007
Email: beijing@oreilly.com

INDIA
Computer Bookshop (India) Pvt. Ltd.
190 Dr. D.N. Road, Fort
Bombay 400 001 India
Tel: 91-22-207-0989
Fax: 91-22-262-3551
Email: cbsbom@giasbm01.vsnl.net.in

JAPAN
O'Reilly Japan, Inc.
Kiyoshige Building 2F
12-Bancho, Sanei-cho
Shinjuku-ku
Tokyo 160-0008 Japan
Tel: 81-3-3356-5227
Fax: 81-3-3356-5261
Email: japan@oreilly.com

ALL OTHER ASIAN COUNTRIES
O'Reilly & Associates, Inc.
101 Morris Street
Sebastopol, CA 95472 USA
Tel: 707-829-0515
Fax: 707-829-0104
Email: order@oreilly.com

AUSTRALIA
WoodsLane Pty., Ltd.
7/5 Vuko Place
Warriewood NSW 2102
Australia
Tel: 61-2-9970-5111
Fax: 61-2-9970-5002
Email: info@woodslane.com.au

NEW ZEALAND
Woodslane New Zealand, Ltd.
21 Cooks Street (P.O. Box 575)
Waganui, New Zealand
Tel: 64-6-347-6543
Fax: 64-6-345-4840
Email: info@woodslane.com.au

LATIN AMERICA
McGraw-Hill Interamericana
Editores, S.A. de C.V.
Cedro No. 512
Col. Atlampa
06450, Mexico, D.F.
Tel: 52-5-547-6777
Fax: 52-5-547-3336
Email: mcgraw-hill@infosel.net.mx

O'REILLY®

O'REILLY™

O'Reilly & Associates, Inc.
101 Morris Street
Sebastopol, CA 95472-9902
1-800-998-9938

Visit us online at:
http://www.ora.com/
orders@ora.com

O'REILLY WOULD LIKE TO HEAR FROM YOU

Which book did this card come from?

_____

Where did you buy this book?
- ❑ Bookstore
- ❑ Direct from O'Reilly
- ❑ Bundled with hardware/software
- ❑ Computer Store
- ❑ Class/seminar
- ❑ Other _____

What operating system do you use?
- ❑ UNIX
- ❑ Windows NT
- ❑ Macintosh
- ❑ PC(Windows/DOS)
- ❑ Other _____

What is your job description?
- ❑ System Administrator
- ❑ Network Administrator
- ❑ Web Developer
- ❑ Programmer
- ❑ Educator/Teacher
- ❑ Other _____

❑ Please send me O'Reilly's catalog, containing a complete listing of O'Reilly books and software.

Name _____ **Company/Organization** _____

Address _____

City _____ **State** _____ **Zip/Postal Code** _____ **Country** _____

Telephone _____ **Internet or other email address (specify network)** _____

Nineteenth century wood engraving
of a bear from the O'Reilly &
Associates Nutshell Handbook®
Using & Managing UUCP.

BUSINESS REPLY MAIL
FIRST CLASS MAIL   PERMIT NO. 80   SEBASTOPOL, CA

Postage will be paid by addressee

O'Reilly & Associates, Inc.
101 Morris Street
Sebastopol, CA 95472-9902